If capitalism survives, which its behavior at the outset of the 21st century makes a matter of doubt, John Elkington will have been one of the contributors to its deserving to do so. Against all the odds, the optimism which imbues this lively and challenging book could be made reality – but only if its lessons are learnt.

Sir Geoffrey Chandler, Chair, Amnesty International UK Business Group, 1991-2001

The Chrysalis Economy is just what my generation has been waiting for: a how-to manual on creating companies we would feel proud to work for. One compelling reason why CEOs and other corporate leaders should listen: the next generation of leaders won't work for you unless you do.

Amy Middelburg, Sustainability Program Manager, PricewaterhouseCoopers, and Co-Founder, CSR Chicks

John Elkington has produced a lively new route map. With an original analysis of the latest pressures, market trends and management frameworks, *The Chrysalis Economy* provides a compass for business leaders aiming not only for social survival but also for reputational excellence.

Robert Davies, Chief Executive, The Prince of Wales International Business Leaders Forum, UK

Any business leader who wants to understand the complex forces impacting the business world of today and tomorrow would be hard-pressed to find a better guide than John Elkington's extraordinary new book. People who care about harnessing the resources of business to create a more just society and a more sustainable economy should read this book - and put a copy in the hands of every corporate decision-maker they know.

Bob Dunn, President and CEO, Business for Social Responsibility (BSR), USA

Is this book in your boardroom, your CEO's briefcase – or better yet, on his/her bedside table? In the search for reliable indicators of sustainability, the presence of *The Chrysalis Economy* in such places may prove to be a lead indicator suggesting how well your company or organization is preparing to face the 21st century challenge of turning sustainability from prattle into practice.

Ralph Hallo, President, European Environmental Bureau, Belgium

With the dot-coms in retreat and the world economy on the brink of recession, the stage is set for the emergence of a new, more sustainable path to prosperity - one which embraces life and includes the entire human community. In this important book, John Elkington helps point the way for the 'corporate metamorphosis' to come.

Professor Stuart Hart, Kenan-Flagler Business School, University of North Carolina, USA

The Chrysalis Economy leaps to the top of the list of 'must-read' books for CEOs and other business leaders of today – and for the professors and deans who are training tomorrow's crop of leaders. John Elkington not only captures the tumultuous changes under way at the global intersection of business and society, but also provides a structure to understand it and a 30-year metamorphosis map leading to a sustainable economic system.

John Prestbo, Editor, Dow Jones Indexes, USA

As he proved with the triple bottom line, John Elkington has been sustainable development's 'Babelfish' to the corporate world, a universal translator. The financial sector can only prosper from the metamorphoses of Corporate Caterpillars and Butterflies into Corporate Honeybees, as well as from the eradication of Corporate Locusts.

Sarita Bartlett, Senior Portfolio Manager and Head of Socially Responsible Research,
Storebrand Investments, Norway

The Chrysalis Economy describes the critical attributes of CEOs of the 21st century if we are to have a sustainable world for our grandchildren to enjoy. The central message: business leaders must have the understanding and courage to broaden their traditional value creation models to address and develop solutions to important social and environmental issues as part of ongoing business strategy.

Paul Tebo, Vice President for Health, Safety and Environment, DuPont, USA

John Elkington has served us up another beautiful banquet of metaphors and analyses of the surprising ways in which the business world is moving toward sustainability. His brilliant presentation of the four types of corporate chrysalids and their transformation, and of the learning flywheel with successive rounds of innovation, are alone worth the price of the book.

Paul H Ray, Ph.D., co-author of *The Cultural Creatives: How 50 Million People are Changing the World*, and Executive Vice President of American LIVES, Inc., USA

The Chrysalis Economy is a can-do book ... John Elkington offers a kind – but firm – guiding hand through the maze of values, responsibilities and accountabilities now facing 'business', whether it operates in for-profit or not-for-profit mode.

Maria Adebowale, Director, Capacity; Member, Sustainable Development Commission; Trustee, Black Environment Network, UK

John Elkington's perceptive analysis provides a clear blueprint for positive - and profitable – corporate action to protect the environment. We await the results!

Steve Warshal, Editor, *Greenpeace Business*, UK

Another book packed full of real cases and unique insights from an author who continues to set the pace in discovering and defining the real potential for sustainability in business.

Dr David Wheeler, Erivan K Haub Professor in Business and Sustainability, Schulich School of Business, York University, Canada

John is simply the field's maestro of incisive and enlightening metaphors – listen for the 'pings' going off in people's heads as they read this, his latest book.

Simon Zadek, author of *The Civil Corporation*; Chair, Institute of Social and Ethical Accountability, UK

For CEOs navigating a path toward a sustainable future, *The Chrysalis Economy* provides insightful lessons from the past; a well calibrated compass for the uncharted future; and some powerful and pragmatic diagnostic tools to assess current positioning.

Jonathan Shopley, CEO, Future Forests, UK

John Elkington's newest work, *The Chrysalis Economy*, offers breath-taking insight into the most important trends of our new century and their implications for business and society. A thinker of extraordinary creativity and depth, he once again demonstrates why leaders all over the world turn to him as advisor and guide.

Robert Kinloch Massie, Executive Director, Coalition for Environmentally Responsible Economies (CERES), USA

The Chrysalis Economy is a beautiful metaphor. Its focus on transformation and on growing concerns about the public realm, not just profits, marks a shift away from the masculine values of late 20th century society, which have done so much damage to our social ecology, towards a more feminized, nurturing and sustainable model of development.

Helen Wilkinson, Founder and CEO, genderquake, UK

JOHN **ELKINGTON**

the Chrysalis economy

**HOW CITIZEN CEOs AND CORPORATIONS
CAN FUSE VALUES AND VALUE CREATION**

CAPSTONE

First published 2001 by
Capstone Publishing Ltd (A John Wiley & Sons Co.)
8 Newtec Place
Magdalen Road
Oxford OX4 1RE
United Kingdom
http://www.capstoneideas.com

British Library Cataloguing in Publication Data
A CIP catalogue record for this book is available from the British Library

ISBN 1-84112-142-8

Typeset by
Forewords, 109 Oxford Road, Cowley, Oxford
Printed and bound by
T.J. International Ltd, Padstow, Cornwall

This book is printed on acid-free paper

Contents

Acknowledgements

Assassinations, barricades, the Viet Cong's Tet Offensive, the Soviets crushing the 'Prague Spring': 1968 certainly looms in the memory. The film *2001* (page 227) first screened and the 21st century seemed a distant dream. 'Red herrings' surfaced in their millions in Placentia Boy, Newfoundland (page 141). 1968 was also the year I met Elaine. We married, raised two daughters, co-founded several organizations. I wrote books, of which this is the sixteenth. Throughout, these three sustained me: Elaine, Gaia and Hania. So, given that *The Chrysalis Economy* commandeered my brain and both kitchen tables for months, I dedicate the book to them, hoping they will feel it worth the effort. My hunch: they will recognize the book for what it is, a manifesto, mapping out another 30 years' work.

A warm thank you, too, to those who helped get the show on the road: my agent, Sara Menguc, my editor at Capstone, Mark Allin, and his colleagues Richard Burton and Katherine Hieronymous.

At SustainAbility, words cannot express my gratitude to Geoff (Lye) and Jodie (Thorpe) for helping me carve out the time necessary to produce the book. Geoff has provided crucial insights and support during recent years, a fact underscored by the fact that two of the key figures in the book are his (Figures 9.2 and 10.2).

In the SustainAbility Core Team, my sincere thanks also go to Seb Beloe, Alex Cutler, Christèle Delbé (now with PIRC), Oliver Dudok van Heel, Lynne Elvins, Shelly Fennell, Julia Hailes, Eliott Jackson, Julia Jobmann, Judy Kuszewski, Tomoo Machiba, Tell Münzing, Eva Okonkwo, Tom Owen, Kavita Prakash-Mani, Jan Scherer, Frances Scott, Nicola Shukla, Katy Terroni, Virginia Terry, Franceska van Dijk, and Peter Zollinger. Many people read various elements of the book while it was in preparation, but I am particularly grateful to Peter and Oliver for their insightful comments.

But the most powerful set of comments came from (SustainAbility council member) Jane Nelson, of the International Business Leaders Forum. Thank you Jane. And thank you, too, to Rupert Bassett, who developed the SustainAbility logos that appear in the following pages.

ERRATA

The publishers would like to draw the reader's attention to the following errors in the text:

Page no.

v	line 10: Are you working for a Corporate Caterpillar, . . .
ix	line 9: One more example of what . . .
	line 10: We will encounter many . . .
x	line 36: London/New York, 23 July 2001
11	line 8: . . . in one of the worst pollution incidents . . .
57	line 14: . . . voluntary organizations.
64	line 3 up: . . . Future Growth Value (FGV) . . .
70	line 9: . . . of 'butterfly'.
77	line 5: . . . difficult to spotlight . . .
84	line 27: . . . metamorphosis still has . . .
123	line 7: . . . and for every one you remove . . .
138	line 4: . . . greed and fear in the . . .
161	line 1: . . . three environmental, . . .
180	line 23: . . . very much harder next time around.
203	line 3: . . . at work developing key performance indicators.
207	line 11: . . . environmental systems; . . .
210	line 32: One interesting question . . .
213	line 23: . . . second largest enclosed space . . .
214	line 32: . . . their shoulders. Fuller's work . . .
228	line 1: . . . 747 Clipper *Maid of the Seas* . . .
230	line 30: . . . no organization can afford . . .
244	line 32: . . . corporate social responsibility (CSR) . . .
264	line 12: . . . to: info@sustainability.com
276	line 7: Alan AtKisson

Others I warmly thank are: Roger Adams, Jacqueline Aloisi de Larderel, Ray Anderson, Matt Arnold, Alan AtKisson, Richard Barrett, Rupert Bassett, Nancy Bennet, Dave Berdish, Thilo Bode, Rebecca Calahan Klein, Sir Geoffrey Chandler, Ian Christie, Ben Cohen, Jill Ker Conway, Roger Cowe, Tom Delfgaauw, Linda Descano, Meredith Doig, Bob Dunn, Ralph Earle III, Murray and Dobrina Edmonds, Pierre Ferrari, Alois Flatz, Adam Ford, Bill Ford, Rob Frederick, Hilary French, Claude Fussler, Jeff Gates, Paul Gilding, Tom Gladwin, Ulrich Goluke, Rob Gray, Josephine Green, Jerry Greenfield, Molly Harriss Olson, Stuart Hart, Paul Hawken, Melanie Hewitson, Julia Butterfly Hill, Paul Hohnen, Helen Holdaway, Jean Horstman, Rupert Howes, Erin Jancauskas, Vernon Jennings, Ian Keay, Brian Kelly, Peter Kinder, Fiona King, Lise Kingo, Frans Knecht, Peter Knight, Niklas Kreander, Dave Larcker, Joe Laur, Elisabeth Laville, David Layton, Mark Lee, Jean-Pierre Lehmann, Tore and Monica Linghede, Kim Loughran, Jim Lovelock, Laurent Marriott Leduc, Bob Massie, Linda McMahon, Charles Medawar, Doug Miller, Sir Mark Moody-Stuart, Titus Moser, Max Nicholson, Diane Osgood, Mads Øvlisen, Alan Pedder, Jacques Pètry, Janet Ranganathan, Jerry Ravetz, Steen Riisgaard, John Roberts, Henry Saint-Bris, Jim Salzman, Hein Sas, Sara Schley, Dave Scott, Peter Senge, Sarah Severn, Bob Shapiro, Jonathan Shopley, Dana Smirin, Andrea Spencer-Cooke, Brian and Delyse Springett, Ulrich Steger, Ab Stevels, Paul Tebo, Teoh Cheng Hai, Sophia Tickell, Wouter van Dieren, Jan Paul van Soest, Steve Viederman, Mark Wade, Rob Walvis, Steve Warshal, Phil Watts, David Wheeler, Jan-Olaf Willums, Des Wilson, Paul Woodcock, Alan Young, Simon Zadek, Jeff Zalla and Debbie Zemke.

Finally, my gratitude goes to everyone else who has been part of the huge number of conversations that fed into to the book. You know who you are. The weaknesses of *The Chrysalis Economy* are undeniably mine; any strengths reflect an increasingly powerful movement determined to ensure we all treat Earth as if we intended to stay.

Foreword

After working with business for over 25 years, I wanted to capture some things I had learned about how transformed business models, companies, value webs and markets can help build more sustainable economies and societies. The target audience: anyone affected by – or interested in – the impacts of business and its capacity to improve matters. And these days that's most of us.

The Chrysalis Economy is about evolution: corporate, technological, economic, political, and above all, cultural evolution. The tension between evolving societal values and different models of value creation is central to my story. This tension is calling forth new styles of business leadership. Indeed, much of the work I have done over the past decade has been at the direct invitation of CEOs and other business leaders. They have included: Mads Øvlisen at Novo Nordisk, Alan Pedder at ICI Polyurethanes and Tioxide, Phil Watts and Sir Mark Moody-Stuart at Royal Dutch/Shell, Bob Shapiro at Monsanto, Jacques Pètry at SITA, Ben Cohen and Jerry Greenfield at Ben & Jerry's, and Bill Ford, Jr. and Jac Nasser at the Ford Motor Company.

In their various ways, they have all struggled with Catch-23. Catch-23? It's now some 40 years since I read Joseph Heller's outrageous novel *Catch-22* in a school dormitory. Despite the tightly-enforced silence rule, I laughed helplessly at Captain Yossarian's misadventures. Much of the humor lay in the 'no-win' aspect of Catch-22, ruling that bomber crew could only be grounded (thereby avoiding dangerous missions) if proved to be crazy. Catch-22, however, noted that a concern for one's own safety on bombing missions was a sign of a rational mind *and* specified that all a crazy airman had to do to be grounded was to ask for permission not to fly. The catch: ask to be grounded and you were clearly no longer crazy.

'Catch-23' surfaced in the 1970s, as a label used by Washington insiders for even more complicated situations. For reasons that will become clear, I will apply the term to the business end of sustainable development (SD). The emerging Catch-23 agenda for business has three main dimensions: economic prosperity (which business knows something about), environmental regeneration (which generally it doesn't) and social equity (which always used to be government's business, didn't it?).

Together, these three dimensions make up the triple bottom line agenda. In retrospect, elements of this agenda have driven my work since the early 1970s. Throughout, the focus has been on helping to make business, markets and the globalizing economy more sustainable. As the work has evolved, my colleagues and I have tried to share our learning. In addition to some 20 reports we have published since founding the international consultancy and think-tank SustainAbility in 1987, I have produced a number of business books focusing on different aspects of SD, most recently *Cannibals with Forks* in 1997, which first introduced the term *triple bottom line*. One more example of Darwinian evolutionist Richard Dawkins has called a *meme*, or the cultural equivalent of a gene. We will encounter any more examples in the following pages (see, for example, page 231).

Once *Cannibals* appeared, our corporate work grew even faster, worldwide, and shifted to a different level in companies. The evolving SD agenda requires companies and other business organizations to focus on – and improve – their performance in economic (not just financial), social and environmental terms. Partly because of the complexity of the agenda, and partly because the necessary tradeoffs often cannot be made at departmental or business unit level, much of that work has been at, or near, board level. Clearly, much of the drama has been in these tradeoffs, but increasingly the spotlight will be on innovative attempts to achieve win–win–win outcomes.

That's part of the story I wanted to tell. But I also want to give some idea of how the necessary corporate and market transformations are best achieved. And that's much harder. It's hard because we are venturing into new territory, where new rules apply. Like the navigators of the great Age of Exploration, and the aviators, astronauts and cosmonauts of the 20th century, the business world is moving into a new realm, a new opportunity space. Unfortunately, many existing corporate vessels were designed for other tasks, other eras, and are highly unlikely to survive the journey.

Just as great navigators set sail before anyone had much of a grip on the nautical sciences, so many early aviators plummeted to earth before we got a real grip on aeronautics. Like it or not, many companies (even entire value-webs) will crash and burn as they attempt some of the challenges outlined below. We will zero in on a number which have already spun out of control, not to gloat but to learn and build upon.

Directly or indirectly, I have been involved in many of these transformation processes. To date, a fair proportion of them, in the words of my friend and colleague Professor Ulrich Steger of IMD, have been "over-promised and under-delivered." True, but much real progress has been made nonetheless. Nor am I and my colleagues alone in the work. Indeed, one feature of the book is a survey of a dipstick sample of those doing similar work around the world (Chapter 13). If we are to sidestep the 21st century version of Catch-23, we must hope that their numbers will expand and their influence increase massively.

One unmistakable sign of success would be growing numbers of companies able, in the words of boxer Mohammed Ali, to "float like a butterfly" in the social and environmental dimensions, yet "sting like a bee" in the commercial domain.

But, as we look for such successes, we should constantly remind ourselves of three things: First, many key demographic, environmental and political trends continue to move in the wrong direction, as Chapter 2 explains. Second, what the top 10 percent of the Fortune 500 are doing (and this is where people like myself often tend to work) is rarely an accurate indication of what the remaining 90 percent are doing, or intend to do. And, third, much of the real action will increasingly happen outside the current rich world, in countries like Brazil, China, India, Indonesia or South Africa. They are not well covered in the following pages, a failing that will look more significant as the years pass.

A final point. Whether we like it or not, and whether we support globalization, localization or some form of 'glocalization', the world will continue getting smaller – and we will all become ever more interconnected and interdependent. This trend will be a central 21st century fact of life. If we ignore the new imperatives, the 21st century could be even worse than the 20th. But this is an optimistic book. It assumes that we can – and will – make a difference, shifting our world onto more sustainable paths. The focus is on Citizen CEOs and their corporations, but their longer term success will depend on the degree to which the rest of us (whether in business, government or civil society) decide to play our part in the biggest transformation our species has yet embarked upon. Having a Citizen CEO – or being profiled in the following pages – is no guarantee of long-term (or even short-term) financial success. To take just one example, Lend Lease – profiled in Chapter 6 – was in real financial difficulties as *The Chrysalis Economy* went to press, its share price suffering badly. We should not be surprised. The uncomfortable fact is that many early corporate pioneers will fall by the wayside, even as some of the paths and navigational tools they developed prove invaluable to those who follow, mapping out and settling the vast new opportunity spaces.

John Elkington
SustainAbility Ltd/Inc
London/York, 2001
www.sustainability.com

Executive summary

The Chrysalis Economy is three things in one. First, it is an early guide to new forms of capitalism that will eventually dominate the global economy (box 1 and Figure 0.2). Second, it is an exploration of the evolving roles of Citizen CEOs and other business leaders (box 2) in making sense of the new business environment – and in breaking through both the Values and Value Barriers (Chapter 4). Third, it is an introduction to three simple management tools designed to help business leaders understand and manage the emerging sustainability agenda.

The three tools are: The MetaMatrix (Figure 0.3), which helps track corporate metamorphosis and distinguishes four main types of company or value web; the Sustainable Business Value Model (see Figure 10.2, page 199), linking 10 forms of value added to 10 different dimensions of sustainable development; and the Learning Flywheel (Figure 0.4), mapping out a path for companies aiming for market-beating triple bottom line performance.

The book's title signals my conclusion that the global economy is entering a protracted period of profound metamorphosis. Economic, social and environmental pressures are converging at a time of growing global interdependence to create the conditions for an era of dramatic technological, corporate and market transformation. As Chapter 5 shows, there are strong parallels between the natural process of metamorphosis and the corporate and market transformation processes described in the following pages.

The subtitle underscores my core message: sustainability is now emerging as the #1 global business challenge. And a key part of the challenge is the growing tension between emerging social values and traditional forms of value creation. Business leaders and companies are racing to assess the associated risks. Many are also positioning themselves to exploit the potential opportunities. But below the surface lies a huge landmine, Catch-23, best stated as a three-pronged paradox:

- *First, Earth's human population has quadrupled over the last century, with a further near-doubling forecast. Meanwhile, the 20:80 nature of today's world, with 20 percent of the world population consuming 80 percent of its resources, is unlikely to be socially and politically sustainable in a world of some 8–10 billion.*

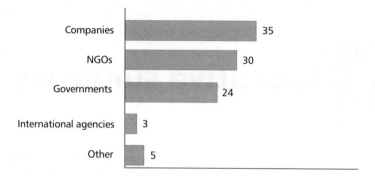

Figure 0.1 Where will SD leadership come from?
Source: GlobeScan survey of experts, Environics International, 2001.

Remember: over 90 percent of these new people will be born into the have-not world.

• *Second, even at today's levels of agricultural and industrial production, the global economy is causing unprecedented environmental problems, including ozone depletion, climate change, deforestation, dramatic species loss and the collapse of major fisheries. We currently consume some 40 percent of the world's plant resources each year; can we expect to consume 70–80 percent without causing utter devastation?*

• *Third, with the collapse of most communist regimes and the relative weakening of governments worldwide, business is increasingly expected to take the lead in delivering sustainable development (SD). Figure 0.1 shows the findings of a recent survey of SD experts. Many business leaders welcome this emerging reality, but this is where the 'catch' comes in. Satisfying the new responsibilities is likely to be impossible without levels of public commitment and support – and government intervention – that are not currently available. As the political heat grows, it will be increasingly clear that new forms of both corporate and global governance are needed.*

The obvious danger is that business will be in the hot seat, landed with responsibility for an evolving crisis that is far beyond its collective capacity to solve or even manage. But every crisis contains opportunity. Indeed, there are grounds for cautious optimism. We have already made striking progress in the areas of environmental and human rights. And, for the more commercially minded, we now stand on the threshold of market opportunities undreamed of in the last century. To have any hope of resolving the Catch-23 paradox, however, we must dramatically accelerate the processes of corporate, technological, economic and – ultimately – cultural metamorphosis.

Box 1: Blips on the Screen

The Chrysalis Economy

In the boom years of the 1990s, many people came to believe that wealth could be created in almost infinite quantities from ever-shrinking amounts of material, thanks to rapidly evolving human ingenuity. At times, it almost seemed that the value of the stock markets had become independent of economic activity. The dotcoms, spawning in huge numbers, were at the sizzling edge of change. Nevada's Burning Man festival (panel 3, page 43) symbolized the wild energy and ambitions of many driving the revolution. But, in retrospect, the sea-change in market sentiment during 2000 heralded the dawn of the Chrysalis Economy.

This new era marks not just the end of the excesses of the first stage of the new economy, but also the beginning of the end for the less sustainable aspects of 20th century capitalism. Figure 0.2 sketches the characteristics of the new order. Some of the crucial economic, social and political characteristics are described in the following pages.

Although we have been tinkering with our technologies, business models and value webs for decades, hoping to achieve anything between 5 percent and Factor 2 (50 percent) improvements in their eco-efficiency, the 21st century's demographic and lifestyle trends will demand Factor 4 (75 percent), Factor 10 (90 percent) and even higher levels of improvement. We will need to innovate both at the level of the *function* (i.e. not just a better car, but better mobility or access solutions) and at the level of the *total system* (i.e. how we design cities and, for example, control urban sprawl).

Nor will the innovations simply be technical or managerial. They will also involve economic, social and moral transitions. Among the key characteristics of the Chrysalis Economy:

- Dramatically greater transparency, as the internet sends the 'CNN World' into overdrive.
- Revolutionary new forms of corporate and political accountability, right across the triple bottom line (TBL) agenda.
- Surprisingly ambitious definitions of social equity and corporate social responsibility.

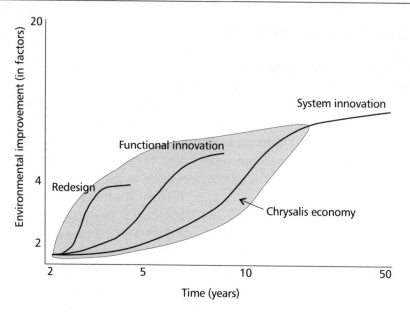

Figure 0.2   The Chrysalis Economy, 2000–2030.
Source: Stevels, Brezet and Weterings, adapted with permission by author.

- Growing tensions between values and traditional forms of value creation.
- Status quo-shaking strategic partnerships between pioneering companies and innovative public interest groups.
- Radical dematerialization, with most of the market-transforming successes being achieved by companies we have hardly (or never) heard of.
- The conscious, strategic incubation by both business and governments of more sustainable technologies, business models and value webs.
- Rapidly evolving financial market interest in relative corporate performance against the triple bottom line – and in the evolving links to long-term value creation.

Box 2: Blips on the Screen

The Citizen CEO

Formal evaluations of CEOs are now commonplace. But how should we assess a business leader's progress in terms of sustainability and its TBL agenda? That's a question we begin to tackle in Chapters 6 and 10. No single CEO or business leader so far models all the desirable characteristics of the Citizen CEO, but growing numbers have been displaying at least some characteristics of the breed.

Based on the cases described in the following pages, and on work done by my friends and colleagues Jane Nelson and Peter Zollinger on what they dub the L.E.A.D.E.R. agenda, these would include:

- A strong vision.
- An acute sense of commercial and political timing.
- The survival skills and stamina to pursue the agenda – whether it is labeled corporate citizenship (CC), corporate social responsibility (CSR) or sustainable development (SD) – through the inevitable market squalls and storms.
- Well-developed peripheral vision – coupled with a real concern for (and capacity to manage) multiple forms of capital.
- An appreciation of diversity in all its forms.
- Unusual sensitivity to the full range of past, present and potential future impacts caused by the company and its value web.
- The wisdom to create a culture of openness, honesty and constructive criticism.
- A readiness to walk the talk, adapting the business not just in compliance with the relevant laws and regulations, but also in response to emerging voluntary standards and societal values.
- An honest assessment of – and willingness to admit to – gaps in his or her understanding and performance, and a determination to remedy them.
- A genuine, inclusive desire to learn from others, inside and outside the company.
- More specifically, the capacity to learn from the inevitable failures – and to help others do likewise.
- Effective networking across his or her sector, and across the wider business community, with a particular focus on enlightening the darker corners of the financial world.
- A capacity to integrate TBL thinking, targets and performance from the boardroom to the workplace.

MetaMatrix	Low impact	High impact
Regenerative (increasing returns)	**BUTTERFLIES** 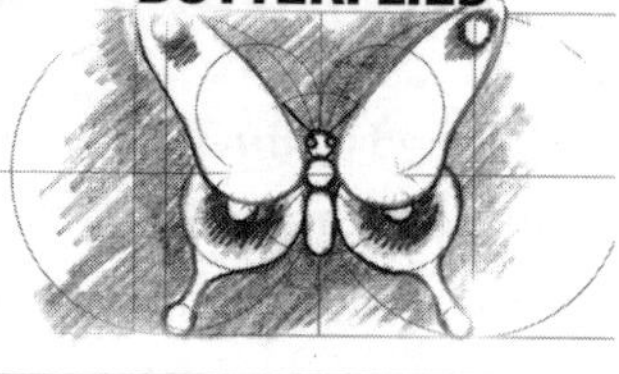 	**HONEYBEES** 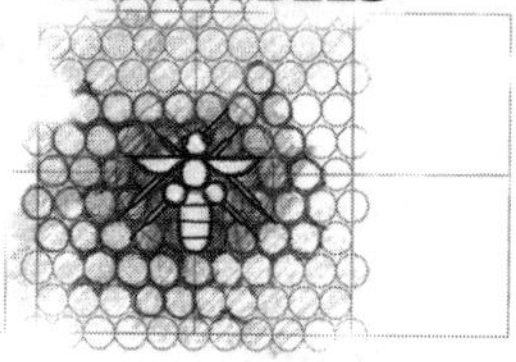
Degenerative (decreasing returns)	**CATERPILLARS** 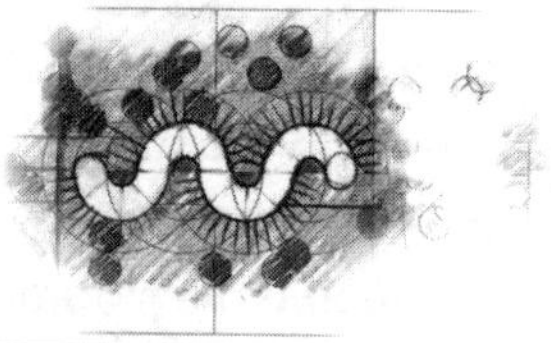 	**LOCUSTS** 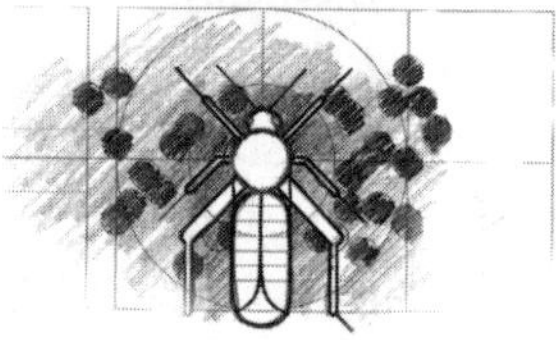

Figure 0.3   The MetaMatrix™. © SustainAbility.

- A willingness to believe that zero (e.g. accidents, health risks, waste, environmental impacts) is both desirable and achievable – and a determination to drive the business in this direction.
- A passion to identify, invest in and incubate more sustainable products, technologies, services and business models.
- A recognition that sustainability is a journey, not a destination
- An interest in legacy.
- A healthy sense of humor: he or she is going to need it!
- And luck, perhaps the most important factor of all.

The Chrysalis Economy is divided into 14 chapters, in five main sections. They cover: the drivers of change (Section I: Chrysalis); the processes of change (Section II: Metamorphosis); the stages of corporate transformation (Section III: Stages); five directions economic evolution may take in the coming decades (Section IV: Migrations); and selected sources of further information (Section V: Sources). Each chapter includes one or more boxes, and a panel, with the panel titles listed on page xx.

The five sections are as follows:

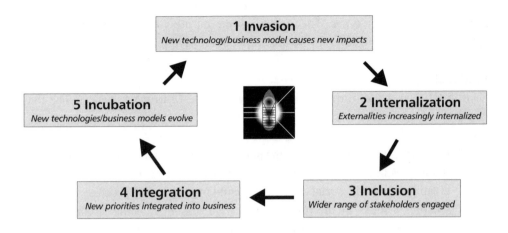

Figure 0.4   The Learning Flywheel™. © SustainAbility.

I CHRYSALI$

Section I introduces Catch-23 and explains how companies that want to overcome it must embark on a cycle of transformation, summarized in the Learning Flywheel (Figure 0.4 and Chapter 1). We then look at two factors that will increasingly drive economic and corporate transformation in the coming decades. The first, discussed in Chapter 2, is the 3P agenda, made up of *Planet* (environmental change), *People* (human rights, broadly defined) and *Politics* (global and corporate governance). Then, in Chapter 3, we review the implications of the 'New Economy' era and its aftermath.

II METAMORPHOSI$

Section II opens by introducing the MetaMatrix, distinguishing between companies or value-webs with either low or high impacts in relation to the degeneration or regeneration of natural and other critical forms of capital (Figure 0.3 and Chapter 4). Chapter 4 explores the two barriers embodied in the Catch-23 challenge: the Values Barrier (page 54) and the Value Barrier (page 66).

Chapter 5 then dives in deeper, comparing companies and value-webs with four insect types: *Locusts*, *Caterpillars*, *Butterflies* and *Honeybees*. Corporate Locusts and Caterpillars are both on the wrong side of the Values Barrier, while Corporate Caterpillars and Butterflies are on the wrong side of the Value Barrier. Corporate Locusts may have pushed through the Value Barrier, creating value for a narrow range of people, but they destroy various forms of capital in the process. Only Corporate Honeybees emerge on the right side of both the Values and Value Barriers.

Chapter 6 then investigates the new breed of 'Citizen CEOs', running companies of all four types. They include some business leaders who are seen as runaway successes, and several who are not – but all have something to teach us.

III STAGE$

Section III then works through the five stages of the Learning Flywheel. The five chapters here run as follows:

- Chapter 7 focuses on *invasion*, the natural process by which an innovation – be it a new technology or a new business model – invades an opportunity space, creating economic, social or environmental impacts in the process.
- Chapter 8 looks at the process of *internalization*, by which a company or value-web absorbs some of the costs previously externalized to society or the environment.
- Chapter 9 focuses on *inclusion*, the process by which a range of internal and external stakeholders are progressively engaged, their priorities established and their legitimate needs met.
- Chapter 10 explores the emerging challenge of *integration*, recalling how companies have handled previous agendas, among them environment, health and safety (EHS), total quality management (TQM), information technology (IT), shareholder value added (SVA) and corporate social responsibility (CSR).
- Finally, Chapter 11 looks at the prospects for *incubation*, considering how more sustainable technologies, industries and even entire economies might be incubated in today's highly unsustainable world.

IV MIGRATION$

Like the monarch butterflies of the Americas, the global economy is going to have to make an extraordinary migration. The Chrysalis Economy is simply the first step in the process.

Section IV, particularly Chapter 12, spotlights ways in which Citizen CEOs and other business leaders currently use scenarios to help them think through the sustainability agenda and its implications. Chapter 13 looks at the perspectives and priorities of some of those who guide companies through the CSR and SD mazes. And Chapter 14, the Afterword, then raises a difficult question: What happens if the world doesn't wake up, and the markets for more sustainable technologies, products and services don't evolve in time?

V SOURCE$

The Chrysalis Economy trawls through a huge amount of information and experience, but literally only skims the surface. So Section V lists references for the rest of the book, and suggests a small number of useful web-sites.

Box 3: Blips on the Screen

Butterfly effects

It's a global cliché. A butterfly flaps its wings in Brazil, the resulting turbulence gradually building to trigger a cascade of effects, including fierce storms in Texas, or along the USA's eastern seaboard. But the cliché gained new life when a laboratory study of the impact of genetically modified corn on America's favorite butterfly, the monarch, suggested that the results could be fatal for this "Bambi of the insect world".

Although the risk was later shown to have been exaggerated by the study's design, and respected scientists now argue that "this is not a very big issue", the monarch helped bring chemical and life sciences giant Monsanto to its corporate knees. Later, in Chapter 6, we hear from Monsanto's ex-CEO about some of the lessons he learned in the process.

Meanwhile, the butterfly effect has become a powerful metaphor for our increasingly interdependent world. Consider the story of asbestos worker Clarence Borel, recalled on page 187. Or remember what happened to American electoral ballot designer Theresa LePore. All she was trying to do was help old people vote. But she ended up throwing American politics into chaos. Angry Democrats even accused her of single-handedly stripping the presidency from Vice-President Al Gore.

LePore had decided that the ballot sheet should be spread across two pages, in what was called the 'butterfly ballot', to allow for larger print. Unfortunately, the new form confused some folk, so they claimed they had mistakenly voted for the wrong candidate. 'Madame Butterfly' got her new name because her form looked like a butterfly, but she also provided another example of the butterfly effect in which small actions lead to mega-impacts.

Meanwhile, whether the economic trend line is up or down, the potential for turbulence is building. Business and markets are mutating, as both old and new economy business models evolve, as they say, at warp speed. Despite the reverses suffered by the dotcoms and other vanguard businesses of the new economy, one thing is clear: new forms of competition are generating new business models, new patterns of value creation. Some will be more sustainable than others, but how do we work out which is likely to be which?

Part of the answer lies in the extent to which business models align with (or change) societal values, present and future. To illuminate the interplay between values and value creation, often powered by unexpected butterfly effects, a series of panels appears through the book. From the snow-capped Alps to the sun-scorched deserts of Nevada, from the worldview of an anti-logging campaigner who spent 738 days up a tree named Luna to that of an astronaut who briefly stood on the Moon and looked back at distant Earth, the panels spotlight ideas, people and trends now driving economic and cultural metamorphosis. They run as follows:

1. Ten Minutes to Save the World – page 9
2. North Sizzles, South Sweats – page 18
3. Storms Blind Burning Man – page 43
4. Interdependence Day – page 68
5. Views from the Moon – page 96
6. Five Labors – page 120
7. Devil's Element – page 141
8. Going for Green Gold – page 163
9. $1 Billion Bet – page 182
10. CEO Mecca Gets Religion – page 203
11. Ray on the Carpet – page 220
12. Transformed Worlds – page 237
13. Pawns in Their Game? – page 256
14. Reexamine the Impossible – page 261

PART I

CHRYSALI$

Chrysalis comes from the Greek for gold, reflecting the fact that many chrysalises have metallic markings.

The chrysalis has come to symbolize transformation, a fleeting stage between different states of being.

As a condition of future development, metamorphosis requires letting go of the past and accepting a new future.

A chrysalis is mysterious, fragile and uncertain in outcome.

So, too, the 'Corporate Chrysalids' as they wrestle with Catch-23.

CHAPTER 1

Introduction
Inside the Chrysalis Economy

Capitalism may have won the Cold War, but there was a catch: Catch-23. As we see in Chapter 2, the emerging global challenge to capitalism can be boiled down into a 3P agenda: People, Planet and Politics. Indeed, the evidence suggests that business leaders and their companies are entering a period unlike anything in their experience.

On the political front, Communism, Socialism and Christianity may be somewhat out of fashion, but their saner champions had a point, indeed several. First, a world of gross, highly visible extremes between those who have access to material wealth and those who don't is unlikely to be sustainable, socially or politically. Second, business cycles periodically make the Market an uncomfortable God: the bursting of the dotcom bubble may prove to have ushered in an unusually challenging period in our economic history. And, third, a global economy which aggressively undermines its own ecological foundations, as ours is doing, will join all previous civilizations in the dustbin of history sooner rather than later.

That's the bad news. The good news is that companies, value-webs and economies can evolve. Indeed, if we know where to look, we can see the process at work all around us. We may argue whether it is for better or worse, but the internet is reaching into every aspect of our lives. It is the most powerful agent yet of globalizing capitalism, which is itself transforming the world economy. Despite the dotcom crash, new technologies, business models and value webs are radically reworking the economic landscape, with profound financial, social and environmental implications. At the same time, powerful values-driven movements are spinning a virtual cocoon of new laws, standards and expectations around the globe, spurring the process of corporate metamorphosis.

So, while the definitions may vary, there is no question that a new economy is evolving. But to simply focus on digital technologies and dotcoms is to miss the key point. Consciously or not, we are incubating a global economy that is dramatically more integrated than anything we have seen to date. With integration come new forms of responsibility and accountability. If we move fast enough, and in the right direction, the resulting forms of economic production should also be more sustainable. In the process, however, business success will be defined and achieved in new ways. Indeed, new forms of economics and accounting are evolving to track and evaluate these trends.

And there is much to track. Globalization has had a spectacular impact over the past decade. Through the nineties, the much-vaunted new economy generated many millions of new jobs from Malaysia to Mexico, and created an extraordinary cornucopia of innovative products for western consumers.[1] Among other things, it brought phone service to some 300 million households in the developing world and drove the transfer of nearly $2 trillion from rich countries to poor through equity, bond investments, and commercial loans. Among the useful (if largely unintended) side-effects, it also helped topple a number of dictators by taking the lid off their regimes.

The downside is that globalization has also resulted in – or exposed – a wide range of labor, human rights and environmental abuses. The demonstrations in the streets of Seattle, Washington, DC, London and Prague in 1999 and 2000 provided a much-needed opportunity to look this gift-horse in the mouth before things went from bad to worse. The current system, as UN assistant secretary-general John G. Ruggie put it, is "unsustainable". As a political economist at Columbia University, he has investigated how previous golden ages of capitalism, such as the one at the end of the 19th century, turned sour. "To survive," Ruggle says, the various forms of capitalism "must be imbedded in broader social concerns."

And that's the way corporate evolution seems to be headed. In a dramatic trend affecting most rich world economies, new forms of corporate accountability are emerging. Companies like Shell, Monsanto and Nike have been hit hardest, but some of them are accepting fast – while many others are now increasingly aware that new forms of responsibility and accountability are being demanded. Some companies, like Unocal with its operations in Myanmar, may still choose to go against the flow, but the trend is clear. A process of corporate and wider economic transformation has begun.

THE METAMORPHOSIS METAPHOR

That said, will the transformation go fast and deep enough to make a real difference? That's the question addressed below. There are many reasons why companies and other business organizations decide to embark upon transformation processes. One is that they know that the public is becoming increasing uneasy about corporate power. In a recent *Business Week* survey, nearly three-quarters of Americans felt business has gained too much power in recent years.[2] Very rarely, a CEO or company owner has an epiphany, a conversion experience, emerging with a transformed vision and set of values. But most transformation processes ultimately link back to perceived market risks and opportunities.

Like caterpillars, many companies and other organizations enter the process of metamorphosis confident they will emerge as something like butterflies. But in the business world, no less than in nature, there are complications. There are competitors to be considered, alongside the commercial equivalents of predators, disease vectors and parasites, making the whole business more precarious and hazardous than optimists might imagine. It has even been suggested that we need a 'Death Valley' with equal status to Silicon Valley to take care of all the companies – old and new – that will die in the coming years, many as a result of unsuccessful metamorphoses. "Organizational death is as necessary a part of our economic system as organizational birth," as Andrew Campbell of Ashridge Strategic Management Centre has put it.[3]

Although a chrysalis may be buffered against external changes for a short time, undergoing metamorphosis in turbulent times can be a dangerous, punishing business. And to make things worse, there are those who argue that the high-tech cocoon we are busily constructing for ourselves has a serious, basic design flaw. Although it may work for a large – even growing – fraction of today's global population of six billion-plus, they argue it won't serve for the population of some 10 billion expected by the middle of the century.

Before I explain the central metaphor used in the book, however, it's only fair to say that *The Chrysalis Economy* itself mutated wildly in the writing. At times, I felt the book was writing me rather than the other way around. It builds on an earlier book, *Cannibals with Forks*, published in 1997.[4] This spotlighted the extraordinary corporate transformations being driven both by emerging societal values and by what I dubbed the triple bottom line performance and targets increasingly demanded by customers and markets.

As the new century dawned, the concept of sustainability shot up the business agenda.[5] Europe, together with countries like Canada and Australia, picked up on it first, but some parts of US business (even under George W. Bush) are now racing up the curve. True, most business leaders still use the term when it suits them, and defined in ways that meet their immediate needs, but the triple bottom line definition of corporate sustainability has gained considerable ground. As a result, high-profile companies are expected to meet not just financial targets, but also a growing range of closely interlinked economic, social, ethical and environmental objectives. Today, sustainable development (SD) is energetically debated both in corporate boardrooms and at meetings like the once secretive Davos Summit, organized each year by the World Economic Forum (panel 10, page 203).

In *Cannibals*, I wondered how the early corporate SD pioneers and champions could sustain their momentum? What I labeled 'corporate cannibalism' was rampant, in the form of a wave of hugely destabilizing corporate merger and acquisition (M&A) deals and the attendant commotion. So powerful was the 'urge to merge' it even sparked party games. Merge Federal Express and UPS, we were told, and you get FED UP. Honeywell, Imasco and Home Oil might come together to create Honey I'm Home. Or, for the really ambitious, you could try welding together elements of Zippo Manufacturing, Audi Motors, Dofasco and Dakota Mining – and end up with Zip Audi Do Da!

No doubt most boards involved in that M&A activity had higher things on their minds, but it certainly made it tougher to keep them – and their employees – focused on anything else. Hang the future, you could almost hear senior executives think: My job's at stake here and now! The corporate citizenship (CC), corporate social responsibility (CSR) and SD agendas have often hung on by their fingernails in the midst of all this corporate restructuring.

Nor have the pressures abated, with major mergers including those between AOL and Time-Warner, and Chase Manhattan Corp and J.P. Morgan & Co. *The Economist* even noted that: "such has been the pace of change in global finance that nothing seems unthinkable anymore."[6] Worse, as *Business Week* put it, "as the number and scale of takeovers soar, the tally and scale of duds are rising spectacularly."[7] With the odds stacked towards failure, commentators began to see many mega-mergers as little more than a side-effect of CEO hubris, coupled with the willingness of boards to rubber-stamp deals.

The merger boom was further fuelled by the advent of the new economy (see Chapter 3). Indeed, for those interested in corporate and value-web transformations, the collision zone between the old and new economies is where such processes have been at their most intense, even frantic. Hence the central metaphor underlying the following pages.

Where (corporate) cannibalism served as the key metaphor in *Cannibals*, in *The Chrysalis Economy* the link is to the extraordinary, natural process of metamorphosis. In its economic equivalent, the resource-intensive, atom-based old economy is mutating into a dematerializing, bit-driven new economy. Only if today's Corporate Locusts and Caterpillars can become Corporate Butterflies and Honeybees can we have any chance of creating truly sustainable forms of capitalism. And in making the transition, successful companies will find themselves moving

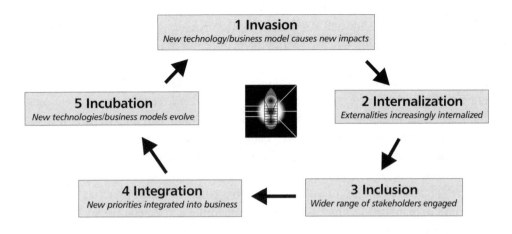

Figure 1.1 Learning Flywheel 1.0. © SustainAbility

through a cycle of change, sketched out in the Learning Flywheel (Figure 1.1) – and explained in Chapters 7–11.

ALL ABOARD THE FLYWHEEL!

As we work around the Learning Flywheel, we will zoom in on ongoing change processes – some successful, some not – in some of the world's best-known companies. When successful, such processes show startling similarities with natural world processes that transform ravenous, earthbound caterpillars into gossamer-light butterflies. When unsuccessful, however, they can tear apart a company, rupturing key links in its value chain. The outcome can be a company or value-web digested by the economic world's version of maggots.

The process of change can start in many different ways. Conversations like that highlighted in panel 1 (page 9) are often critical first steps. Having looked at some of the outcomes of their work in earlier chapters, we consider the role of change agents in more depth in Chapter 13. But this is not an attempt to redo the work of

'When you have to turn into a chrysalis – you will some day, you know – and then after that into a butterfly, I should think you'll feel a little queer, won't you?' (Alice to the Caterpillar, in *Alice's Adventures in Wonderland*)

people like Art Kleiner, with his insightful study of the role of 'corporate heretics' in *The Age of Heretics*.[8] Indeed, it's interesting that Kleiner ends his book by talking about the sustainability-focused work of people like Paul Hawken and Amory Lovins.

No, the aim here is to build on such work and show how leading companies are evolving in this area. As Kleiner notes, "corporate heretics may be the closest thing we have, in our self-contradictory time, to genuine heroes. They provide the unsung conscience of our civilization." These are the people that my colleagues and I seek to help in the process of corporate transformation. Fine, but why label the cycle of transformation as a flywheel?

The answer is that a flywheel, a rotating wheel designed to act as an energy store and to regulate machinery, builds up momentum and kinetic energy with every successive stroke of a reciprocating engine. In the same way, if successfully handled, each successive move around the Learning Flywheel can build up a store of kinetic energy in a company or other business organization.

The reciprocal expecation is that once an organization starts along this path of transformation, helping the entire world go round in more sustainable ways, the easier it becomes to continue – and the harder it becomes to shift back to old, unsustainable patterns of behavior. We will look at the evidence, some of which supports the thesis, some of which does not.

Meanwhile, the very survival of our industrial species depends on our ability to accelerate the conversion of today's caterpillar economies and corporations into the sustainable economies and value-webs that tomorrow's world will demand. This conversion process will initially be driven not so much by governments as by business. And business, in the end, will be driven by the interests, concerns and passions of individuals and communities. Few will go as far as Julia 'Butterfly' Hill (panel 4, page 68), but growing numbers are prepared to take a stand – to selectively target or avoid companies they see as being in the wrong.

In response, as part of a generational shift now transforming the top levels of business, we see the emergence of a new breed of 'Citizen CEOs'. As a result, we are seeing some early-stage changes in corporate behavior. For example, the demerger document issued by Denmark's Novo Nordisk in preparation for splitting its business into Novo Nordisk (health care) and Novozymes (enzymes) explicitly referred to top management's determination to carry forward Novo's triple bottom line philosophy into the new order.[9] Chapter 6 spotlights this Citizen CEO trend – and some of the hopes, fears and ambitions that drive these people.

PANEL 1

Ten minutes to save the world

This 'Dear John' e-mail came through while I was working on the book. It spotlights the challenges that internal, values-oriented champions face in getting across their messages to value-focused CEOs and other business leaders. I have anonymized both the correspondent (Chrys) and their company, dubbing it Amoeba Inc, but have left the language to speak for itself. The only words I have changed would have given away the company's identity.

Dear John,

Next week, I will likely have all of 10 minutes to convince our company's No. 2 to incorporate sustainability/social responsibility considerations into the fabric/DNA of our company.

As background, we are listed on the relevant stock exchanges, are expanding rapidly in our region, and are building a presence in China. We provide a range of financial services, but Amoeba is still a fairly small player. We are seeking brand recognition, differentiation and, of course, to maximize shareholder value. But we have no well-developed values/ethics at group level, despite having offered ethical finance services for some time.

Values are there at some level, of course, though they are viewed differently in the different regions where we operate. They are not explicit and no employee could tell you with confidence what they are. We do a few things that can be described as philanthropic, but we have no community/social policy, no environmental strategy. Value is very much defined as financial (I'm sure you've heard all of this before!). The company is not badly run – but it could be so much better!

I believe passionately that this is a leadership opportunity in our sector and markets that is not incompatible with the stated objectives of our company. It is not incompatible with our brand, either. The brand's goals include innovation, passion and dynamism.

The No. 2 is responsible for the development of the brand and we are about to spend millions on promoting it in our markets.

So I have to act now to make a difference. I am not a lone voice here, indeed an influential ally has helped get me this meeting, but we don't yet have critical mass. As for our No. 2's social conscience, he/she seems to be of the old school of thought that says that "the business of business is business," with corporate progress measured in $.

To push our No. 2's button, I have to talk his/her language – to make this thing seem like a financial 'no brainer'. I want him/her to think, 'Hey, this has substance and warrants serious investigation before big $ are spent.' China may push a button, too. Our competitors are pouring into the country, with high expectations of a huge future market. But what will influence the purchase decisions of young Chinese people? So many have experienced first hand human rights abuses, pollution and corruption – will they seek out socially responsible companies to provide their pensions and other financial services?

I can only count on 10 minutes. What can I tell him/her that will blow his/her socks off?

I need evidence that sustainability pays, is not a fashion, and offers a sustainable, low risk strategy that will deliver shareholder value. And I also want to convince him/her that this does not mean 'back to square one', that we can work with brand principles that we already have and achieve many of the objectives that are already in place – for example, attracting and retaining talented people.

I will contact you over the next day or so, and hope that you can spare a few minutes to help set my course.

With thanks,

Chrys

We will return to the role of CSR and SD champions, and to the Amoeba Game, in Chapter 13. The gist of my answer to Chrys is captured in Chapters 7–11, which is why 10 minutes is rarely enough time to get the message across. But Chrys was successful. A new task-force was formed to review the challenge, chaired by the company's CEO.

CHAPTER 2

Beyond the limits
Planet, people and politics

It's an extraordinary story, and may even be true. It came to mind as I lunched with a director and several other top executives of a giant drug company in Basel, Switzerland. Novartis was in the news again. The business press was praising the company's chairman and CEO, Dan Vasella, for launching a new cancer drug.[10] And for those who don't track the industry, the company originated in the merger of two long-established Swiss chemical giants, Ciba-Geigy and Sandoz. Neither had an unblemished environmental reputation. But, of the two, Sandoz was the most notorious, because of its involvement in one of the worst pollution incident of modern times.

The disaster occurred in 1986, barely six months after the devastating Chernobyl nuclear accident in the Ukraine. And now, I recalled, a former CIA officer was claiming the Sandoz 'accident' was no such thing, indeed that there was a direct link back to Chernobyl.[11] The official – and media – stories after the Schweizerhalle disaster largely followed the same lines. Following a fire in Sandoz's giant storage halls, they were flooded by firefighters with about 13,000 cubic meters of water. As a result, tonnes of dangerous chemicals and a great deal of highly toxic mercury were flushed into the Rhine, killing millions of fish. Less than a week later, more than 150,000 dead eels surfaced – and the Rhine was dubbed the 'River of Death'.

It took almost a decade for the river to recover, and the accident's cause was never fully determined. A few weeks before that lunch, however, the former head of counter-terrorist operations for the CIA was quoted as saying that the Soviet Union had caused the disaster to distract world attention from the horrifying aftermath of Chernobyl. The KGB, it was alleged, had instructed the Stasi, East Germany's security police, to carry out "diversionary activities". The Stasi, we were told, had used the Sandoz contingency plan, filed with a Zurich insurance company, to plan the sabotage.

It was suspicious, the Novartis director mused, that the fires almost exactly followed the worst-case scenario laid out in the contingency plans. The same period had also seen a series of accidents affecting all the major German chemical companies, with the perhaps unintended effect of boosting the fortunes of Germany's Green Party. Cock-up or conspiracy? Well, whether or not we choose to believe the story, and the Novartis folk certainly weren't pushing it, one thing is clear. Major companies don't need any extra help from governments, friendly or hostile, when it comes to causing disasters.

But then neither are most governments blameless. Too often, we focus our concerns about the world's future on business, forgetting – or choosing to overlook – the fact that many of our most urgent problems are caused by megacities, power generation, farmers, fishermen, state industries, military activities and so on. They, too, are helping push the world's ecosystems beyond their limits. But, while the focus on business may be unfair at times, it still makes sense. If we can convert business to the sustainability agenda, the potential political and economic leverage on these other sectors could be dramatic.

PLANET, PEOPLE, POLITICS

This is an optimistic book, but looking deep into the third millennium there is plenty to be worried about. Physicist Stephen Hawking recently warned that humanity may well not survive the next thousand years, because of an asteroid impact, war or climate change.[12] Even so, a question I am often asked by business people is: How confident can we really be that the problem trends will continue? Clearly, a great deal will depend on the public and political responses.

One reason why the direst predictions of studies like 1972's *Limits to Growth* haven't come to pass, yet, is because at least some people heeded the warnings. The growing interest in sustainable development (SD) has been another contributory factor. The most popular definition runs as follows: "Development which meets the needs of the present without compromising the ability of future generations to meet their own needs."[13]

A phrase I coined some years ago to explain the triple bottom line agenda was 'People, Planet, Profit'. It was later used as a conference title in places as far apart as Sweden and South Africa, also turning up as the title of Shell's second sustainability report in its *Profits & Principles* series.[14] But in what follows I want to focus on a slightly different 3P agenda. This time, it kicks off with the *Planet* (in the form of the environmental agenda), whose health provides the ultimate bottom line. It then moves on to *People* (the human rights agenda, broadly defined), before parting company with the original 3P formula by spotlighting the world of *Politics* (represented by the rapidly mutating corporate and global governance agendas).

Switched-on readers will have spotted that this chapter's title is lifted from the 1992 book of the same name, a 20-years-on report from the team that gave us *Limits to Growth*.[15] The point made below, however, is not simply that our rapidly globalizing economic system has ruptured a succession of natural limits, like a runaway truck crashing through police road-blocks, but that it is also now thundering into a minefield, in the form of human rights and governance agendas. There are profound implications for both companies and the worlds of national and international politics.

Once again, the evidence is all around us. Even in a world of DVD-driven color, Hollywood still likes to present things in easy-to-grasp pitch-black and snow-white. So anyone who has watched the Columbia Pictures film *Erin Brockovich* will know that companies can behave badly, very badly. Despite odds heavily stacked against her, Brockovich, played in the film by Julia Roberts, fought for the rights of pollution victims – and won. The US utility Pacific Gas & Electric (PG&E) had to pay out $333 million to those suffering the health effects of hexavalent chromium pollution from its Hinkley plant. PG&E, in short, was branded in the courts as what we will later describe as a 'Corporate Locust'.

But this is not simply a feel-good story about latter-day Davids (in the form of Brockovich, aided and abetted by her legal partner, Ed Masry) taking on the might of corporate Goliaths. Increasingly, too, there are those who are determined to take on the globalizing capitalist system as a whole. To understand why, we need to understand why the cumulative impacts produced by Corporate Caterpillars and Locusts are seen to be potentially so dangerous.

Some scientists, most notably professor James Lovelock, have encouraged us to think of our home planet in terms of *geophysiology*, of planetary medicine, as though the planet were alive.[16] His theories may still be controversial, but the chances are that they will massively transform the way in which we view our planet in the coming century.

So if Earth were like any other patient, how might we set about reading her state of health – and that of her six billion-plus (going on seven) human inhabitants? Three possible answers: flip through the 276 pages of *State of the World*,[17] produced by the Worldwatch Institute, the 300 plus pages of *World Resources*,[18] by the World Resources Institute (WRI), or the 290 pages of the *Human Development Report*,[19] by the UN Development Program (UNDP). Let's do all three. By the end of this chapter, you'll be ahead of many experts. Frankly, even professionals are unlikely to have more than skimmed one of these volumes. So, to speed things up, here's a reader's digest. And to make things simpler, let's cluster the findings under three headings: environment, human rights and governance.

In each case, the world has made real progress in recent decades, although the

21st century challenge still looks daunting. We will focus on 21 priority areas: seven critical environmental issues; seven key human rights issues; and seven emerging priorities in the area of governance. Explicitly or implicitly, we are talking of various forms of capital that will need to be accounted for and managed. They include natural and environmental capital, human and social capital, and cultural and institutional capital.

PLANET

Seven environmental priorities

From the perspective of an astronaut or cosmonaut, Planet Earth is still a beautiful blue orb, shining with rude good health (panel 5, page 96). But things are not always what they seem: even to the non-professional eye viewing the world in close-up, our home planet seems to be in deep trouble. It is running a temperature, in addition to having a severely ulcerated ozone layer and a range of other potentially life-threatening complaints.

A key cause of the ozone hole over Antarctica turned out to be the use of CFCs. These are chemicals that have played a crucial role in refrigerators, air-conditioning equipment, and firefighting equipment, in addition to a wide range of other applications, including the manufacture of some drugs and the foaming of plastics such as polyurethane. Having worked with the polyurethanes industry through the 1990s, I have to say I was reasonably impressed at how fast the world economy shifted away from most ozone-depleting substances, but – though unbelievably complex – the ozone issue was relatively simple compared to climate change or the loss of species and biodiversity.

The Antarctic ozone hole woke many people up. By 2000, the hole covered 11 million square miles, three times the size of the United States.[20] "The ozone hole is the first clear manifestation of global environmental change," said professor Alan O'Neill, who chaired a recent conference to track progress since the 1987 Montreal Protocol. The aim of the Protocol was to shift the world economy away from CFCs and other ozone-depleting substances. The news from the Buenos Aires event was reasonably good: the hole in the southern hemisphere's ozone layer would start to shrink within ten years, we were told, and heal completely within 50.[21] As French skeptics might say, *On verra*.

The rate of progress is shown by the fact that the European Union cut its use of CFCs from 300,000 tonnes in 1986 to 4,300 in 1998, while Japan cut its usage from 118,000 tonnes to zero. Not all the trends have been going in the right direction, however. China's CFC consumption went from 29,000 tonnes in 1986 to 51,000 in

1997 – and there has been a roaring black market in some parts of the world, to meet demand from those with older equipment. Business is far from the only culprit, of course, but the globalization process is increasingly forcing major corporations into the spotlight.

So what does the current environmental agenda look like in the early years of the 21st century? The global doyen among world-watchers is Lester Brown of the Washington-based Worldwatch Institute, which he founded in 1974. Ten years on, he launched the annual *State of the World* series of reports, now translated into some 30 languages. In 1992, he followed on with a parallel annual series of *Vital Signs* reports, subtitled 'The Trends That Are Shaping Our Future'. Over the years, these publications have oscillated between pessimism and highly qualified optimism.

Strikingly, he kicked off the 2000 edition of *State of the World* by noting that even our ancestors are signaling a growing environmental crisis.[22] Warning that some of the biggest surprises of the new century may well come from climate change, he spotlighted the fact that as the world's glaciers start to melt, they are giving up the preserved bodies of long-dead humans. One popped up in Canada's western Yukon Territory, after an estimated 2,000 years in the ice, following the earlier discovery of a 5,000-year-old 'ice man' protruding from an Alpine glacier. "Our ancestors are emerging from the ice with a message for us," Brown warned: "Earth is getting warmer."

Brown was in a pretty glum mood as the century turned. "When the first edition of *State of the World* was published," he explained, "the year 2000 seemed a long way off. Record rates of population growth, soaring oil prices, debilitating levels of international debt, and extensive damage to forests from the new phenomenon of acid rain were all causing concern. By the end of the century, we then hoped, the world would be well on the way to creating a sustainable global economy."

But that wasn't how things turned out. As the Worldwatch team put the 2000 edition to bed and the clocks ticked towards December 31 1999, Brown concluded that "we are about to enter a new century having solved few of these problems, and facing even more profound challenges to the future of the global economy."

Not that he was blind to the progress achieved in the 20th century. "As we look back at the spectacular achievements of the century just ended," he noted, "the landing on the Moon in July 1969 by American astronauts Neil Armstrong and Buzz Aldrin stands out. At the beginning of the century, few could imagine humans flying, much less breaking out of Earth's field of gravity to journey to the Moon." In fact, it took just 66 years from the day in 1903 when the Wright brothers wobbled into the air at Kitty Hawk, North Carolina, to the moment when Armstrong took "one small step for a man, one giant leap for mankind."

Caught up in the excitement of such technological achievements, and in thrall to the much-vaunted new economy, Brown feared that western consumer societies had "lost sight of the deterioration of environmental systems and resources. The contrast between our bright hopes for the future of the information economy and the deterioration of Earth's ecosystem leaves us with a schizophrenic outlook."

So what was keeping Lester Brown awake at night? He listed seven key concerns. Here they are in headlines:[23]

- *Population growth.* Between 1950 and 2000 (the period during which your author grew from a 1-year-old baby to a 50-year-old adult), world population increased nearly 150% from 2.5 billion to 6.1 billion, a gain of 3.6 billion. Birth rates may have fallen, but recent forecasts suggest that human numbers will grow another 45% to 8.9 billion by 2050, a gain of 2.8 billion. According to the UN, 98 percent of world population growth to 2025 will be in the developing world. As a result, Europe's population (25 percent of the world total in 1900) will drop to just 7 percent in 2050.[24]

- *Global warming.* When the Industrial Revolution began over 200 years ago, the concentration of carbon dioxide (CO_2) in the atmosphere was some 280 parts per million (ppm). By 1959, when I was 10, detailed measurements using modern equipment showed that level had reached 316 ppm, a 13% rise over two centuries. By 1998, when I was verging on 50, it had reached 367 ppm – a jump of 17% in just 39 years. In parallel, global average temperatures have risen, from 13.99°C in 1969–71 to 14.43°C in 1996–98, a gain of 0.44 degrees. If CO_2 levels double during the 21st century, forecasters had warned that temperatures could rise by at least 1°C, and perhaps as much as 4°C. Early in 2001, the Inter-governmental Panel on Climate Change (IPCC) said the warming could be nearly 6°C by 2100.[25] The Panel also confirmed that human activity is a key contributory factor.

- *Water tables.* One of the most striking symptoms of these changes is falling water tables. Over-pumping of underground water in China, India, North Africa, Saudi Arabia and the United States exceeds 160 billion tons of water. Given that it takes roughly 1,000 tons to produce a ton of grain, this is equivalent to 160 millions tons of grain, or half the US grain harvest. On this basis, the food supply of at least 480 million of the world's 6-plus billion people is now being produced with the unsustainable use of water. Under the north China plain, which provides some 40% of that populous country's grain, the water table is falling by a staggering 1.6 meters (5 feet) a year. Such changes will spark future conflicts.

- *Cropland.* As human numbers have grown, the average area of cropland available per head has shrunk. Since the middle of the 20th century, grainland area per person has halved, from 0.24 hectares to 0.12 hectares. Even if the total grainland area were to remain the same over the next 50 years – despite growing losses to urbanization, industrialization and soil degradation – the area per head would fall by another third to 0.08 hectares by 2050.

- *Collapsing fisheries.* We also depend heavily on the world's oceans and seas for food, particularly animal protein. The globalization of Japan's *sushi* industry has been just one factor driving rocketing world fish demand.[26] Between 1957 and 1997, the oceanic fish catch grew nearly five-fold from 19 million tons to over 90 million tons. Most marine scientists say that the oceans cannot sustain a total catch of more than 95 million tons, suggesting that all future growth in demand will have to be met from land-based or fish-farming sources. In the UK, the fishing fleet has already shrunk by two-thirds over the past 50 years. Now the fishing quotas are being radically reduced once again, to try to protect collapsing fish populations.[27] Unfortunately, global warming and pollution trends are also having a disastrous impact on the world's oceans, seas and reefs – which are key to marine productivity.

- *Disappearing forests.* No one who watches TV or reads the newspapers needs to be told that the world's forests are in trouble. According to recent research, the area devoted to crops worldwide has increased six-fold since 1700, mainly at the expense of forest and woodland.[28] And the forested area per person globally is forecast to fall further, from 0.56 hectares today to 0.38 hectares in 2050. In many countries, growing demand for forest products – lumber, paper and fuelwood – has already reached unsustainable levels. And the impacts of pollution, urbanization and allied factors on forests are very much headed in the wrong direction.

- *Species loss.* But the trend that could have the greatest impact on the human prospect is the irreversible and accelerating loss of plant and animal species. The percentage of birds, mammals and fish under immediate threat of extinction is now reckoned in double digits: 11% of the world's bird species, 25% of its mammal species, and some 34% of all fish species. "As more and more species disappear, local ecosystems begin to collapse," Brown warns. "At some point, we will face wholesale ecosystem collapse."

It's interesting that Brown doesn't even manage to get around to mentioning nuclear risks. The Chernobyl disaster, for example, is now estimated to have cost over 4,000 lives among the clean-up workers alone.[29] A further 70,000 have been crippled by radiation, according to Ukrainian government figures. To make matters worse, an estimated 3,400,000 people – including 1,260,000 children – are suffering from fallout-related diseases. Unofficial figures put the health impacts even higher. A recent WHO study predicts a further 50,000 cases of thyroid cancer among children, for example.

Despite such tragedies, the overriding challenges in the new century, Worldwatch concludes, are to stabilize both the climate and the human population. Success in these two areas would make it easier to tackle other priority issues. The alternative is utterly bleak: "If we cannot stabilize climate and we cannot stabilize population," Brown concludes, "there is not an ecosystem on Earth that we can save. Everything will change."

PANEL 2

North sizzles, South sweats

In the late 1970s, our eldest daughter – Gaia – suffered 'febrile convulsions' when she ran fevers as a baby. The process is relatively common, indeed I also went through it at a similar age. It happens when a rapidly rising temperature (caused by infection) overwhelms the ability of a child's nervous system to cope. The process may even help the body shake off excess heat. Now we may be seeing the same process at work at the planetary scale.

Coral cores from the Pacific show an acceleration of the El Niño current cycle, which can trigger powerful hurricanes as far away as the Atlantic, plus devastating droughts in southern Africa and Indonesia (causing, among other things, fires and famine). In the 19th century, it happened every 10–15 years. Since the late 1970s, however, it has shifted to a four-year-cycle. During the last century it has been stronger than at any time for 130,000 years.[30] The change may be driven by higher sea surface temperatures, linked to global warming and greenhouse gases.[31]

Like geophysiologist Jim Lovelock (father of that hugely powerful meme, the 'Gaia Hypothesis'), future generations may come to see a fevered planet as inevitable symptoms of a "people plague". So what will be the impact on tomorrow's politics and markets? What liabilities will cascade to industries that have helped cause the problems? And, perhaps most seriously, will we learn to cope – or will our political systems also go into spasm?

Few controversies so powerfully illustrate the growing interconnections between the environmental, human rights and governance agendas covered in this chapter. So, for example, climate change will likely hit the poorest parts of Europe hardest, according to research commissioned by the European Union – itself an attempt to evolve governance systems at a new, regional level.

The richer nations of northern Europe and North America may largely be to blame for the greenhouse emissions that are driving climate change, but the worst impacts will be felt elsewhere, from Bulgaria to Bangladesh. "The wealthy metropolitan centers such as London, Paris and Frankfurt will be resilient and may even benefit," explains Martin Parry, part of the University of East Anglia study team.[32] Although the risk of flooding may increase, rising temperatures are likely to improve agricultural and forestry productivity, and reduce energy needs for heating. In the north, cold winters are forecast to be half as frequent by 2020.

In the south, by contrast, hot summers are likely to double in frequency by 2020. This will boost the need for air conditioning, hit water supplies and cut farm output. The study also forecasts deteriorating air quality in southern European cities, coupled with reduced summer demand from tourists due to excessive temperatures and the growing problems caused by forest fires.

Once, it was said that when General Motors sneezed, America caught a cold. Perhaps tomorrow's equivalent will be: When northern industrial economies sizzle, the south sweats. Or, to put it another way, the emissions from our cars help trigger tornadoes and floods a world away. Ask yourself: How long will the exploding populations of the South – from Bulgaria to Bangladesh – put up with it?

PEOPLE

Seven human rights priorities

People are at the very heart of the Catch-23 agenda. And it's an uncomfortable fact of life that throughout human history pretty much every society has known at least some degree of racism, sexism, authoritarianism and xenophobia. As a result, in all

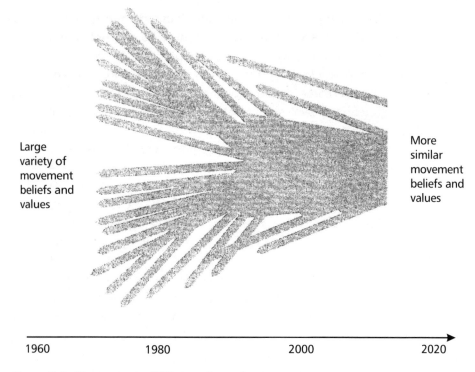

Large variety of movement beliefs and values		More similar movement beliefs and values

1960   1980   2000   2020

Figure 2.1 Convergence of TBL agendas and movements.
Source: The Cultural Creatives.

regions and cultures, the struggle against oppression, injustice and discrimination has been ongoing. But whereas it would once have been a case of out of sight, out of mind, in today's world human rights – civil, political, economic, social and cultural – are moving to center stage.

The business world has had to come to grips with a range of new discriminations, from ableism (discrimination in favor of able-bodied people), ageism (against the old) and sightism (against the blind) through to smokeism (against smokers) or weightism (against the overweight).

Underneath all of this, the human rights and sustainable development agendas, once more or less separate, have been converging (Figure 2.1). This diagram, taken from *The Cultural Creatives*,[33] was designed to show the social and consciousness movements converging in the US, but could also be used to illustrate the ways in which campaigning communities and their priorities are now converging right across the triple bottom line agenda. The 'Battle of Seattle' illustrated the trend.

Indeed, it is no accident that business people are increasingly finding that the agenda they face is a highly complex, constantly shifting amalgam of environmental, human rights and a wide range of other socioeconomic and political issues. Triple bottom line imperatives are becoming an inescapable – if often highly uncomfortable – fact of business life.

The total amount of human suffering in the world beggars the imagination. Some 2.4 billion people lack basic sanitation, a billion are without safe water, nearly 800 million people are undernourished, 250 million children are used as child labor, and 1.2 million women and girls under 18 are trafficked for prostitution each year. More than 12 million Africans have already died from AIDS and by 2010 it is estimated that Africa will have 40 million AIDS orphans.

Nor are things always getting much better on the economic front. More than 30 countries – with more than half a billion inhabitants – had a lower per capita income in 2000 than they did two decades earlier. Even in the rich OECD world, more than 130 million people lived in 'income poverty'.

Grim though these statistics are, however, the picture is far from totally black. Indeed, looking back, one of the less visible achievements of the last century was its very real overall progress in human rights. In 1900, for example, more than half of the world's population lived under colonial rule, and no country gave all its citizens the right to vote.[34] Today, some three-quarters of the world live under (at least nominally) democratic regimes.

The daily press and other media may brim over with genuine horror stories, from Rwanda (where perhaps a million people died) to Bosnia and Herzegovina (with an estimated death toll of up to 250,000), but it is also worth looking behind such grisly scenes. Since 1948, when the Universal Declaration of Human Rights was adopted (page 162), there has been great progress in eliminating discrimination by race, religion and gender – and in advancing the right to schooling and basic health care.

By 1990, 10 percent of the world's countries had ratified the six major human rights instruments, but by 2000 – in just 10 years – this had zoomed to nearly half of all countries. All but one of the six core covenants in the Universal Declaration had each been ratified by more than 140 countries, while all but one of the seven core labor rights conventions had been ratified by 125 or more countries.

And a good deal has also been going on at the national and regional levels. Since ending apartheid, South Africa has placed human rights at the heart of its development strategy. India's Supreme Court has insisted on the rights of all citizens to free education and basic health care. And the expanding European Union is making human rights a key priority, with its European Court of Human Rights.

Of course, democracy is no guarantee of progress toward SD, but experience suggests that it is the only political regime compatible with respect for all five main categories of human rights: civil, political, economic, social and cultural. Democracy, as UNDP points out, has four defining features in terms of human rights – and these tend to be self-reinforcing.

First, democracy involves the holding of free and fair elections. Second, it requires free and independent media, as a guarantee of freedom of expression, thought and conscience. Third, the separation of powers among different branches of government helps protect citizens from human rights abuses. And, fourth, an open civil society encourages participation, protecting the right to peaceful assembly and association.

So what are the current human rights priorities? According to UNDP, the struggle continues in seven key areas:

- *Freedom from discrimination.* The central principle of human rights is equality – in opportunities and choices. A succession of powerful social movements has propelled a range of issues (related to discrimination by gender, race, religion, ethnicity or age) up the political agenda. But huge problems remain in some countries. In South Africa, for example, 98% of whites live in houses, while more than 50% of Africans live in traditional dwellings or shacks. And the plight of indigenous peoples remains grim in many parts of the world.

- *Freedom from want.* Human poverty is a major barrier both to achieving a reasonable standard of living and to realizing the full range of human rights. Although countries like China, India and Malaysia have made considerable progress in cutting poverty, some 1.2 billion people worldwide live on $1 or less a day, nearly half of them in South Asia. More than a billion people live in inadequate housing and about 100 million are estimated to be homeless. Even in the United States, something like 750,000 people are homeless on any given night.

- *Freedom to develop potential.* Many developing countries have made significant progress in recent years in respect of the rights to food, health and education. But these achievements should not mask the real problems that remain. Nearly 18 million people die every year from communicable diseases – and nearly 30 million from non-communicable diseases, mainly in the OECD countries. About a third of children under five suffer from malnutrition. About 90 million children are out of primary school, and over 230 million out of secondary school. What an unbelievable waste of human potential!

- *Freedom from fear.* In poor and rich nations alike, people face various forms of actual or threatened violence. There are threats from one's own state (including arbitrary arrest, detention and torture), from other states (war, support for oppressive regimes) and from other groups of people (ethnic conflicts, crime, street violence), in addition to threats specifically directed at women (rape, domestic violence) and children (child abuse). As an indication of the scale of these threats, the 1990s saw 5 million people killed in civil wars and 50 million forced to flee their homes – this last figure representing 1 person in every 120 on the planet. During the decade, more than 300,000 children were soldiers and 6 million young people were injured in armed conflicts.

- *Freedom from injustice.* "I can tolerate poverty," said one poor farmer in Bangladesh, "but not to get justice in the eye of the law in my own country just because I am poor, that I will not tolerate." Like it or not, though, huge numbers of people have to put up with just such injustices – and much worse. In Bangladesh, the anti-corruption NGO Transparency International showed that nearly two-thirds of those involved in litigation paid bribes to court officials. Too often, it seems, justice has become a commodity that only the rich and powerful can afford.

- *Freedom of speech.* This heading includes freedom of participation, expression and association. The last century's brutal one-party states committed some of the worst abuses of human rights, but also catalyzed powerful resistance movements. As a result, most have given way to some form of democracy. Today, the state retains its monopoly on the media in only 5% of countries. Among our best hopes, the growth of non-governmental organizations (50,000 in Hungary and 45,000 in Poland, for example) and the reach of the media (there are more than 10 million internet users in China). But democracies remain fragile: about 40 countries do not have a multiparty electoral system. And in 1999 alone, according to the International Press Institute, 87 journalists and other media people were killed while doing their job.

- *Freedom from exploitation.* Finally, productive and satisfying lifestyles enable people to buy goods and services. They empower people politically by enabling them to influence decision-making in their workplaces and beyond. The Universal Declaration of Human Rights recognizes the right to work, to freely choose employment and to enjoy just and humane working conditions. Even so, there are some 250 million child laborers. At the other end of the spectrum, there are those who might even welcome at least a degree of commercial exploitation. At least 150 million of the world's workers were unemployed at the end of 1998, and as many as 900 million were underemployed. About 35 million people were unemployed in OECD countries alone.

The range of industries affected by such human rights issues is growing. Diamond companies, particularly De Beers, have been under fire because of so-called 'conflict' or 'blood' diamonds from Angola and Sierra Leone. De Beers now talks of ensuring that it provides only 'clean' stones.[35] And pressure from the UK government forced the controversial diamond mining company Oryx to halt its UK flotation.[36] Oryx was linked with the Democratic Republic of Congo, which has been torn by a bloody civil war.

In the future, too, new forms of human rights abuse will surface. Already, for example, the mining and oil industries have come under massive challenge in this area. At the same time, too, companies like GlaxoSmithKline and Novartis have been attacked for allegedly failing to provide affordable drugs to AIDS victims in countries that cannot afford state-of-the-art drugs.[37] Some campaigners are now framing such issues as abuses of human rights.

New surveillance technologies will also bring new concerns. There is no doubt that they can help cut crime: a CCTV surveillance system installed at one housing estate in Hull, UK, for example, cut crime by almost half.[38] But where will this end? Companies like Bull, the French computer maker, and Racal Research, the British defense contractor, are working on 'smart' cameras and software which will enable the police and security services not only to watch what you are doing but also, by observing your body language, to predict what you are about to do.[39] "You and I don't have to be paranoid about it," was the way one closed-circuit-TV-repair company put it, "but our children and grandchildren should be scared to death."

Another possible future issue focuses on the health impact of 'electronic smog', which has been growing exponentially. A study of microwave workers in the US found that certain groups with long-term exposures suffered from a progressively raised risk of brain tumors. And research on a Latvian town called Skrunda raises even more worrying possibilities.[40] It was sprayed for more than 30 years by Russian over-the-horizon radar. Scientists investigated the health of 900 children conceived, born and raised in the path of those incoming signals. Many turned out to have defective attention, working memory and motor coordination compared to those not exposed. Although companies using microwave signals tend to dismiss the risks, neurology professor Ross Adey is among those warning that in the future, "wherever we go, we will be immersed in a sea of low-level, pulsed microwave signals."

But what, you may still ask, has all of this got to do with *business*? Is this simply something for drug companies, mobile phone makers or CCTV companies to worry about? No. The fact is that, whether they like it or not, the world's major corporations are increasingly being expected not only to respect a growing array of human rights but also to champion them. "By virtue of their global influence and power," UNDP argues, "they must accept responsibility and be accountable for upholding high human rights standards – respecting the rights of workers, protecting the environment, and refraining from supporting or condoning regimes that abuse human rights."

A range of voluntary initiatives have pushed the envelope for years, but the launch of UN Secretary-General Kofi Annan's 'Global Compact' signaled that these issues are now on the agenda as never before (page 159). New forms of governance are being experimented with. The key questions for companies: what are the priorities for our business – and how far and how fast should we move? The answers will very much depend on what happens next in the linked fields of global and corporate governance.

POLITICS

Seven governance priorities

Not long ago, it looked as if economics would crowd out politics. Now, as *Time* magazine put it recently, "Politics is coming back into the global economy."[41] Some of the pressure is coming from companies. Take Nokia, Finland's largest company. "We are being expected to solve problems which business enterprises are not meant to solve," protested the company's CEO, Jorma Ollila.[42] "It's politicians who should solve social problems."

Whatever your views on the matter, it is hard to deny that our ability to tackle the SD agenda is being massively hampered by our inability to tackle the governance agenda effectively. But, as the environmental and human rights movements fight their way from the periphery into the mainstream, the issue of governance is surfacing repeatedly. The political links between the environmental and human rights agendas on the one hand, and the global and corporate governance agendas on the other, are increasingly evident.

But it is still often easier to point to unsustainable – rather than sustainable – governance. Take an extreme case, Russia. The country's president at the dawn of the 21st century, Vladimir Putin, was previously chief of the FSB, the successor to the KGB. In that role, he accused environmental organizations of being, in effect, anti-Russian. Once he was president, he went as far as dissolving the Federal Forest Service and the State Commission on Environmental Commission.[43] As a result, there was no longer any state organization to stand in the way of the State and Corporate Locusts, which are rapaciously exploiting the country's forests, oil or minerals. Russian Aluminum, spotlighted in Chapter 4, is one Corporate Locust taking advantage of the situation. Among other things, the company has been accused of such corporate crimes as murder, death threats, fraud, bribery and money-laundering.[44]

A good person to ask about the problems that weak governance systems bring is Aleksandr Nikitin, a former naval officer and environmental whistleblower. After spending ten months in jail, Nikitin was acquitted of high treason. The charge: that he helped write a report for the Norwegian environmental group Bellona on the threat of radioactivity from Russia's aging fleet of nuclear submarines. Despite the fact that Nikitin's work was based on published sources, the state accused him of a capital crime, divulging state secrets. On his release, Nikitin established a new organization, the Coalition for the Environment and Human Rights.

No one should doubt the importance of such initiatives. Countries that lack basic democratic processes and where secrecy prevails suffer as a result. Visit Yekaterinburg in the Urals, for example, and you will find a city where over 60 people died when anthrax bacteria escaped from a Soviet germ warfare complex in 1979.[45] The authorities insisted that the source of outbreak was infected meat, but local people suspected something more sinister – particularly when it became known that the victims had been buried in metal coffins.[46]

On the other hand, there are those – even in the West – who see some of Nikitin's western supporters as enemies of free markets. "It started just about when the world's capitalists were congratulating themselves on the defeat of communism: a new wave of anticorporate populism," as self-declared 'capitalist tool' Forbes magazine put it.[47] "What happened to tobacco companies, what is happening to genetic engineering companies, is beginning to happen to the drug industry." From the activists in the streets of Seattle, Washington, DC, London and Prague, to those who sell knock-off versions of major drugs, Forbes sees a huge growth in what it lumps together under the grab-all label "corporate saboteurs".

Certainly, you don't need to be a rabid capitalist, or even a Forbes reader, to acknowledge that the forces of anti-capitalism are growing in strength. Quick: what are these? N30, A16, S11, S26. "If you are part of the anti-capitalist resistance," as The Economist put it, "these terms will need no explaining. Each denotes a day of protest against 'corporate-led globalisation'."[48] Many of the protestors, it continued, "know little about the organisations they are attacking – but not all of them, by any means, are in it merely to vent incoherent rage or have a fun day out. The more thoughtful among them recognise that street protests are only a convenient tactic in a larger war, and that if their movement is to grow it will need a vision – positive proposals, that is, as well as a list of things it hates."

There is no doubt that the signals sent by the protests have been heard. Within months of the Seattle protests, I found myself in the boardroom of the International

Finance Corporation (IFC), part of the World Bank group. The growing pressures on such institutions were the main topic of conversation. But it's worth asking what are the deep currents under all the spume and frothing in the world media? The answer may be that, for those with eyes to see, these are just more symptoms of an inexorable trend towards world governance.

One of the most convincing treatments of this theme I have read is Robert Wright's *Nonzero: The Logic of Human Destiny*.[49] He tracks what he describes as "the arrow of life" from the primordial soup to the World Wide Web – and thence into the deep future. The underlying message: In 1500BC there were some 600,000 autonomous polities on the planet, whereas now – after centuries of nation building – the number has shrunk to less than 200. The inevitable trajectory: world government, or at least world governance.

Not that we should expect everything to go smoothly. During the 1990s, Benjamin Barber identified two emergent and competing 'world orders': *Jihad* and *McWorld*.[50] On the one hand, in the Jihad future, the world is seen as increasingly 'tribal', fragmenting along lines of ethnicity, language, religion or economic interest. An extreme case is Afghanistan's Taliban. The implosion of Yugoslavia and the push for secession by French-speaking Canadians are two other examples of this trend. The outlook: growing tension, fuelled by overpopulation and environmental stress – and given a fierce twist by new forms of terrorism, empowered by deadly new technologies.[51]

By contrast, the problem in McWorld isn't chaos so much as "a spooky kind of order," as Wright puts it, "emanating from the multinational corporations and globetrotting financiers who animate McWorld. They swear allegiance, not to any nation, but to profit alone, and they've implanted their values into such supranational bodies as the International Monetary Fund (IMF) and the World Trade Organisation (WTO), whose tendrils threaten to engulf slowly, and then smother national self-determination." In this view, the alphabet soup of supra-national organizations – IMF, UN, WTO – is the harbinger of a coming planetary authority.

Given so many people of diverse backgrounds implacably oppose this trend, how might all of this come about? Hollywood likes to depict the world coming together as a result of alien invasion, but what happens if the aliens don't come?

The answer is that a host of pressures are building that will create a growing sense of global security problems, in the process driving us towards global governance. Robert Wright again: "They range from terrorists (with their menu of interestingly spooky weapons) to a new breed of transnational criminals (many of whom will commit their crimes in that inherently international realm, cyberspace) to environmental problems (global warming, ozone depletion and lots of merely regional but still supranational issues) to health problems (epidemics that exploit modern thoroughfares). They all imply supranational governance in one sense or another."

Current trends suggest that future governance will have at least seven key characteristics:

Joined-up experience

First, a sustainable world will be driven by the normal – if accelerating – succession of disasters and other surprises, helping to keep politicians and business leaders off-balance. In the 'CNN World', the problems and interests of people on the other side of the planet increasingly become our concern. Ozone holes, climate change and the proliferation of germ warfare technology are just some trends that will help give at least some of us a shared sense of identity and common purpose.

The key question here is whether the sustainability transformation will be smooth, with a succession of easy-to-negotiate steps, or whether – as with the world wars of the last century – the changes will come in more dramatic forms. The answer will depend on what happens in each of the six areas identified below, but most of my money would be on a series of sudden, unexpected jumps, the punctuated equilibrium form of political evolution.

Joined-up decision-making

The purpose of governments is to connect the unconnected. Governments may seem out of fashion, but a sustainable world will be impossible without joined-up politics, governance, and decision-making. One of the biggest problems we face globally is what we might call 'the governance gap'. Governments, and other governance systems, will mutate rapidly as new pressures evolve right across the triple bottom line agenda.

On the social front, changing demographics, with some societies aging and others seeing massive baby booms, will transform politics and, eventually, governance systems and processes. New intra- and intergenerational issues will surface, focusing on economic, environmental and social justice. New international government and governance systems will evolve to handle the pressures.

The economic pressures will also grow tremendously. Take the case of Gazprom, the huge Russian energy producer. A recent visit by western financial experts shocked the Russians. Gazprom, they were told, was worth dramatically less than 1 percent of its market potential – because of the country's desperately poor governance systems.[52] Valued at $4 billion late in 1999, Gazprom could have been worth $1,960 billion on the basis of accepted western multiples, had it been based somewhere with good governance. In short, good governance pays.

Joined-up campaigning

Governments can't do it all, however. At times, global governance will be highly diverse, a game for multiple players. These will include the usual suspects, among them multilateral organizations (e.g. UN, IMF, World Bank), international associations (G8, OECD, Commonwealth, NATO), inter-regional groups (APEC, Trans-Atlantic Partnership), regional bodies (EU, NAFTA, ASEAN, Nordic Union, OAS, OAU), private governance processes (companies, standard-setting institutions like ISO, trade unions, NGOs), national governments (of which there are some 230) and subnational governments (such as US or Australian states, Canadian provinces or the German Länder).[53] But the game will also be played – or attempted – by new entrants we have never heard of.

Expect the evolving governance system to be increasingly dependent on networks. These may seem disconnected, but – like the 'imaginal cells' in the chrysalis – they are not. Networks, says Manuel Castells, author of three thought-provoking books on the theme,[54] "are extraordinary, dynamic, lean structures that have no personal feelings. They kiss or kill."[55] And one of the most surprising things about the Information Age "is that it's not correcting inequality." The new economy as it is now, he concludes, is not sustainable." At the same time, however, the network is having a profound impact on our world: "The network becomes the social structure of everything," Castells says. And that fact will have profound implications for future governance.

Love them or hate them, a sustainable world will be impossible without joined-up campaigning by NGOs, governments and business. The internet, web-sites and e-mail 'listservs' have played a crucial role in pulling campaigners together and ensuring new levels of coordination in their increasingly global protests. The art of network politics will be to pull all these disparate forces and agendas together into something rather more coherent and workable.

Joined-up mental models

A sustainable world will be impossible without joined-up thinking – and without radically different mental, business and development models. The disconnects in our current mental models often play out in the real world, sometimes with disastrous economic, social or ecological effects.

The perils can be seen in what has happened to the Aral Sea. For the five million people who live near the now-shriveled shores of what was once the world's fourth largest lake, the experience has been, in the words of a former schoolteacher in the area, "a fairytale in reverse".[56] "When I was a child," she says, "I used to swim in the sea. Now it isn't there." Few disasters have so powerfully illustrated the triple bottom line impacts of getting things wrong.

Environmentally, a vast ecosystem has been turned into a poisonous desert, contaminated by pesticides used to grow cotton. Socially, local people suffer from extraordinarily high rates of such diseases as asthma, cancer, pneumonia and kidney disease. Economically, completing and accelerating the vicious cycle of decline, local industries such as fishing, canning, tourism and construction have collapsed like a deck of cards.

Interestingly, those taking a greater interest in climate change and related issues include the military. The UK Ministry of Defence, for example, sees a real risk that climate change will spark future wars.[57] In a report called *Global Trends 2015*, the US National Intelligence Council concludes that the coming decades will see the lack of fresh water, among other issues, becoming a potential trigger for regional wars.[58]

Markets do not guarantee that we will escape such disasters. Indeed, if we are to ensure that the 21st century does not create even worse problems, we need new business models and new development models.

Joined-up markets

The disconnect between market and other realities scarcely needs emphasis. A sustainable world will only be possible with joined-up markets and pricing signals. To some extent, markets can evolve under their own steam. But the international haggling over the carbon trading systems proposed as part of the solution to the climate change agenda has spotlighted the vital role that governments will often play, nationally and internationally.

Markets also need even more basic forms of jump-starting. While the current institutions of world governance push western-style capitalism as the only recipe for economic success in the rest of the world, the evidence suggests that successful capitalism depends on social, political and institutional factors that are often absent or precariously weak in other parts of the world.

As Hernando de Soto of Peru's Institute of Liberty and Democracy puts it, capitalism works in the west but usually fails everywhere else not simply because there are weak legal systems but, more specifically, because Third World and former communist countries do not have the necessary property laws. De Soto notes: "The poor inhabitants of these nations – the overwhelming majority – do have things, but they lack the process to represent their property and create capital. They have houses but not titles; crops but not deeds; businesses but not statutes of incorporation." [59]

Once markets do exist, a tremendous amount of work needs to be done to ensure that the valuations and pricing signals reflect emerging social, environmental and economic realities. Organizations like the WTO often seem to resist market experimentation designed to promote more sustainable natural resource exploitation, but if the WTO won't do it there will be a gap in the market for more switched-on institutions to fill.

Joined-up fiscal policy

A sustainable world will be impossible without joined-up approaches to taxes, subsidies, incentives and other forms of fiscal policy. For example, we must phase out public subsidies for unsustainable activities, including fishing fleets, inefficient irrigation systems and the unsustainable logging of forests.[60] Environmental scientist Norman Myers has estimated that the global subsidy for unsustainable practices in agriculture, energy and transport is over $1 trillion a year.[61]

Such 'perverse subsidies' can warp any new sustainable resource management regimes. Western governments are being pressured to set an example by switching subsidies towards sustainable resource use, redesigning processes used to produce economic valuations of natural resources, developing positive financial incentives for investment, and linking aid to developing countries to the progressive removal of their own damaging subsidies.

Joined-up moralities

Finally, and this may prove to be the toughest challenge of all, a sustainable world will be difficult, if not impossible, without joined-up ethics. This is where the real crunch comes between values and unsustainable value creation. The tension between the worldviews represented, for example, by *McWorld* and *Jihad* will not ease any time soon. But the hope must be that globalization, combined with the new risks and opportunities it raises, will drive us towards a shared ethic based on human, civil and environmental rights. Sustainable capitalism is extremely unlikely without common values. If the UN can get its act together, the Global Compact (page 159) launched by Kofi Annan may provide a useful spur in this direction.

If the central challenge is to redesign the global economic system, as Lester Brown argues, what's going to make this happen? He notes approvingly that "high-profile CEOs have begun to sound more like environmentalists than representatives of the bastions of global capitalism." We will focus in on some Citizen CEOs in Chapter 6. But, however many of their corporations start the arduous transition from caterpillar and locust behaviors to more sustainable forms of value creation, a still more fundamental shift is needed. The necessary next step is what Thomas Kuhn called a 'paradigm shift'.

When I read Kuhn's *The Structure of Scientific Revolutions*[62] in the 1960s, it literally changed the way I saw the world. And that is what the book is essentially about: the ways in which today's reality morphs – or explodes – into tomorrow's. One of the best-known examples of such a shift involved the uncomfortable transition from the old Ptolemaic worldview, in which the sun revolved around the Earth, to the Copernican worldview, in which we rotate around the sun. Once the shift had happened, the whole universe looked – felt – different. The environmental revolution of the second half of the 20th century, spurred along by the outside-in images brought back by the first generation of astronauts and cosmonauts, has triggered a paradigm shift of almost equal proportions.

Already, there are some hopeful signs. Over 30 countries, including almost all of industrialized Europe, plus Japan and Canada – have succeeded in stabilizing their populations. Another, much larger group of countries, has reached the so-called 'replacement level' of fertility of 2.1 children per couple. But this can take a long time to translate into population stabilization, largely because of the huge numbers of young people entering their reproductive years. This group contains two of the most populous countries, China and the United States.

Two other hopeful trends are the growing interest in 'decarbonization' and in the solar/hydrogen economy. "Restructuring the world energy economy," Brown argues, "is the greatest investment opportunity in history." And the second, linked trend is the somewhat erratic progress in restructuring tax systems to drive innovation and investment in more sustainable technologies and other forms of value creation. A key task here will be to get major corporations to use their political muscle to actively campaign for tax reform.

Business people may think it unfair that they are increasingly expected to deliver against this massive agenda, but business is not just the main source of many of the impacts discussed above and in Chapter 7, but is also our primary engine of change. As Chapter 4 explains, business and companies come in multiple forms, from low impact, degenerative 'Corporate Caterpillars' through, potentially, to high impact, regenerative 'Corporate Honeybees'. To understand how we can best leverage change, we need to know what sorts of business organisms we are dealing with.

But to conclude our survey of the state of the world, a final word from Lester Brown. "There is no middle path," he says. "The challenge is either to build an economy that is sustainable or to stay with our unsustainable economy until it declines. It is not a goal that can be compromised. One way or another, the choice will be made by our generation, but it will affect life on Earth for all generations to come."

CHAPTER 3

Extreme economics
The real new economy

"Extreme skiing is my sport, my thinking and life itself," said Davo Karnicar after skiing non-stop down Everest. The 38-year-old Slovenian, exhausted but triumphant, had virtually plummeted down the mountain, with stretches of ice collapsing beneath his speeding skis. Part-way down, he was shocked to pass the frozen body of a dead climber, one of over 160 people who have died on the mountain. Karnicar, who had already skied down Mont Blanc, took a month to climb up to the world's tallest peak, but came down in less than five hours. Thanks to strategically placed cameras, hundreds of thousands of people in over 70 countries watched his descent on the internet.[63] For many entrepreneurs and investors, this was like watching the New Economy in action.

But why is this relevant? The answer is that this is at least part of the economic context in which we must now address the priority issues highlighted in Chapter 2. And, to put it mildly, an already complicated task is being made even more difficult. Indeed, as I finished *The Chrysalis Economy*, more stock market wealth was being destroyed across the new economy than at any time in history. Optimists no doubt could see these events as the economic counterpart of self-digestion inside the chrysalis. True, the process may prove to have boosted the long-term sustainability of our economies, but close up the self-digestion part was ugly.

Despite many earlier assurances that this was no bubble economy, the collapsing fortunes of leading new economy pioneers told the real story. Microsoft's Bill Gates fortune had dropped 64 percent from $87 billion to $32 billion, Softbank's Masayoshi Son's plummeted 94 percent from $69 billion to $4 billion, WorldCom's Bernard Ebbers' slumped 77 percent from $1.7 billion to $388 million and Apple's Steve Jobs, who was one of the early pioneers in this field, saw his stake in the company crash 80 percent from $1 billion to $212 million.[64]

Was it an accident that so many new economy pioneers had looked forward each year to the Burning Man festival (page 43)? Hardly. Like Karnicar, these people live on the edge, on adrenaline. The ride up the curve was wildly exciting, but what is it like to lose $10 billion – as both Amazon.com's Jeff Bezos and Yahoo's Jerry Yang did in the dotcom stock collapse of 2000? There were plenty of old economy folk who enjoyed a sense of revenge as the new economy world was rocked on its heels. As company valuations shifted, old economy companies that had been relegated from top company listings clawed their way back, past the corpses of dead or dying new economy competitors.

But the excitement isn't over yet, not by a long shot. The end of the e-bubble doesn't mean that the new economy – and 'extreme economics' – are dead. Long term, the network economy brings new customer dynamics, offering new value levers and opening up the prospect for new value propositions.[65] As Kenichi Ohmae explains, it is if an "invisible continent" is forming, where the "commanding heights" of the economy will be very different.[66] Nor is IT the only game in town: the new long wave of economic change is also being driven by great suites of technology, among them biotechnology and nanotechnology.[67]

The more exuberant dotcom pioneers have claimed that their technologies and business models would bring an end to business cycles: Don't count on it. Every economic era turns out to have its own unique curse. The old economy business cycle was based on housing and autos; the new economy business cycle is more likely to be driven by technology and by financial markets.[68]

None of this means that the new economy was a myth.[69] But one lesson that has to be learned over with every new market bubble is that most new business models don't work.[70] Just as most genetic experiments fail in nature. And during periods when financial capital is underpriced, as it unquestionably was during the internet bubble, vast numbers of wobbly 'me-too' experiments are tried, which increases the casualty rate when the cycle turns.

Pessimists like Michael Mandel predict that the result of the dotcom crash could even be an "Internet Depression".[71] The upside of the tech cycle, he has argued, is a long, low-inflation boom, with soaring tech spending, rapid innovation, and a buoyant stock market. The downside is that all this is very likely to turn into a deep, pervasive downturn. The expansion phase is marked by the rapid introduction of new technologies and new business models, while the contraction phase sees technological stagnation. Contraction is likely to bring a raft of old economy problems, among them weak productivity growth, falling investment, depressed stock markets and rebounding inflation.

If Mandel proves to have been right, none of this is going to be particularly helpful in the short term for those promoting the corporate social responsibility (CSR) and sustainable development (SD) agendas. But, paradoxically, whether the outcome is recession or depression, this shift in economic cycles is a necessary precondition for the emergence of the Chrysalis Economy.

DESTROYED, CREATIVELY

The Chrysalis Economy is already at work all around us. Again. Every so often, our economies experience waves of discontinuous change, what economist Joseph Schumpeter dubbed "creative destruction".[72] Now it's happening once more, as the world finds itself caught between two economies, an old industrial economy based on the amplification of muscle power and a new one based on the amplification and expansion of the human mind.[73]

That said, there was no way many new economy companies could be sustainable in the longer term. Enthusiasts argued that new business models meant that the economy would become radically more efficient, while the resulting downward pressure on prices meant that "inflation is dead – dead as a doornail".[74] Even the idea of supplying goods at cost to consumers was seen as brilliant strategy. FreePC was lauded for giving a free PC to the first 10,000 customers who signed up for its ad-funded services. "In all probability," said one Harvard Business School professor, "it will not be long before companies go beyond free and start paying people to use products and services".[75]

Dotcoms touted their mounting losses as evidence that they were successfully growing the business, but at what cost? A study by management consultants McKinsey showed that many e-tailers were losing considerable amounts of money on every transaction, even before the crash.[76] In the last quarter of 1999, for example, the online toy store Etoys had lost $4.04 on every order, the online grocer Webvan lost $12.90, and Drugstore lost $16.42 on every non-prescription order. They were literally paying customers for their custom.

Making money on the Net, such companies soon found, was far trickier than they had expected. "You had a bunch of companies running into this chasing quick money," said Toys'R'us.com CEO John Barbour. "But they didn't have a business model, they don't have a path to profitability and they don't have a compelling consumer benefit." [77]

Some commentators were slightly more upbeat, however. Irwin Stelzer was among those who compared the dotcom mania to the tulip mania that shook 18th century Holland.[78] He quoted venture capitalist Bill Davidow to the effect that "there was a tulip business even after the tulip mania." A few years later, once the speculators had gone, the trade in tulips regained a sort of equilibrium. Among other things, tulip traders shifted from seasonal to year-round production, and also learned how to control the viruses that periodically destroyed their businesses. But the 'irrational exuberance' was not entirely squeezed out of the system: there was a spurt in hyacinth prices later in the century and another in dahlia prices in 1838.

So count on further outbreaks of irrational investor exuberance in the world of the Net, the Grid, or whatever it eventually evolves into. And in other areas of technology. Even so, useful evolutionary work *is* being done. The new economy, both in boom and bust, is signaling new forms of value creation. The key characteristic of the new economy has been lower transaction costs, although the dreams of "frictionless capitalism" now seem more remote than they did a few years back.

But the online trading of everything from books and tulips to electricity and broadband capacity will have a massive, permanent impact on the global economy. OK, but what conclusions can we draw from all of this for our prospects of achieving more sustainable forms of value creation? To simplify radically, let's look at three trends: in business models, footprints (ecological, economic and social), and accounting.

TREND 1: TBL BUSINESS MODELS

The internet, says Gary Hamel, has "spawned a Cambrian explosion of new competitive life forms."[79] This makes a lot of sense in evolutionary terms. "Swarms of start-ups serve a Darwinian purpose," as Professor Amar Bhidé puts it. "Their experiments enable the 'fittest' new products and technologies to emerge."[80] It may be messy, but the end result is a lot more creative than anything you would get with command-and-control.

So fast will be the pace of change, Hamel argues, that "every company that was 'built to last' must now be 'rebuilt to change'." The pace of economic evolution, he notes, has always been a function of the number and quality of interconnections between individuals and the ideas they hold. New technologies like the telegraph, railroad, the telephone, the car, the airplane and now the internet "allow ideas to circulate, combine, and recombine in ways never before possible."

Business concept innovation will be key. Indeed, Hamel argues that "business concept innovation will be the defining competitive advantage" in what he calls "the age of revolution."[81] The companies that will flourish in the internet age will be different. They will be – have to be – capable of radical, continuous change. "It is not so much that these companies embraced the internet as that their organizations mirrored the internet," Hamel explained. "They are democratic, open, experimental, highly networked, non-hierarchical, and malleable." Nostalgia is out: like a caterpillar digesting old organs to build the new, a company like Nokia succeeds by selling off all its 'heritage' businesses to pour its energy into mobile phones.

Some startling, heady predictions were being made. Over at consultants PricewaterhouseCoopers (PwC), they talked of 'MetaCapitalism', driven by new e-business models.[82] They predicted that global capital market value would grow from $20 trillion to $200 trillion in less than a decade. Writing before the e-crash got into its stride, the PwC team concluded (the italics are theirs) that: *"The period from 2000 to 2002 will represent the single greatest change on worldwide economic and business conditions ever, and most of the impact will occur during the next 18 months."*

MetaCapitalism, they argued, will create much more dynamic behaviors – indeed, they used the term "It's Alive!" to describe the nature of what they dubbed the 'MetaMarket'. The basic idea here is that MetaMarkets are "outsourced, managed networks that continuously replace elements of the supply chain with more efficient players. Participants at various points along the demand or supply chain will be essentially free agents, easily replaced to improve performance at that point in the value chain." Another key characteristic is that they are awash in real-time, online information.

This has been a key factor in the success of such business models as that used by Michael Dell of Dell Computer, allowing what Dell calls "virtual integration" through the supply chain.[83] A key feature of Dell's business model has been *scalability*, enabling rapid – indeed, *hyper* – growth. The company achieved over 50 percent annual compounded sales growth from 1992 through the 1990s. Among the factors that Dell says have driven his company are "a sense of destiny," good crisis management and learning skills, and "productive fear," ensuring that business decisions are based on sound risk assessments.[84]

We have also heard much talk of B2C (business to consumer) and B2B (business to business) models. Perhaps most fundamentally, the power of the internet makes it possible to do things outside the company that were once done inside.[85] As a result, we are seeing growing interest in so-called 'business webs', or b-webs. Indeed, Don Tapscott argues that b-web will be as routine a label for economic actors in the internet age as 'corporation' was in the industrial age.[86]

"The most important thing about what we call the new economy," Tapscott stresses, "is that business-model innovation is the key to success. The beauty of it is that it applies to banks, chemical and mining companies as much as anyone else." He instances the case of Enron, a traditional US utility that reinvented itself as a marketplace for energy, telecom bandwidth and a range of other services. He suggests that the process of taking companies apart and putting the pieces back together with the internet at their heart has hardly even begun.

A key impact of these sort of b-webs is 'disintermediation', the process by which businesses involved in distribution go to the wall as direct channels open up between content providers and their customers. "What excites me most about the new economy," said technology forecaster Paul Saffo who heads the California-based

Institute for the Future, "is that we're in the middle of a fundamental change in the nature of commerce, in the nature of capitalism. Commerce isn't about buying stuff, it's about interacting with people in different ways." [87] We are involved in a whole "renegotiation of culture". Brace yourself, he suggests: "We're at the beginning of a transformation that will continue for a couple of decades."

Optimists see the process as more or less inevitable. "Corporate citizenship is an essential feature of the new economy," says Simon Zadek. [88] "Successful companies in the new economy will engage effectively with their stakeholders in the markets for goods and services, finance, labour and political patronage. Corporate citizenship implies a strategy that moves from a focus on short-term transaction to longer-term, values-based relationships with these stakeholders."

By contrast, social critic Jeremy Rifkin is characteristically gloomy about the way things are likely to pan out in what he dubs the "experience economy" of the future. [89] We are seeing a long-term shift from industrial production to cultural production, he argues. In this new era, every business wants to be like Nike, which owns no factories and has relatively few physical assets. Instead, the company operates as a design studio and distribution network. "Nike's real capital," Rifkin explains, "is the image it weaves around its shoes. When a child pays £70 for Nike shoes, he is really paying to 'experience' the Nike story."

In what he dubs the emerging Age of Access, businesses will rapidly move away from owning things. Car companies, film companies, music companies and book publishers no longer simply sell physical products. Instead, we buy access to experiences, as when we rent a video or lease a car. In the process, Exxon, General Motors, USX and other old giants of the industrial era give way to the new giants of cultural capitalism, such as Bertelsmann, Disney, Microsoft, News Corporation, Sony and Time-Warner.

What worries Rifkin most, however, is that each person's lifetime potentially becomes a commercial market. In business circles, he growls, "the new term is the life time value (LTV) of the customer – the theoretical measure of how much a human being is worth if every moment of his or her life were to be commodified in one form or another in the commercial sphere."

Could we beat back the tidal wave of change, even if we wanted to? Maybe, but we would need to operate with a degree of foresight and discipline that is rare even in wartime. And the pressures for ever-more change are growing all the time. Over the next three decades, it has been forecast, computing power will grow by a factor of one million. Astonishing. Computers will become so powerful, so easy to use, so invisible, that they will change our lives in ways that are inconceivable today. [90]

Technology is not automatically benign. The way in which it is used determines its impacts. IBM, for example, has been accused of supplying punchcard calculating machines to the Nazis, which were subsequently used to automate the Holocaust. They were used to identify Jews, for example, and to run concentration camps.[91]

And as Bill Joy of Sun Microsystems explains, a factor of a million "shrinks a millennium to nine hours, a lifetime to 40 minutes, a year to 30 seconds. A jet plane is less than 1,000 times faster than walking, yet even that drastically reshapes our perception of the world." He notes: "The last major man-made overlay on civilization's landscape was the automobile. Even though we love our cars, we did a horrible job with them – they pollute, they isolate, and they have changed the landscape in ways that make them both incredibly frustrating and absolutely essential."

If we are to overlay a new digital design in a way that doesn't lead to such high order of dysfunction, we are going to have to learn to practice design at a radically different level. The key question here: How do we set about creating a wide range of TBL business models to test out in the marketplace?

TREND 2: TBL FOOTPRINTS

A basic assumption has been that the new technologies and business models will more or less automatically be good for the economy, society and the environment. Having worked several times for BT through the 1990s, I have found this attitude to be widespread in the IT industry. People in the industry talk about the way in which teleconferencing will replace road and air transport, and – still – about the paperless office.

You also find this unspoken confidence in the intrinsic sustainability of the new order in the biotechnology world. Here, as with Monsanto, the assumption is that that new knowledge will enable us to replace toxic atoms (pesticides) with sustainable bits (DNA-encoded biopesticides, engineered into crops). New GM golden rice strains, we are told, will protect or even restore the sight of children. Clearly, we stand on the threshold of a new age of miracles.

But read books like *The Nudist on the Late Shift*, which provides the inside story of Silicon Valley, and you will find extreme forms of blinkering.[92] The focus is almost always on your value proposition, not your values. OK, new economy folk admit, so places like Silicon Valley may get a bit congested, but in the big scheme of things the e-economy will press much more lightly on the earth. Really? How do we know? Can we count on things getting better? Only, it seems, if we decide to make it happen.

Indeed, anyone who assumes that the new economy will take yesterday's Corporate Locusts and Caterpillars and transform them almost overnight into Corporate Butterflies or Honeybees should take a reality check. Try dipping into the work of Jim Salzman, professor of law at American University. A long-time friend and colleague, he notes that amid all the hype about the information revolution and deindustrialization, we are seeing some rather surprising trends.

Rather than assuming that the transition to a service economy is automatically benign, that all service companies are going to be Butterflies or Honeybees, he distinguishes between 'smokestack services' and 'cumulative services'.[94] Smokestack services, he argues, include relatively high-impact activities such as electric utilities, airlines, Federal Express, and hospitals. Cumulative services, on the other hand, tend to be less visible, but collectively may still have considerable impacts. They include dry-cleaners, dental surgeries, hotels and fast-food chains such as Burger King or McDonald's.

Some of these new services may be helping along the dematerializing trend, he accepts, but they are often creating new problems. San Francisco Bay, he notes, is registering growing levels of silver pollution. When the problem first came to light, the authorities looked for silver mines or factories using the metal. Instead, the most important source of the problem turned out to be dental surgeries.

Among the most profound impacts, Salzman concludes, are those flowing from what he calls 'leverage services'. These are businesses, like Amazon.com, B&Q or Wal-Mart, that act as funnels between suppliers and consumers. The specifications they impose on their supply chains can have a huge impact on the ecological, social or economic footprints produced. That's why such businesses as Home Depot are attracting increasing attention from campaigners, who recognize the potential to leverage huge changes across such supply chains, once they get the attention of the central leverage service company.

New economy technologies and business models will also produce social and economic footprints, both positive and negative. In a joined-up, CNN world, companies will find that they are increasingly held responsible for what happens way upstream – and way downstream – of the activities over which they have direct control. Such pressures will drive the evolution of triple bottom line accounting (see below), but they will also drive the evolution of new forms of project, technology and business portfolio assessment (Figure 11.1, page 218).

In the process, we will learn to think differently. Figure 3.1 plots the TBL impacts of an oilfield through its productive life.[95] Increasingly, we will need to ask ourselves how a similar plot might look for each new technology, product or other business venture proposed – whether the life-time is likely to be measured in decades

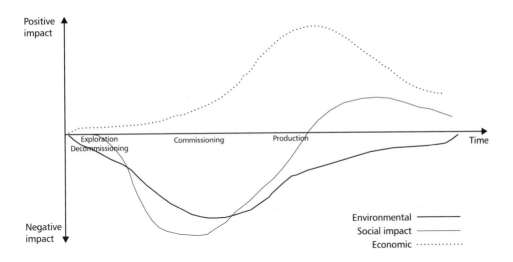

Figure 3.1 Economic, environmental and social impacts of hydrocarbon activity.
Source: T. Moser, Ph.D. Dissertation (Cambridge, 1998).

(as with an oil-field), years, hours, minutes or (in the case of some physics experiments) nanoseconds.

TREND 3: TBL ACCOUNTING

One service sector whose direct social and environmental impacts are often thought of as small is accounting. But, at the same time that accountants are getting to grips with the new economy, they are also having to get their brains around the triple bottom line. So expect to see the third great metamorphosis happening in the rarified world of accountancy.

Let's start with the basic task of valuing a company. Once upon a time, a company's market value was roughly equal to the sum of its physical assets – the land, plant and capital it owned. These were the assets that industrial age companies used to produce cashflows and profits.[96] In the new economy, despite its very real hiccups, even older companies tend to rely less and less on physical, or tangible, assets to create value. In fact, value is increasingly produced by so-called 'intangible' assets. Things like brands, know-how, intellectual property, R&D, human capital and relationships.

Before the dotcom crunch, for example, just 10 percent of the $300 billion valuation of Microsoft was backed by traditional physical assets recorded on the company's balance sheet. The things that most directly contribute to value creation in Bill Gates' empire do not appear on the balance sheet at all, a fact which Gates himself has noted "is probably not very enlightening from an accounting point of view."

In the new, connected economy, the economic action is shifting from the tangible to the intangible. This has enormous implications in terms of potential wealth creation. "Long term," say Stan Davis and Christopher Meyer of the Ernst & Young Center for Business Innovation, "the information economy's form of capital – information, knowledge, and talent – can be leveraged indefinitely at much lower costs than can the financial capital needed to build steel mills in the industrial age. The amount of financial capital required is much smaller, which is lowering the amount of capital needed and thus its cost. And, unlike a factory, information's capacity is almost unlimited. The wealth from movies or computer games comes from almost pure margin as more and more people use them, a phenomenon often called 'increasing returns'."[97]

They argue that companies should be valued in terms of their growth potential, not the growth achieved. "Assets tell you where a company has been," they note; "income, where the company is; market capitalization, where a company is headed; and risk, at what rate of acceleration. A company overflowing with tangible assets may be too heavy to run the race."

Victory, in this analysis, will eventually go to the virtually weightless, to the Butterfly or Honeybee, not the Caterpillar or Locust. Whatever happens in dotcom-land, however, it seems certain that dissatisfaction with traditional accounting methods will grow. Old economy accounting was backward looking, rooted in the needs of statutory financial reporting. As the new economy boomed, however, it was increasingly clear that traditional forms of accounting were losing touch with emergent reality. Of course, much of the 'value' created by the new economy and related business models was illusory, reflecting hope and hype. But it also became clear that current cashflows were becoming less useful in predicting the longer-term performance and value of new economy players.

Accepted accounting principles often encourage companies to do the wrong things, at least as far as the new market rules are concerned. None of that has stopped companies like Amazon recognizing that 'weightless' assets and intangibles are the very foundation of the new economy, of course, but growing numbers of accountants now accept the need for new accounting models. Accounting firms like PricewaterhouseCoopers are now scrambling to develop and introduce methods that help capture and value hidden forms of value. PwC calls its approach *ValueReporting*, branding it with an iceberg. The message is that many essential measures of corporate well-being lurk beneath the surface of a company's published accounts.[98]

In parallel, there has been a huge growth in work on ethical, social and environmental accounting. Groups like the World Resources Institute (WRI) have been developing new ways of valuing environmental risks, for example. In a recent study of the pulp and paper industry, WRI found that at least half of the companies it studied expected the financial impacts of impending environmental issues would be at least 5 percent, with several expecting impacts approaching or exceeding 10 percent. In some cases, however, the expected impact on stockholder equity ranged as high as 15 or 20 percent.[99]

Expect this experimentation in accounting to continue. In parallel, too, there has been an explosion of new standards to help companies manage their aspects of their triple bottom line performance – and to help accountants capture at least some of the value created in the process. A brief survey of a sample of 21 evolving standards can be found in box 11 (page 157). One conclusion would be that early single-issue standards are giving way to new contenders which, like the Global Reporting Initiative (GRI), aspire to embrace all three dimensions of business performance: economic, social and environmental. The adrenaline rush may not quite be on a par with skiing down Everest, but the importance of the work in trying to capture the value created or destroyed by the four main business models covered in Chapter 4 is difficult to exaggerate.

 PANEL 3

Storms blind Burning Man

Before the dotcom crash, there was no better place to take the raging pulse of the new economy than at the Burning Man Festival in Nevada's Black Rock Desert. Burning Man first ignited in 1986, when a landscape architect built an eight-foot-tall wooden effigy and set fire to it on Baker Beach, San Francisco. A tiny wing-beat in the bigger scheme of things. Part of the idea was that the blazing figure would help re-ignite the "suppressed and depressed counterculture".[100] It did that – and more.

The spectacle mutated into an annual fantasia. In 1990, this was relocated to the Nevada desert. Burning Man really comes alive at night, when the desert glows with glow sticks and electro-luminescent outfits, while flame-throwers and lasers light the star-studded sky. "If the multidimensional spectacle can be reduced to one single concept," says journalist Daniel Pinchbeck, "it is transformation; transformation of consciousness, transformation of artistic creativity into ecstatic communion, of sculptures into flames and ash, of visible fields of electricity into a death-defying game, of all kinds of energy into new forces. And transformation of the self: After the event, many Burners change jobs, start new relationships or end old ones, or begin anew in other ways."

In retrospect, the dust-storms that plagued and blinded Burning Man Y2K presaged the financial market storms that would wipe billions of dollars from the valuations of the dotcoms. But if the spirit with which the 'burners' dusted themselves off once the storms had passed through is anything to go by, the new economy may have more staying power than some critics have allowed. "Calamity binds a community together," said John Perry Barlow, a former Grateful Dead lyricist and founder of the Electronic Freedom Foundation.

Anyone wanting a listening post to keep tabs on the metamorphoses reshaping our companies, value webs and economies – and prepared to put up with more than a little nudity and public sex – should have at least one eye trained on the Black Rock Desert. But the dotcom crash brought a message that many of those beating a path to Burning Man would rather not have heard.

Here, as elsewhere, the laws of economic and financial gravity still apply, as Sun Microsystems chairman and CEO Scott McNealy put it. "Startups may put rapid growth ahead of profits for a time," he said, "but eventually they will have to return to the true nature of business. They will have to charge more than the cost of the goods and services they deliver, and make a profit. They will have to add value to people's lives – same as always. And they will have to be trustworthy, conduct their businesses with integrity, and guard their reputations."[101]

PART II

METAMORPHOSI$

In fiercely competitive markets, businesses can move to higher or lower states.

Once metamorphosis starts, however, the old life-forms are digested, the new assembled.

To avoid the process is to risk extinction.

But there are also tremendous risks for the growing number of Corporate Chrysalids.

CHAPTER 4

Value versus values
Penetrating the values and value barriers

What color is your dream? Anil Kapur found a highly individual way of communicating the core values of his biotechnology-based company. Given that he works at the Indian subsidiary of a Danish group, this was always going to be something of a challenge. The values embraced by most Danes, we might assume, are at least half a world away from those espoused by most Indians. But, again, the evidence suggests otherwise – and Kapur radically simplifies the complexity that so often fogs this area. Each employee, each new recruit, at Novo Nordisk Pharma India receives a tool box containing just seven items. They are:

- *A rope.* This, employees are told, signifies freedom. You can use it to climb up and achieve a successful career. It is a connecting bond to the core values. But be careful, employees are warned: you can misuse it to hang yourself.
- *A mirror.* Whatever you do, you should be able to look yourself in the face.
- *A piece of sandpaper.* Without friction, everything would slip by. With too much friction, nothing moves. Open, honest, constructive criticism is necessary for change and progress.
- *A watch.* Timeliness is crucial for success, so plan to do things on time and to deadline.
- *A pen.* Team success depends on each individual's willingness and ability to give good feedback.
- *A piece of canvas and a brush.* Employees are told: 'Learn to paint your own dream'.[1]

These values are spotlighted at all large company gatherings – and potential new recruits are tested against them, to see whether they are likely to fit in with the company's culture. Not that this culture is totally new. Indeed, Kapur notes that these values had existed for some time in the organization, as unspoken principles. But commercial success and the resulting growth meant that growing numbers of employees needed to be brought into the culture.

The tool box brings the core values to life in a very tangible way, signaling the need to be open, accountable, honest and willing to share improved practices. Before focusing on six values likely to be key stepping stones in the sustainability transition, let's briefly look at the nature of the external and internal challenges facing companies in relation to the values agenda.

GROWING TENSIONS

The tension between value creation and values is not new. Think of the historical controversies surrounding empire-building, slavery or the working conditions imposed during the Industrial Revolution. Nor have such problems gone away. Slavery – in both old and new forms – is now said to be more common than at any time in human history, including the Roman Empire.[2]

And new or mutated values are continually surfacing. Consider what happened with Huntingdon Life Sciences, the UK-based animal testing company. Campaigners brought HSL to brink of bankruptcy, after intense pressure focused on individual managers, investors and shareholders forced a number of the company's financial backers to pull out: fund managers Phillips & Drew sold its HSL stake, WestLB Panmure stepped down as broker, and HSBC stopped holding HSL shares on behalf of its clients.[3] At the eleventh hour, and fifty-ninth second, just as the Royal Bank of Scotland was about to call in a £22.6 million loan, a US backer said it would bail out HLS.

An interesting question: would closure have helped cut animal suffering? Apart from the fact that the tests are required by government laws, HLS supporters stressed that UK test rules are much stricter than those in some other countries where the work might otherwise be done.[4]

Sensitivity to animal welfare issues may be greatest in the UK, but this controversy illustrates how values-based campaigns can bring highly profitable businesses to their knees. It also illustrates the new tactics being used by some activists: at least two dozen bankers say they were called at 3am in the morning, accused of supporting animal torturers and warned that their family could be targeted.[5] A worrying case of a legitimate end being used to justify questionable means.

Now the new economy is adding new dimensions to the debate, intensifying the collisions between value creation and values. Yahoo! may not automatically spring to mind in this area, for example, but perhaps you recall a recent French court case? The central issue was this: Should an American internet services provider take responsibility for preventing French citizens from gaining access to online auctions of

Nazi memorabilia? French law forbids the sale or exhibition of objects likely to incite racial hatred, including such memorabilia.[6] A Paris court ruled that Yahoo! had not gone far enough to keep offensive objects out of the hands of French citizens. It gave the company three months to block access for French e-surfers to the relevant parts of its site. Failure to do so, Yahoo! was told, could result in punitive fines.

Worried by the implications for its business model, Yahoo! queried whether national laws should apply to a global medium? It challenged the technical feasibility of excluding certain types of internet user. It stressed that even the use of key words and programs designed to screen out anyone identifying themselves as French would leave a huge number of opportunities for abuse. But, at least in retrospect, one of the most interesting aspects of the Yahoo! defense was this: the company's lawyers noted that any such changes might put it in breach of the US constitutional right to freedom of speech.

In the worst case, they argued, internet service providers would end up having to comply with the most restrictive controls in all the legal jurisdictions potentially affected by such services. Would Yahoo! have to shape its global offering to satisfy Chinese, Hutu, Iranian or Libyan sensitivities? Lawyer Mike Pullen warned that pressure groups could attack any web-site, choosing the most restrictive laws in force anywhere in the world. "Anti-smoking groups could have a go at the tobacco manufacturers' sites, using advertising legislation. Environmental groups could attack sites over GM food. The list is endless," he protested.

Later, in a dramatic U-turn, Yahoo! said it would obey the court order and self-censor.[7] Whatever the final legal outcome, the arguments and counter-arguments underscore the fact that companies and other business organizations must often bridge yawning chasms between the values of different individuals, age-groups, countries and cultures. And that is one of the strongest reasons why growing numbers of companies and other business organizations are starting to carry out regular values audits (box 4, below). In the process, they would be well advised to think through the implications of two key impediments to real progress in this area: the Values Barrier and the Value Barrier. Let's look at each of these in turn.

Box 4

The soul at work

Corporations are not machines, or at least most aren't. They are made up of people, of relationships, of learning processes. As a result, new business metaphors often compare corporations to living systems, biological or ecological. There is growing talk of 'emotional intelligence', of corporate values and cultures, even of the 'corporate soul'.

Someone who is not shy of using such language is Richard Barrett, former values coordinator at the World Bank. He distinguishes between corporate change and corporate transformation.[8] In his book *Liberating the Corporate Soul*, he sees change as a different way of doing, "doing what we do now, but doing it in a more efficient, productive, or quality-enhancing way."

By contrast, transformation results in "a different way of being." It involves changes at "the deepest levels of beliefs, values, and assumptions." Transformation, Barrett believes, occurs most readily in systems that "are vulnerable, learn from mistakes, are open to the future, and can let go of the past and their rigid beliefs."

Successful companies tend to: have strong, positive, values-driven cultures; make a lasting commitment to learning and self-renewal; continually adapt, using both internal and external feedback; build strategic alliances with internal and external partners, customers and suppliers; be willing to take risks and experiment; and have a balanced, values-based approach to targeting and measuring performance.

Rather than leaving things there, however, Barrett has developed a suite of transformational tools, designed to take companies through the five main stages of transformation. These lead from unawareness, through awareness and the learning and practicing of new behaviors, to the most fundamental stage of all, a change in values.

The approach defines four types of human need (physical, emotional, mental and spiritual), seven levels of employee consciousness and motivation (safety and health, relationships, self-esteem, achievement, personal growth, meaning, making a difference, and service), and seven matched levels of corporate consciousness (survival, relationships, self-esteem, transformation, organization, community, and service).[9]

The bottom three levels of employee or corporate consciousness, as shown in Figure 4.1, are basically driven by self-interest, the top three by a growing interest in the common good.

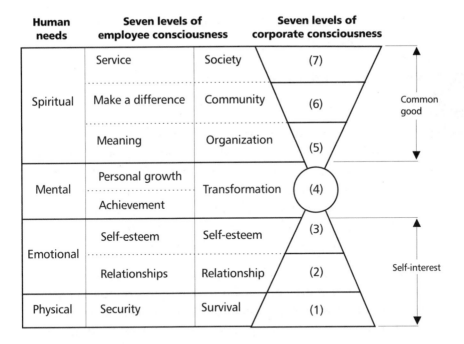

Human needs	Seven levels of employee consciousness		Seven levels of corporate consciousness	
Spiritual	Service	Society	(7)	Common good
	Make a difference	Community	(6)	
	Meaning	Organization	(5)	
Mental	Personal growth	Transformation	(4)	
	Achievement			
Emotional	Self-esteem	Self-esteem	(3)	Self-interest
	Relationships	Relationship	(2)	
Physical	Security	Survival	(1)	

Figure 4.1   Seven levels of corporate consciousness.
Source: Richard Barrett.

The sustainability imperative, in different ways, can operate at each of these seven levels.

Nor is the values audit step the end of the road. Barrett suggests that since "organizational transformation begins from the top," companies need to carry out a 'leadership values assessment' and create a 'balanced needs scorecard'. The last of these he has built on the work of people like Stephen Covey (of *The Seven Habits of Highly Effective People* fame[10]) and Robert Kaplan and David Norton (with their Balanced Scorecard, designed to "translate strategy into action"[11]).

So what are the implications for would-be Citizen CEOs and other business leaders? Even the best may need to go through a three-stage development process, says Barrett. In the first stage, personal transformation, they connect with their deepest self. During stage 2, emotional intelligence, they learn to connect with their colleagues to create a more cohesive organizational culture. And stage 3 involves learning the importance of connecting with stakeholders, including customers, suppliers, the local community, and society at large.

Box 5: Blips on the screen

Touchstones

Growing numbers of companies are revisiting their business principles, as Shell and Ford have done, or are realizing for the first time that they need their own set. Clearly articulated business principles create standards that help to bind an organization together, as Business for Social Responsibility (BSR) puts it, and to guide employees in decision-making.[12] Among the reasons why companies head in this direction are the following:

- They want to create a corporate culture 'touchstone', with companies variously describing their business principles as the 'glue', 'touchstone' or 'moral backbone' of the organization.
- They see the draft principles as a focus for evolving internal conversations, with an initial 'straw man' version drawn from existing policies, codes and principles being used to stimulate internal debate and engagement.
- They see such principles as the best way of embedding values throughout the organization, with the next step being to integrate them into, among other things, strategic planning, decision-making processes, business practices, management systems, employee performance reviews, and succession planning.

THE VALUES AND VALUE BARRIERS

Values are fundamental to the process of wealth creation, whether or not it is sustainable. Indeed, a strong case can be made that the best forms of capitalism – like other more traditional forms of value creation – have always depended on values.

Some years back, in *The Seven Cultures of Capitalism*,[13] two respected business researchers reached a surprising conclusion on the basis of an investigation of the business cultures and value systems of countries around the world. Wealth creation, Charles Hampden-Turner and Fons Trompenaars argued, "is in essence a moral act," driven by values. And these values, we were told, flow from national and corporate cultures. "In any culture," they explained, "a deep structure of beliefs is the invisible hand that regulates economic activity. These cultural preferences, or values, are the bedrock of national identity and the source of economic strengths – and weaknesses."

Each of the countries they studied turned out to have its own unique combination of values. "This value set is an economic fingerprint," we learned, which "correlates with specific types of economic achievement and failure."

So it is plain wrong, *The Economist* argued recently, to say that capitalism "is 'value-free'. It is anything but. Capitalism exalts individual freedom and voluntary, rather than obligatory or customary, interaction among the members of society. It is difficult to have capitalism without freedom and almost impossible to have freedom without capitalism. Whether or not you agree with its values, capitalism is a system positively bulging with moral content."[14]

Greater levels of corporate transparency and accountability mean that the 21st economy will develop its own unique fingerprints, with a mutated set of values at its core. However it is defined and managed, the triple bottom line of sustainability must increasingly set the minimum requirements for successful business.

The sustainability transition will require growing numbers of companies, value webs and economies to shift from degenerative to regenerative forms of value creation (see Chapter 5). In the process, they must first cross the 'Values Barrier', or they will end up stuck in Caterpillar mode – or shift into highly damaging Locust forms of value creation. Second, they face the 'Value Barrier', which involves creating sustainable value on a sufficient scale to satisfy a reasonably equitable world of 8–10 billion people.

THE VALUES BARRIER

The Values Barrier is illustrated in Figure 4.2. This introduces the MetaMatrix, featured in greater detail in Chapter 5. The MetaMatrix sorts business models, companies, value webs, and even entire economies, on the basis of whether they have a net regenerative or degenerative impact on the economic, social and, perhaps most importantly, ecological systems of which they are part. The vertical columns then distinguish between those producing low-level TBL impacts and those producing much greater impacts.

It is sometimes possible to make a great deal of money by flying in the face of society's established or emerging values, but such forms of value creation risk growing counter-pressure.

Like the sound barrier that shook many would-be transonic aircraft to pieces, the Values Barrier represents a major hurdle for companies embarking on transformation processes. Just as pressure waves build up around an aircraft approaching the speed of sound, so companies moving towards and through the Values Barrier trigger a series of internal and external shock-waves that can create massive instability. Monsanto's unsuccessful efforts to shift from the Locust to Honeybee mode of operation are a striking case in point (page 108).

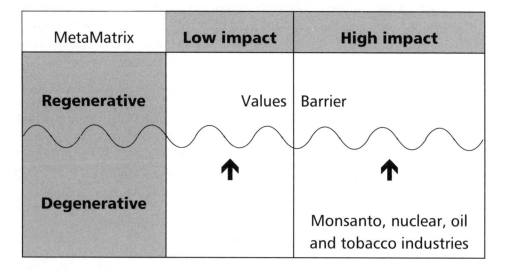

Figure 4.2 The Values Barrier. © SustainAbility.

As the shock-waves build around a business, so does the drag factor. In some cases, the reason may be that the financial markets resist the transition, because they cannot see where sufficient financial value will be created. In other cases, companies may find that their notion of a regenerative business model is out of line with wider societal perceptions and priorities. Instead of a gradual increase in pressure, for example, aircraft and companies alike can sometimes experience a sudden increase in pressure across the shock-wave.[15]

Interestingly, too, an aircraft that holds its speed at or around the speed of sound, at Mach 1, experiences the greatest drag. The same is true of a business that operates at or near the Values Barrier, rather than breaking through – and operating well beyond – it. Staff spend a high proportion of their time trying to work out what they should do in particular circumstances, rather than having a clear picture of right and wrong.

That said, there is an interesting difference between aircraft designers working on aircraft able to penetrate the sound barrier with ease and those designing new business models (or adapting old ones) to ensure that they can pass through the Values Barrier. Aircraft designers go for radical streamlining, with special features like swept wings helping to reduce drag. By contrast, as we see in Chapter 9, businesses that successfully operate around – and across – the Values Barrier often do so by evolving more inclusive forms of governance.

According to conventional business thinking, processes and systems that bring outside stakeholders inside should increase drag, whereas the experience of companies spotlighted in Chapter 9 suggests that the reverse can often (if not always) be true. Indeed, to bend the analogy somewhat, some stakeholder processes provide companies with the equivalent of a wind tunnel. They can test new business concepts against the emerging priorities of those who can limit or boost those companies' license to operate and to innovate.

Based on our experience with such processes, the following six values will be among the conditions for sustainable business success in the 21st century.

1. Ultra-transparency

Although we are unlikely to reach anything like total transparency, dramatically increased levels of corporate accountability and disclosure will be a necessary condition for sustainable capitalism. Coming decades will see business exposed to levels of global transparency unimaginable today. Some people may try to build 'stealth' corporations and value webs, sometimes successfully, but for most companies the assumption must be that they need to operate as if conditions of almost total transparency prevailed.

This is desirable. Transparent markets tend to be more efficient, adapting continually to new needs and offering open access to innovators.[16] The corporate sustainability reporting trend has a central role to play in this respect. But total transparency raises new issues for companies, which is why Microsoft now has a Chief Privacy Officer, charged with helping the company to get its brain around the ethics of privacy in a world of free-flowing information.[17]

2. Open governance

'Stop the world, I want to get off' was a phrase that gained currency in the Sixties. But, however much some people may want to turn back the tide of globalization, the broad trend is unstoppable. As a result, we will generally do best when we embrace the potential of the future with open arms and open minds. Open systems, like the World Wide Web, are the wave of the future.[18] Unfortunately, however, capitalism is globalizing ahead of the capacity of global governance systems to cope, as is explained in Chapter 2.

The shock-waves that have built up around such organizations as the World Trade Organization (WTO), the World Bank and the International Monetary Fund (IMF) signal growing concerns about this governance gap. The response could evolve in a number of directions, as illustrated by three scenarios published by the World Business Council for Sustainable Development (Chapter 12).

3. Equal opportunity

Free market fetishists may not like it, but sustainable capitalism will often evolve most readily where there is real equality of opportunity. Such opportunity must embrace all the different forms of capital discussed below. Meanwhile, most definitions of SD are based around concepts both of intra-generational (i.e. justice within a generation) and of inter-generational (justice between generations) equity.

The intra-generational equity agenda spotlights the need to ensure equality of opportunity across generations currently alive, while the linked inter-generational agenda focuses on the need to ensure equality of opportunity between today's generations and tomorrow's.

4. Multiple capitals

Sustainable capitalism will depend on the management, regeneration and evolution of many different forms of capital. Capitalism has traditionally focused on financial capital, however, in the belief that natural and manufactured forms of capital are interchangeable. As a result, companies have mainly paid attention to manufactured and financial forms of capital. Manufactured capital, which includes all our technology, buildings and other forms of physical infrastructure, facilitates production processes – but is not embodied in the final product.

Now, however, the business world is being asked to measure, value and manage new forms of capital.[19] Skandia has been one of the companies leading the charge, focusing on intellectual capital (a measure of brainpower and creativity), structural capital (including corporate culture, management processes, IT systems, databases, reputation and brands) and customer capital (the value of customer relationships and loyalty). But even Skandia's pioneering approach does not cover key aspects of sustainable capitalism, for example natural and social capital. Three basic forms of capital which sustainable capitalism must increasingly focus on are:

* *Human capital.* Each of us is part of the world's human capital. In the past, nations went to war over land and natural resources; in the coming decades, the competition will be for intellectual capital and talented people. As Skandia's approach acknowledges, our brains, knowledge and experience are

crucial inputs to the processes of wealth creation. Among the key contributors to human capital are the knowledge, skills and motivation needed for wealth creation. Education and training are the most obvious form of investment in this area. Poverty prevents many hundreds of millions of people from achieving their full potential and poverty alleviation will therefore be a central priority in sustainable capitalism.

- *Social capital.* This is the net value added to social and economic activities by human relationships and co-operation. High levels of trust in an organization or society can reduce the amount of non-productive friction caused during wealth creation.[20] SD will be most likely – and will be achieved at the lowest overall cost to the economy and to nature – in societies where there are the highest levels of trust and other forms of social capital. Key contributors include families, communities, schools, businesses, trade unions, and voluntary organization. True, many business leaders see social capital as a concern for governments, but they have huge impacts in this area.

- *Natural capital.* This is the really critical form of capital, the ultimate bottom line. In the simplest terms, natural capital measures stocks or flow of energy and matter yielding valuable goods and services. Given that it took a $200 million investment to keep eight people alive in the Biosphere 2 complex for just two years, the value of the natural systems that produce Earth's oxygen, purify air and water, decompose natural wastes and regulate the climate is obviously going to be high. One attempt at measurement put the annual value of such environmental services at between $36 trillion and $58 trillion, in 1998 dollars, compared to the Gross World Product that year of $39 trillion.[21] Go figure.

In terms of social capital, research in Japan, South Korea and the USA has shown that building trust through supply chains really does pay off in terms of increased efficiency and substantially lower costs.[22] So how does this work? Well, it turns out that positive impacts flow from investment, job creation, or products that help develop social capital (e.g. telephones, software), and negative impacts from disinvestment, layoffs, or products that potentially undermine social capital (e.g. alcohol, firearms).

One tricky question raised by the existence of different forms of capital, however, is whether they can be traded and even substituted for one another? Our industrial economies have been built by entrepreneurs and corporations wedded to the notion that their sole purpose is to convert natural capital into various forms of financial, manufactured, human and social capital. That assumption is now being challenged.

As the sustainability agenda has evolved, some of the more switched-on economists have begun to talk in terms of 'weak sustainability' and 'strong sustainability'. The weak variety reflects the idea that the main focus of enterprise and the economy must be on maintaining the overall stock of capital, with no effective limits on the substitution of one capital for another. So, for example, the clear-cutting of an old-growth forest may be justified by the jobs and wealth generated. The strong variety of sustainability, by contrast, holds that some forms of capital – 'critical' natural capital – cannot (or should not) be traded or substituted. This has major implications for how natural resources and other forms of capital are valued.

5. Real diversity

It's a fact: most human eyes and brains tend to prefer diverse environments, and with good reason. Monocultures may be highly productive in areas like agriculture or manufacturing, bringing useful economies of scale, but they can also be highly unstable. Urban monocultures may be cheaper to build and, at least on paper, to operate. But everywhere we have tried to develop such monocultures, they have caused unexpected (but not unpredictable) problems.

Just as natural ecosystems and agriculture depend on genetic, biological and ecological diversity for their continued resilience and health, so our economies create wealth by drawing upon – and, less often, generating – economic, social and cultural forms of diversity. Like it or not, social and ethnic diversity is going to be a given. In the UK, the number of people from ethnic minorities has risen from a few tens of thousands in 1950 to more than 3 million today.[23] And by 2055, non-Hispanic whites are predicted to be a minority in the USA.

A sustainable world will be highly diverse: sustainable business models and lifestyles won't come off the production lines like early Fords. Instead, just as plants evolved a huge variety of shapes, colors, and reproductive strategies around their common core of chlorophyll-based photosynthesis, so future business models and lifestyles are likely to be highly diverse, even as they converge around radical improvements in eco-efficiency – and in the conservation and generation of multiple forms of capital.

In the energy industry, for example, we see a new diversity in micro-power solutions, rather than the mega-schemes (nuclear power plants, dams) favored in the past.[24] The trend started with new technologies like the highly flexible gas turbine. Now major companies are responding to the trend. Swiss-Swedish power engineering company ABB, for example, is refocusing its entire business away from mega to micro business, with a growing focus on wind turbines and fuel cells.

6. Shared learning

Learning, invention and innovation will be core values of a sustainable economy. And our learning needs will very much depend on what it is that we are trying to sustain (box 6, page 60). Sustainable capitalism will be built on brave experiments, rapid prototyping, and the wide communication of lessons learned from both successes and failures. The sharing will need to happen not just in the products of learning, but also in the processes themselves. This is a key benefit of well-designed and well-run stakeholder engagement processes. All of that said, the 'precautionary principle' will mean that some high-risk experiments will need thorough vetting before they are allowed to proceed.

Peter Senge, long-time champion of the 'learning organization', has helped drive things forward in this area by founding the Society for Organizational Learning (SoL) and its Sustainability Consortium. His 'five disciplines' of organizational learning provide useful guidance on how to prepare corporations for the sustainability transition.[25] They are:

- *Personal mastery.* This involves learning how to expand our personal capacity to create the results we most desire, and creating the organizational environment in which our colleagues can also develop themselves towards the goals and purposes they choose.
- *Mental models.* Here the focus is on reflecting on and continuously clarifying and improving our internal pictures of the world, and on working out how they shape our actions and decisions.
- *Shared vision.* Personal visions are unlikely to change the world unless shared. Groups can build shared images of the future they are seeking to create, shaping targets and guiding subsequent actions.
- *Team learning.* There is nothing automatic about the ways in which teams learn. Floods of highly relevant and up-to-date information may fail to improve performance unless conversational and collective thinking skills are developed – and team values emphasize sharing, learning, appropriate action and prompt feedback.
- *Systems thinking.* Intuition can get us a long way, but we also need ways – and a language – to describe the forces and interrelationships shaping the economic, social and environmental systems on which we depend. Systems

thinking is a necessary condition for penetrating the Value Barrier and developing Honeybee forms of wealth creation.

Box 6: Blips on the screen

What do we want to sustain?

A tricky question to answer. Current definitions of SD are far from value-free. It is possible, for example, to imagine a sustainable world which is neither equitable nor democratic, though both are central to the 1987 Brundtland Commission definition.[26] And it all depends on what we are trying to sustain. A technology? A company? An economy? A society? A natural resource or ecosystem? Let's take each in turn.

A sustainable technology

Like new species, new technologies compete against the old. Few have the capacity to survive indefinitely, although some – like archery or pottery – hang on in craft, museum or recreational niches. Technologies that are successful in meeting key needs at one point in time may cause unexpected problems when scaled up. So, for example, CFCs offered real safety and health benefits, but later proved to have totally unexpected effects on the planet's stratospheric ozone layer. Life-cycle thinking and management are crucial in sustainable product design, but so is careful monitoring of any impacts, coupled with a willingness to pull products off the market if danger signs emerge.

A sustainable company

For most CEOs and boards, this is the Big One. To succeed, a company must sustain its license to operate and to innovate. Different studies tend to discover the same things about long-lived companies with a strong financial performance [27]. Among other things, they:

- Have a strong, positive, values-driven culture.
- Maintain an ongoing commitment to learning and self-renewal.
- Adapt continually to internal and external feedback.
- Form strategic alliances with internal and external partners, customers and suppliers.
- Are willing to take risks and experiment.

- Use a values-based approach to measure economic, social and environmental performance.

A sustainable economy

Some economies, like some based on biomass energy or slave labor, have been fairly long-lived. In an accelerating world, however, static economies or economic units are doomed, even if they are museums. Successful economies are dynamic, able to manage successive waves of creative destruction. They will also tend to have governance systems favoring sustainable companies – with a high proportion of Corporate Caterpillars, Butterflies and Honeybees, rather than Corporate Locusts. Critically important here is the pricing of natural resources, together with the shifting of taxes from things we want (like more jobs) to things we want less of (like pollution or species loss).

A sustainable society

Some cultures and societies, like those of the Australian Aborigines, have lasted over thousands of years. But most societies, and all previous civilizations, have collapsed at some point, because of disease, war or environmental change, often triggered by poorly considered farming or forestry practices. To be sustainable in the 21st century, a society must not only manage natural resources sustainably and help protect the global ecosystem, but also remain competitive. Among other things, this requires investment in education and in sustainable technologies and infrastructure. There is also a growing recognition of the degree to which dynamically sustainable economies depend upon the governance, legal and broader cultural contexts within which investment, enterprise and business evolve.

A sustainable natural resource or ecosystem.

Many of us assume that ecosystems, and the flows of natural resources they provide, are stable over long periods of time. A few are, but most are not. Indeed, one key characteristic of sustainable ecosystems, particularly those we rely on for resources, is a capacity to ride out and recover from massive change. New ecosystems would establish themselves even in the radioactive ruins of a collapsed industrial civilization, but if we want to sustain

even a proportion of the ecosystems we depend on we have our
work cut out.

THE VALUE BARRIER

If the Values Barrier can seem impossible for unethical companies to break through,
the Value Barrier can also be exceedingly hard for some of the world's most ethical
companies to penetrate. The challenge for genuinely sustainable value creation in the
coming decades will be to deal *profitably* with the problems and opportunities thrown
up by a world of 8-10 billion people.

It is easy enough, meanwhile, to show unsustainable value management. The
asbestos story, for example, seems to go on and on. The stocks of companies with
even a remote connection to the material have tumbled as investors tried to work out
the implications of further waves of litigation.[28] With some 25 US companies already
in bankruptcy protection due to potential asbestos exposure, investors have been
worried that lawyers will sue companies that never made the material, but either used
it in their workplaces or transported related products. The year-to-year slump in
company values has been unbelievable: as asbestos-related concerns grew,
Federal-Mogul shares lost 87.9% of their value, Owens Corning's 96.1%, W.R.
Grace's 81.4% and USG's 53.2%.

While it is undeniably true that corporations exist to produce a competitive
return for shareholders, the parallel trend is also now clear: 21st century business will
have to be increasingly values-conscious, if not always driven by the values that the
rest of us embrace. Even the internet, as the Yahoo! trial illustrates, is beginning the
long haul from its wild west era to something more evolved. The online health
industry, for example, is developing new ethics standards to help consumers evaluate
the flood of medical information now found on the Net.[29]

So what does this imply? Investors, entrepreneurs and corporate managers
have got used to focusing on the 'burn rate' of their companies, the speed with which
they are consuming financial capital. But tomorrow's successful companies will also
have to be acutely sensitive to different forms of burn rate throughout their value
webs. They will need to monitor and actively manage the rates at which they generate
or destroy not just physical and financial capital but also, for example, human,
intellectual, social and natural capital.[30]

None of this will be easy. Indeed, one interesting question is who is going to
pay? Most of us take the process of wealth creation for granted, assuming that
business and the economy can take all of this in their stride. Certainly, the numbers
look impressive. The US economy, for example, began from an almost standing start

after World War II and yet by 2000 had passed the $10 trillion (that's $10,000,000,000,000) a year mark in terms of gross domestic product.[31] The early years of the new century will bring recessions, potentially even a full-blown depression, but there is no reason to think that more sustainable forms of capitalism won't emerge in the coming decades.

They will evolve in a world of intense, often bruising competition. The process of creative destruction will sometimes sweep away companies and value-webs which, at least on the surface, look perfectly healthy right across the triple bottom line. So, whether we like it or not, 21st century business will also have to be value-driven. To put it bluntly, companies that fail to deliver the levels of value that their shareholders and the financial markets expect will fade or die.

The 30:3 syndrome

And the uncomfortable fact is that rich world companies are simply not operating on a level playing-field. They are often undercut by cheaper competitors from other parts of the world. As if that were not enough, it turns out that most customers are more concerned about quality, price and delivery than they are about the values of the producer or the TBL impacts of the production process.

Look at the results of a recent study by one of the world's most consciously ethical businesses, the UK Co-operative Bank. They commissioned what was billed as "the most in-depth research into ethical consumerism."[32] And what did they find? Not remotely what they hoped to find. The results showed that while most people claim they take social and environmental issues into account when shopping, those concerns seem to evaporate by the time they reach the checkout.

Even though 88 percent of those questioned claimed to be ethical shoppers, when challenged, only 23 percent could name anything they had done to justify that claim. At a time when the media were brimming over with coverage of anti-capitalism protests in Seattle, Washington, London and Prague, only one in three respondents believed that the environmental impact of a product was important. Over three-quarters rated brand name, value for money and customer service above ethical considerations.

As a result, the Co-operative Bank has identified what it calls the '30:3' syndrome among consumers. A third of consumers say they care about environmental and social issues, yet the ethical market so far only translates into around 3 percent of sales.[33] The work focused in on five clusters among consumers:

• The largest group, at 49 percent, is the *Do what I can* group, who tend to be older, a quarter of them over 65. They have ethical concerns, but do not hold them very strongly.

•   Second, there is the *Look after my own* group, at 22 percent of consumers. They tend to be younger and on lower incomes, and are least likely to make choices based on ethical factors.

•   In third place, at the 18 percent mark, there are the *Conscientious consumers*, who will consider ethical issues once price and quality are removed from the equation. They are more likely than other groups to be car and home owners, and more concerned about quality than brands. Few are happy to be described as 'ethical' or 'caring', however.

•   Fourth, there is the *Brand generation*, at around 6 percent. These people are most concerned about brands, product quality, service and value for money. One in three is under 25, and this group is the only one that prefers to describe itself as 'ethical' rather than 'caring'.

•   And, fifth, at 5 percent, there are the *Global watchdogs*. They are professionals, aged 33-55, and concentrated in the wealthier regions. They think of themselves as ethical consumers, and two in five seek out information on products, brands and companies.

Value mantras

No surprise, then, that ethical concerns have been fairly slow to engage in the marketplace, nor that financial value has been the main business mantra. But how can companies pay more than lip service to the concept of creating value for customers and, even more importantly, shareholders? One answer has been to use techniques like the Economic Value Added (EVA) and Market Value Added (MVA) tools developed by the management consultancy Stern Stewart.

Calculating a company's EVA is relatively easy. Essentially, it involves measuring the difference between the profit it makes and the cost of the capital it uses. The idea is that as everyone involved in a business becomes aware of the cost of capital, shareholders, management and workers can all begin to pull together. In its MVA surveys, Stern Stewart aims to work out to what degree companies have created or destroyed value. Put simply, MVA is the difference between a company's current market value, including equity and debt, and the money invested in the business and retained by it over the years.

Stern Stewart has also recently added a new measure to EVA and MVA, Future Growth Value (FVA). This aims to assess what proportion of a company's market value results from investor expectations that it will grow in future. So, for example, the hope has been that some dotcoms would create spectacular value, justifying a higher-than-normal valuation today. But tobacco companies, facing tougher regulation and declining markets in the rich world, will tend to score a lower-than-average FGV.

Another, collaborative approach to valuing the intangible assets typical of the connected economy has been produced by Ernst & Young's Center for Business Innovation and the Wharton School for Business, working with *Forbes ASAP*. It is called the Value Creation Index. Those involved, including Wharton's Professor Dave Larcker, express surprise at how strongly sensitivity to community and environmental issues ranked in the survey results.[34]

Even so, if the sustainability transition is to develop at a sufficient pace, entrepreneurs must develop business models that can break through the Value Barrier. And the financial markets are going to have to work out how to discriminate those sustainability-focused business models that are most likely to create higher-than-average FGV, or whatever other measures evolve in the coming decades.

The implication is that the sustainability transition is going to need something more than several thousand new Corporate Butterflies. We are going to need Honeybee Corporations and value webs to do the real heavy-lifting. The key problem here, at least for Caterpillar and Butterfly businesses, is to break through the Value Barrier – and to do so in the right way. It is quite possible for a Caterpillar Corporation or value web to slide across into the Locust domain, for example, creating much greater financial returns – but at the expense of running down other forms of capital.

Increasingly, shareholders and other stakeholders will ask what a given enterprise can do to break through the Value Barrier (Figure 4.3), not only creating greater financial returns but doing so in ways that are both sustainable and, desirably, regenerative. The examples given here are ethical investment, organic agriculture and renewable energy, all of which are in the process of scaling up from their Butterfly stages to something closer to Honeybee mode.[35]

Both/and: values and value

Clearly, whether we look at companies in trouble, like Pacific Lumber/Maxxam or Yahoo!, or at companies that are some way down the path to solutions, like Novo Nordisk, it turns out that we shouldn't be thinking of values and value creation in terms of either/or, but of both/and. In Sweden, for example, a high-profile debate about ethical practices in farming is now seen as a key reason why the country appears to have avoided the staggering costs associated with 'mad cow' disease.[36]

But we should also pay attention to the ways in which values are surfacing in the new economy. In their book *Blur*, Christopher Meyer, director of Ernst &

MetaMatrix	Low impact	High impact
Regenerative	Ethical investment Organic farming Renewable energy →	V a l u e
Degenerative	→	B a r r i e r

Figure 4.3   The Value Barrier. © SustainAbility.

Young's Center for Business Innovation (CBI), and Stan Davis, a CBI research fellow, describe a world in which connectivity, speed and intangible assets come to dominate the social and economic landscapes.[37] In this blurring world, we obviously have to pay attention to how the nature of value is changing, with new ways being found to price goods, information, emotion and even attention.[38] Apart from the fact that these trends transfer power from producers to consumers, we are seeing every buyer-seller exchange increasingly colored by values – which may be economic, informational, emotional and/or ethical.

As the interplay between values and value creation moves further into the spotlight, companies aspiring to world class ethical behavior must get a grip on what their own employees think, perceive and believe. Such attitudes and behaviors are going to be fundamental for any company, any organization, wanting to be part of the sustainability transition.

Interestingly, more than 80 percent of executives questioned in a survey in Europe and North America by consultants Arthur D. Little (ADL) believed that their

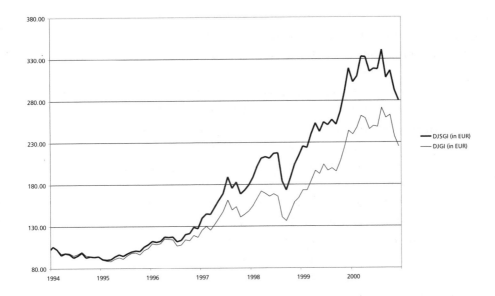

Figure 4.4 Dow Jones Sustainability Group Indexes performance (1994–2000).

companies would be able to extract value in moving towards sustainability, although most felt that their companies had made limited progress to date.[39] Once the need for transformative changes is finally recognized by a given company, we tend to see a rapid take-up by business of what Debra Meyerson calls 'tempered radicals'.[40] We will look at the attitudes, beliefs and experience of a sample of these people in later chapters.

Box 7: Blips on the screen

Play it again, Sam

When New York-based Dow Jones & Company linked up with Zurich-based Sustainable Asset Management (SAM), you could almost feel a shift in the global economy's center of gravity. Other major players had been involved in the socially responsible investment field for some time, among them mainstream players like Salomon Smith Barney, but this alliance seemed to signal something new. With the launch of the Dow Jones Sustainability Group Indexes, investors could more readily track the triple bottom line performance of leading sectors and companies.

Among the companies identified early on as sustainability leaders were BMW, Bristol-Myers Squibb, Credit Suisse, Deutsche Telekom, Fujitsu, Procter & Gamble and Thames Water. They were rated in terms of sustainability risks and opportunities.[41] Different companies may have very different views on how such assessments should be made, and on the ways in which social and environmental performance relate to financial performance, but the fact that they are now being made underscores the way in which the worlds of values and value creation are now converging. Of course, all such statistics should be taken with a big pinch of salt, but the out-performance of the shares of sustainability leaders in Europe (back-cast for the period 1994-99) is shown in Figure 4.4, against the overall Dow Jones Group performance. At least on this evidence, values-driven investing not only doesn't destroy financial value but helps create it.

PANEL 4

Interdependence Day

Daughter of a preacher, Julia 'Butterfly' Hill chose as her pulpit a 200-foot redwood, dubbed 'Luna' by the Earth First! activists who first organized the sit-in. But what started as a fairly routine protest quickly metamorphosed into one of the most extraordinary protests of recent years, pitting a lone young woman and her ragtag supporters against the might of a US logging company, Pacific Lumber, part of the rapacious Maxxam Corporation.

When Julia first climbed Luna, she thought of staying days; in the end, she spent a total of 738 days up the tree. "If I had seen what the Luna tree sit had in store when I first got involved," she admits, "I would have run screaming in the opposite direction." But in the process, she says, she became the "ultimate poster child" for the growing clash between emerging social values and old economy forms of value creation.

So, I ask, what made her climb Luna in the first place? "Most people assume I had an environmental background," she replies, "or that I had hippy parents." Neither, in fact, was true. Remembered as a stubborn child, she was raised with few possessions, but "plenty of convictions". She notes, however, that a severe bang to the head may have helped reinforce her strong sense of mission! When a car she was driving was rear-ended by a Ford Bronco in 1996, she suffered brain damage.

"When your life is threatened," she recalls in her extraordinary book *The Legacy of Luna*, "nothing is ever the same again."[42] But she also muses that the injuries had been to the left, analytical side of her brain, perhaps letting the right, more creative side take over. "It became clear to me that our value as people is not in our stock portfolios and bank accounts," she explains, "but in the legacies we leave behind."

A defining moment was when she first found herself in the California redwoods. She told me her "heart burst wide open". She fell in love with the giant trees – and, within a few weeks, also witnessed first hand the destructive activities of Pacific Lumber/Maxxam Corporation. The die, as they say, was cast.

"Tree sitting is a last resort," she insists. "When you see someone in a tree trying to protect it, you know that every level of our society has failed. The consumers have failed, the companies have failed, and the government has failed." Like other activists, she saw an urgent need to "put my body where my beliefs are." Once up the tree, she found that Luna gave her the sense of purpose she had long sought. And Pacific/Maxxam, a Locust company if ever there was one (read Julia's description of their napalming of clear-cut areas), unwittingly managed to reinforce her resolve.

Concerned that her growing (if unlooked-for) celebrity status was shining an unwelcome spotlight on its activities, Pacific/Maxxam sent in tree-climbers, air horns and even helicopters to force her down, all to no avail. One activist was killed in the anti-logging protests and several others badly injured, but still she clung on. She found herself repeating a mantra: "Julia, your inaction is as much part of shaping the world as the actions of others."

Tree-sits, she explains, have three purposes: "to protect the tree and hopefully a few around it, to slow down the logging while the people who work within the legal system do their work, and to bring about broad-based public awareness." Thanks to mobile phones and other technology, she worked the media and took the battle to her corporate antagonists. From her perch, for example, she took part in a live CNN debate with Pacific Lumber's president, John Campbell. Indeed, her descriptions of her handling of the media should be required reading for anyone trying to make sense of – and communicate in – the CNN World.

I asked where the 'Butterfly' came from? Simple. Asked whether she had a 'forest name' on her arrival at the activists' base camp, which was disbanding for the winter, she could only think of butterfly'. The name felt "sissy", she says, so she experimented with tougher-sounding alternatives, including 'Monarch'. But, in the end, "Butterfly it was."

Appropriate, too. She describes the butterfly visions that have accompanied her since childhood. "At one point, when I was feeling extremely despondent, a vision came to me of a butterfly poking out of a cocoon. When it finally broke free it was a magical butterfly with prismatic colors." A vision encapsulating her most deeply held values. And she believes there is a message here for anyone and everyone living a caterpillar lifestyle, attached to consumerism and the material world. Personal transformation, she argues, is a necessary step towards the wider sustainability transformation. Richard Barrett would be the first to agree (page 50).

In the end, she got her legal agreement. Luna was protected "in perpetuity", together with a 200-foot buffer zone. A tremendous symbolic victory, but still one skirmish in the long drawn out war against unsustainable forestry. As I was completing this book, news came through that someone had taken a chainsaw to Luna, cutting through enough of the trunk to endanger the tree's future.

So I ask Julia: Is she hopeful that the corporate world can be transformed? Only, she says, if consumers and citizens allow no other option. So maybe one of this Butterfly's most powerful wing-beats will turn out to have been her idea of declaring July 3 Interdependence Day, celebrating the interconnectedness of the web of life. A true meme. That, and the inspiration she has given to a new generation of activists, young and old.[43]

CHAPTER 5

Inside the cocoon

Are you working for a Corporate Caterpillar, Locust, Butterfly or Honeybee?

Ours is a Caterpillar Economy. But, just in case this sounds acceptable, have you ever watched caterpillars at work on a leaf? Their pudgy, well-rounded look betrays their insatiable appetites. Two enthusiastic caterpillar-watchers are Claude Nuridsany and Marie Pérennou, best-known for their award-winning film *Microcosmos*.[44] They describe a caterpillar this way: "It is basically an intestine disguised as an animal, with a few extra appendages – three sets of claw-like legs and five sets of abdominal suckerlike pads that propel it towards an unceasing supply of food." Within hours, the largest leaf is reduced to a ragged lacework.

Viewed from the right angle, many of today's companies and value-webs are like that. But instead of the cabbage leaf, think of the world's biosphere or the social fabric of our communities. So is the only difference between a Caterpillar Economy (which has the potential and time to evolve into something more sustainable) and a Locust Economy (which faces a far bigger challenge, if it can adapt at all) simply one of scale? Well, Caterpillar companies and value-webs scaled up to a world of 8–10 billion would certainly be every bit as damaging globally as some locust infestations are regionally, but there is a fundamental difference. While locusts are locusts throughout their lives, caterpillars have the potential to become something very different. And the same is true of Caterpillar companies and value-webs.

That said, it's often much harder to spot the process of metamorphosis in companies than it is in caterpillars. For one thing, you can put a caterpillar in a jar. Later, having eaten twice its body weight every day and shed its skin a number of times as its body grew, you will find it has increased its weight by several thousand times. At that point, it stops eating, seems distracted, wanders off right and left. Then it picks a spot, weaves itself a cocoon and begins the process of transformation.

After a while, a series of violent, wavelike movements uncover the chrysalis. If you were to cut through the chrysalis at this stage, you would find a disappointing, shapeless mess. This is the result of self-digestion. Some of the caterpillar's existing organs, like its silk-producing glands, have been completely digested by enzymes and the nutrients recycled for new uses. Other organs, including muscles and the circulatory system, are remodeled.

Interestingly, even at 'birth' – or hatching – a caterpillar contains shreds of the butterfly it will become. These are small clusters of cells called 'imaginal buds', from the word *imago* (referring to the adult insect). Inside the chrysalis, these islands of cells suddenly awake, exploding outwards to create the structure of the butterfly. Along the way, some exceptionally powerful hormones get to work in the 'mess', catalyzing metamorphosis.

Then, when all is finally ready, a whole new set of organs and features appear: wings, compound eyes, antennae, proboscis. The butterfly gradually extracts itself from both its chrysalis and cocoon, stretching and flapping its wings a few times as a test, and then launches itself forth into its new existence. The process has many similarities with those on which 'Corporate Chrysalids' embark.

Box 8: Blips on the screen

Corporate chrysalids

Fact: BP, DuPont, Ford, Interface and Shell may all be high profile Corporate Locusts (or at least companies showing strong residual Locust tendencies), but they have been showing signs of becoming Corporate Chrysalids. Logical follow-up question: What's a Corporate Chrysalid?

Well, in his classic sci-fi novel *The Chrysalids*, John Wyndham described a world paralyzed by genetic mutation.[45] Nuclear conflict had left a world in which the mutation rate was so extreme that the chances of breeding true were less than 50 percent. People with mutations – including children – were hunted down and destroyed. Then came a new form of mutant: The Chrysalids.

The Chrysalids were able to communicate telepathically, and (because they were harder to detect) were seen to pose a new order of risk. On the last page of the story, the background hum of voices for those connected in this new way is described as "not unlike the buzzing of a hive of bees." These people are able to "think-together." They "are alert, corporately aware of danger to their species."

Corporately aware: what a great description for the Corporate Chrysalids. Early on, these people – and their companies – are often seen as mutations in their world. Ray Anderson at Interface, Sir John Browne at BP, and Bill Ford, Jr. at Ford are just three cases in point. Indeed, the notion of the Corporate Chrysalid first popped into my brain while I was taking part in a boardroom meeting at Ford, outside Detroit. During the meeting, co-chaired by Ford CEO Jacques Nasser and Chairman Bill Ford, Jr., BP CEO Sir John Browne was beamed in by video link from London. He held the assembled executives spellbound for over an hour as he explained how he saw the SD challenge evolving for companies like BP and Ford.

Citizen CEOs may not be telepathic, but they sense the same threats, see the same sort of opportunities to transform their businesses, and – as the Ford meeting showed – communicate among themselves in novel ways. As they network and spread best practice in the emerging field of sustainable capitalism, they pose new orders of risk for those who cling to old, unsustainable business models.

They also face risks themselves, as we will see in Chapter 6. Today, inevitably, the focus is on the highest profile corporations and their leaders, but increasingly the spotlight must also pick up all those other corporate species in the economic eco- system – including large private companies and even the Mafia and other 'black' and 'gray' market actors (see Figure 6.1, page 100).

COCOONED

It's human nature to want to look inside things. At present, though, it's impossible to cut into the global cocoon of laws, taxes, standards, values and other market drivers that is beginning to reshape capitalism. It's as much in our heads as it is out there in the real world. Indeed, it's hard to look inside one of today's Corporate Chrysalids and get any real sense of what is going on. But anyone who has worked with one or more Corporate Chrysalids will probably recognize similarities between their work and natural metamorphosis.

So, for example, the notion that a company or organization already contains 'cells' representing a future, more sustainable state, would make sense to any of the change agents we focus on in Chapter 13. The need to digest the old and create the new is a major challenge, particularly when you have to do it in the same space at the same time. And the new features required by the butterfly also have their counterparts in the new structures, systems, processes and skills evolved by companies as they emerge from the corporate cocoon spun around them by legal constraints, market standards and changing societal values.

As companies and other business organizations work towards breaching either the Values Barrier or the Value Barrier, either of which can 'cocoon' a business at a lower level of evolution, they need navigational tools. We will use two simple ones. First, the MetaMatrix, already introduced on pages 54 and 65, helps plot business models, companies and value-webs in terms of their impacts on the regeneration or degeneration of various forms of capital – natural, social, human, intellectual, institutional, cultural, and so on (see Figure 5.1). Featuring four types of insect (three of which can fly), the MetaMatrix should be seen as version 1.0. And, second, the Learning Flywheel maps out five fundamental stages in the process of corporate transformation (page 7).

Even so, you can almost hear the disbelief. What can CEOs and other business leaders possibly learn from *insects*? Or insect metaphors? The answer is a good deal, both directly and by analogy. Insects don't think much about tomorrow, so far as we can see, but their history has so powerfully shaped their behavior that they are well adapted for most possible futures. Indeed, if you are looking for the business case for SD, a key reason why insects have much to teach us is that they have been here a lot longer than we have – and will presumably be here long after we are gone. In the process, they have had plenty of time to learn life's lessons, hard and soft.

Humans of one sort or another have been around for about a million years. Insects, by contrast, have been around for some 400 million years. Compared to an estimated 24,000 vertebrate species, there are between 5 and 30 million invertebrate species.[46] They do ecologically vital – and economically significant, for good or ill – work. Indeed, there are somewhere between 130,000 and 200,000 invertebrate and vertebrate species that regularly visit flowering plants, many of which totally depend on them for cross-pollination. These include huge numbers of butterflies and bees, which we will use as our symbols for a sustainable economy.

However you look at them, insects are one of evolution's wildly successful experiments. As a result, there are many more of them than there are of us. The world's human population may recently have passed the 6 billion mark, which certainly is beginning to feel like a lot of people, but a single swarm of African locusts in the 1950s was estimated to contain 8 billion insects.[47] And a 19th century estimate of another swarm put the number of individual locusts at 50 billion.[48] Unfortunately, just as locusts and other insects can cause tremendous damage to ecosystems and economies alike, so can people – and the Corporate Caterpillars and Locusts that help sustain them.

So how do we distinguish problem technologies, business models or value-webs from those offering real-world solutions? Some early answers are signaled in the MetaMatrix. This sorts business models, companies, value webs, and even entire economies on the basis of whether they have a net regenerative or degenerative impact on the economic, social and, perhaps most importantly, ecological systems of which they are part. The vertical columns then distinguish between those producing low-level impacts and those producing much greater (and often cumulative) impacts. Remember, however, that any given company or value web can exhibit several of these behavioral styles simultaneously. ABB, for example, in investing in new sustainable energy systems like microturbines and fuel cells, but at the same time faces huge financial liabilities because of asbestos.[49] So let's start with the degenerative line of the MetaMatrix.

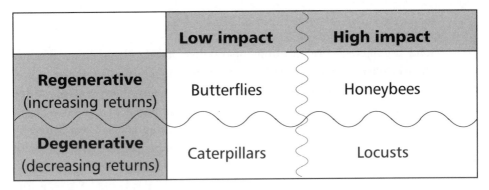

	Low impact	High impact
Regenerative (increasing returns)	Butterflies	Honeybees
Degenerative (decreasing returns)	Caterpillars	Locusts

Figure 5.1 The MetaMatrix. © SustainAbility.

DEGENERATION

Corporate Caterpillars and Locusts are both in the degenerative domain, on the wrong side of the Values Barrier (page 54). In the natural world, the caterpillar has long been a symbol of greed and destruction. Facing many threats, caterpillars have evolved extraordinary defenses. They mimic owls or scorpions, bristle with spines, signal foul tastes and poisons. But the basic law is: No caterpillar, no butterfly. The same is true of Corporate Caterpillars, but Corporate Locusts are another matter entirely. And Corporate Maggots (characterized, for example, by high levels of corruption) are to be avoided at all costs.

	High impact	Traits
Degenerative (decreasing returns)	Locust 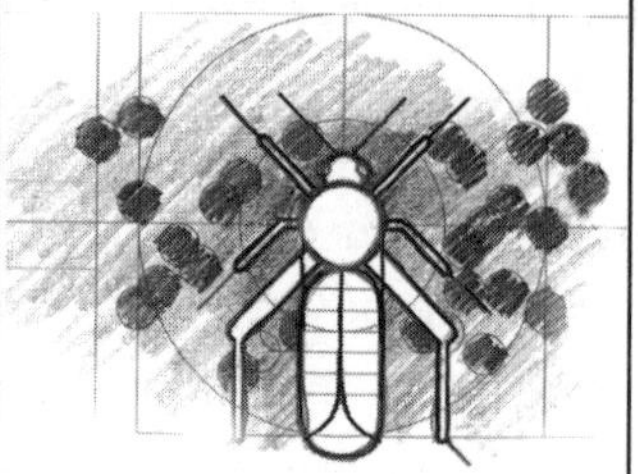 	• Highly unsustainable business model • Tendency to swarm, overwhelming habitat • Destroys various forms of capital • Zero cross-pollination • Blind to early warnings

Figure 5.2 The Corporate Locust: potentially high negative impact. © SustainAbility.

Some commercial organizations operate as Locusts throughout their life cycles, whereas others display Locust-like behaviors from time to time. In the natural world, locusts can serve as a nutritious food, but they have long symbolized the ultimate destructive scourge. Indeed, it is no accident that they are recorded as one of the biblical plagues that tormented Egypt and neighboring lands. Long feared by agricultural peoples, swarms of locusts can strip a landscape bare in a matter of hours.

Immense swarms devastated the Great Plains of the United States in the 1870s: "The locusts are said to have left fields as barren as if they had been burned over," wrote one observer. "Only holes in the ground showed where plants had been. Trees were stripped of their leaves and green bark. One observer in Nebraska recorded that one of the invading swarms of locusts averaged half a mile in height and was 100 miles wide and 300 miles long." Corporate Locusts may be on the right side of the Value Barrier, in the sense that they can be highly productive, financially at least, but are very much on the wrong, degenerative side of the Values Barrier.

Interestingly, however, locusts in the wild show two distinct phases: the *solitaria* phase (when they operate on their own) and the migratory *gregaria* phase (when they come together in those great swarms). The same can be said of the equivalent commercial activities: one gold-mine, paper mill or oil refinery may be tolerable, but dozens of them working at close quarters can turn an entire region into a wasteland. If you put locusts in an uncrowded environment, they adopt the *solitaria* type of behaviors. If you crowd them, they switch into the *gregaria* phase – and swarm. This behavior must have provided survival advantages to locusts, but it can put one hell of a strain on affected environments. Great Plains pastures devastated by locusts took years to recover. As far as Corporate Locusts are concerned, think of gold rushes, boom times.

When it comes to naming names, it's clearly difficult to spotlighting Corporate Locusts without running the risk of being sued. And having almost been sued by McDonald's on the basis of the challenges in an earlier book, *The Green Consumer Guide*, I am not particularly keen to repeat the experience.[50] But in the following pages we will come across a number of companies and industries that have shown strong Locust tendencies.

That said, for every Corporate Locust or set of Locust-like corporate behaviors, that we can readily name, there are literally thousands of other Corporate Locusts out there destroying economic, social and environmental value. Some parts of Africa, Asia, Latin America and the regions once covered by the old Soviet Union are literally crawling with them. I have flown over Siberia, for example, and looked down on massive forests being eaten away literally as we flew overhead. Many of these organizations are more like Corporate Maggots.

Corporate Locusts are very much part of the 'decreasing returns' world, where the more you do of something the worse things get. As gold-miners exhaust richer ore-bodies, for example, the effort needed to produce gold can go off the scale. Along with the growing amount of energy required for digging, lifting and air-conditioning as mines go deeper, we need to consider the spoil produced as poorer ores are processed, and the growing range of environmental impacts caused by deep mining, chemical ore processing and spoil disposal.

One such Corporate Locust has been Russian Aluminum, the world's second-largest aluminum producer.[51] In a lawsuit filed in New York, the company has been accused, among other things, of murder, death threats, fraud, bribery, and money laundering. Wherever they may be based or operate, such lawsuits suggest that the pressures on Corporate Locusts are going to grow.

The extraordinary US tobacco lawsuits have also encouraged activists to explore how similar tactics might be used to tackle other industrial locusts. In the climate change area, for example, they have been focusing their attention on such carbon-intensive sectors as oil, steel, cement and coal-fired electricity companies. The evidence suggest that a much wider spectrum of industrial activities will be targeted as Locust-like in the coming decade.

Spotting Corporate Locusts

Like it nor not, locusts are an integral part of many natural ecosystems. In the same way, Corporate Locusts are often found in commercial ecosystems. But, whatever form they take, they tend to be uncomfortable (and often dangerous) neighbors. Historically, Locust-like economic activities have often created social and cultural capital, but it is much rarer for them to generate real natural capital. One accidental example of this happening, however, was the evolution of Britain's highly diverse Norfolk Broads from massive peat-diggings that subsequently flooded. A more recent, intentional example has been René Haller's creation of a thriving ecosystem out of a run-down cement quarry at Bamburi, Kenya.[52] The economic value created in the process has been striking, but was really incidental to the original activities.

More typically, locust infestations – whether natural or commercial – have to be controlled. Indeed, as the sustainability transition proceeds we will see a growing number of companies – and their value webs – being branded as Corporate Locusts and treated accordingly. Obvious examples have included the asbestos, persistent chemical insecticide, illegal drugs, and child prostitution industries. At times, too, even relatively low-impact companies can suddenly begin to display locust-like characteristics. Among the key characteristics of a Corporate Locust are the following:

- An unsustainable business model, even in an equitable world of 6 billion-plus
- Periods of invisibility, when it is hard to discern the impending threat
- Based on exploitation of non-renewable resources, or unsustainable use of potentially renewable resources
- A tendency to swarm, overwhelming the carrying capacity of social systems, ecosystems or economies
- The destruction of natural, human, social and economic capital
- Collectively, an unsustainable 'burn-rate', potentially creating regional or even global impacts
- An incapacity (conscious or not) to foresee negative system effects, coupled with an unwillingness to heed early warnings and learn from mistakes.

Apart from Russian Aluminum, the list of Locusts is long. Think of the industrial fishing and logging industries. Think of Pacific Gas & Electric (page 13) or Pacific Lumber/Maxxam (page 68). Some cases of extreme degeneration are well known, like Chernobyl, the Rhine disaster (page 11), or the rising salinity of Australian soils caused by land clearance and various forms of agriculture. Others may only become clear with the passage of time.

Want another example? Well, around 3,000 pharmaceuticals are discharged into European sewers and deposited on farmland in sludges and manures.[53] Given that up to 90 percent of the active ingredients of medicines or drugs are excreted unchanged into the environment, it seems very likely that we will also see growing concerns in this area in the coming years. Meanwhile, here are seven examples of Corporate Locusts:

- *British Nuclear Fuels.* Indicted for "systematic management failure", BNFL has been an object lesson on how not to run high-risk businesses. The operator of Sellafield, described as "the nuclear dustbin of the world" by its critics, BNFL has been the source of endless bad news. In an attempt to save its long-planned privatization, the company said that it would attempt to remove the "treacle layer" in its management structure that had resisted change.[54] Despite the cull of board members and executives, however, the bad news kept flowing. Increased liabilities of at least £5 billion were announced only months after a published review estimating liabilities (largely associated with environmental clean-up) pushed estimates of the cost of decommissioning Sellafield at between £27 billion and £34 billion.[55] "One of the reasons we are in the mess we are in today," said the man drafted in to turn the company around, "is because there was not enough focus on the seriousness of compliance."[56]

Watch this space, however. If climate change really accelerates, the nuclear industry may begin to be seen rather differently.

- *Brown & Williamson.* Spotlighted in the Oscar-nominated film *The Insider*, Brown & Williamson's behavior was probably not unusual for Big Tobacco companies. It was accused of manipulating the nicotine content of cigarettes to 'hook' young smokers.[57] Much of the background became public knowledge owing to whistleblower Jeffery Wigand, originally hired by the company to work on a safer cigarette. The damaging evidence led to a massive court settlement in 1997 that forced leading tobacco companies to agree to pay $246 billion to US states over 25 years. Now even healthy smokers are suing the US industry, claiming $500 million to pay for medical tests.[58]

Some tobacco companies are now diversifying into less damaging sectors, as in the case of Phillip Morris buying Nabisco. Maybe some of these Locusts can begin to meta-morphose into something more sustainable?

- *Esmeralda Exploration.* A 50 percent partner in the Baia Mare mine, along with the Romanian state firm Remin, Western Australia's Esmeralda went into voluntary liquidation in 2000. The mine had been the source of a massive pollution incident, involving the release of 100,000 cubic meters of cyanide-polluted water into river systems in Romania and Hungary. In addition to killing fish, the incident poisoned the drinking water of more than two million people.[59]

No chance of Esmeralda becoming anything but a dead Locust. But will others learn from its mistakes?

• *Freeport-McMoRan Copper & Gold.* This giant US mining corporation was badly caught out by the shifting business environment in West Papua, formerly Irian Jaya, Indonesia. Freeport's $4 billion mining project worked well enough under the repressive Suharto regime. At the time, the company's combative chairman, James R. 'Jim Bob' Moffett, knew how to work the system.[60] Now Suharto is disgraced, however, and the Indonesian government wants to reclaim billions of dollars his regime pilfered.

  Freeport managed to impact on all three dimensions spotlighted in Chapter 2. On the environmental front, the mine dumps 200,000 tons of silt into local rivers every day, turning a 230-square-mile delta into a desert. On the human rights front, the company has been accused of complicity with the Indonesian military's detention, torture and murder of civilians. And on the governance front, the Amungme tribe that claims traditional title to the mining area says Freeport doesn't share enough of the wealth created. In response, Freeport has commissioned an outside audit and appointed a special counsel on human rights, Judge Gabrielle MacDonald.

I met Judge MacDonald late in 2000. She faces a huge task, but my reading at the time was that she could well help begin the process of turning this Locust around.

• *Pacific Lumber/Maxxam Corporation.* Spotlighted by the defiance of Julia Butterfly Hill, this company became one of the world's better known Corporate Locusts (panel 4, page 68). Given that some of the most dramatic corporate turnarounds have followed companies suffering a punch in the corporate nose, maybe there's some hope here – but I for one will not be holding my breath.

Not yet the subject of a Hollywood film, but that seems only a matter of time.

- *Prosper de Mulder.* The company which makes meat and bone meal from animal carcasses, for feeding to farm animals. Now at the epicenter of the "mad cow" disease disaster. Britain's exports of contaminated meal were allowed to continue despite warnings from the government's own chief medical officer that this was "short-sighted." An attempt to ban meal export was stalled by the agriculture ministry, which argued that meal exporters would challenge any ban in the courts.[61]

To a vegetarian, like the author, the very idea of feeding animal meal to herbivores seems obscene. But if companies are going to do this sort of thing, which seems against the natural order, they owe it to us to be ultra-sensitive to early, weak signals that things are going wrong. Prosper de Mulder was anything but.

- *Railtrack.* Few industries are as critical to a sustainable economy as the railways. Privatized in 1996, the company responsible for Britain's railway infrastructure was set up in such a way that it had limited incentives to invest. A key reason was that the civil servants responsible for privatization assumed that the rail network would continue to decline, so prioritizing maintenance over network expansion. Subsequent growth led to massive problems, aggravated by a series of fatal accidents. Bringing the network up to the standards of continental operators will cost an estimated £55 billion over the next 10-20 years.[62]

  Prime Minister Blair accused Railtrack of "arse-covering" tactics.[63] Railtrack bosses allegedly knew of "life-threatening" metal fatigue problems in rails, but failed either to inform the regulator or replace the rails.[64] But the government itself was largely to blame for privatizing the railways at speed – in ways virtually guaranteeing fragmentation and a lack of co-operation. A key flaw that emerged after the accidents: weak links between Railtrack and rail operators, freight operators, rolling stock leasing companies, and the myriad of contractors (notably, Balfour Beatty) and sub-contractors that maintained the network.[65]

Several reviewers of this chapter queried whether Railtrack was really a Locust? "It was certainly blind to early warnings," said one, "but it seems that short term management and an inability to reconcile shareholder value with health and safety regulation were the real problems." Fine, but whatever the motivation the system-level impacts were devastating.

Ask a Corporate Locust to consider the business case for SD and it will have little idea of what you are talking about. The short-term interests of financial stockholders (particularly big ones) are its top priority. The business case thinking outlined in Figure 10.2 (page 202) would seem light-years away, although younger executives (and non-executive directors) might well see the light. More optimistically, however, we are seeing sectors like the mining industry getting together to work out how they collectively could help shift the world onto a more sustainable path.[66] Will others follow suit?

	Low impact	Traits
Degenerative (decreasing returns)	Caterpillar 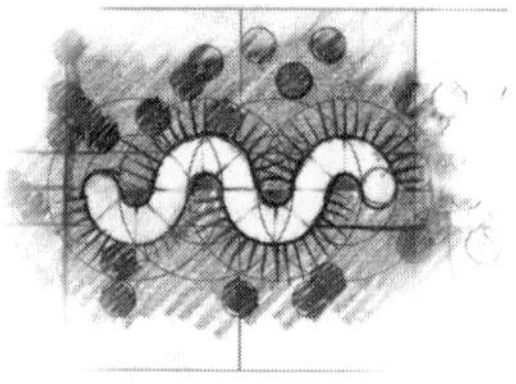	• Longer-term, an unsustainable business model • High 'burn rate' • Relatively local impacts • Potential for switching to regenerative mode

Figure 5.3   The Corporate Caterpillar: low negative impact. © SustainAbility.

In some ways, these are the most interesting companies of all. They often are based on novel business models, with high potential to provide long-term value – if only they can penetrate the Value Barrier. In the near-term, however, they may chew their way through a good deal of financial, social or environmental capital. Indeed, it should come as no surprise that the caterpillar has had an odd, double symbolism.

On the one hand, because it numbers among the crawling creatures, the caterpillar has been an emblem of greed and destruction. Anyone who has had their gardens attacked by caterpillars will probably sympathize. Interestingly, too, these feeding machines can have unsuspected appetites: some caterpillars are carnivorous, feeding on ant larvae, aphids or scale insects.[67]

When caterpillars swarm, they can cause extraordinary problems. In New Zealand, for example, hundreds of thousands of migrating moth caterpillars once so crowded a railway line that their crushed bodies brought a train to a slimy, slithering halt.[68] In the same way, large numbers of small and medium-sized enterprises (SMEs) operating in damaging ways can result in government clean-up plans losing traction. Cumulatively, their impacts can be at least as great as those caused by major corporations.

On the other hand, caterpillars have long symbolized the shift from a lower to a higher state. The process by which the caterpillar first turns into a chrysalis and then into a butterfly is one of the most mysterious processes humans have ever witnessed. The Corporate Caterpillar is on the wrong side of both the Values Barrier and also of the Value Barrier, but has the potential to break through both.

So, while the Corporate Caterpillar may be destructive, it typically contributes to a value web that creates something of higher value – or has the potential to metamorphose into something dramatically more sustainable.

Spotting Corporate Caterpillars

Usually, Caterpillars are much harder to spot than Locusts. Unless, that is, you live or work right next door. If you do, it may be hard to detect the metamorphic potential of the particular business, but some extraordinary commercial activities have evolved into well-known and moderately civilized international companies. So here are some characteristics of Corporate Caterpillars. They tend to:

- Be based on an unsustainable business model, particularly when projected forward into an equitable world of 8-10 billion people
- Have the potential for transformation into a more sustainable guise, often based on a mutated business model
- Generate relatively local impacts, most of the time
- Show single-minded dedication to the task in hand
- Depend on a high 'burn-rate' although usually of forms of capital that are renewable over time
- Operate in sectors where there is evidence that pioneering companies are already starting to metamorphose towards more sustainable forms of value creation.

Among possible candidates for Corporate Caterpillar status are:

- *3M.* Known for its product innovation, Minnesota Mining & Manufacturing with its Pollution Prevention Pays (3P) Program – has long been a poster-child of the corporate environmentalism movement. Indeed, its 3P Program gives it characteristics of a Corporate Butterfly. The highly diversified company makes everything from telecommunications connectors and inkjet printers to pharmaceuticals and Post-It notes.[69] Roughly 50,000 3M products have their roots in one original product: sandpaper. Having sorted out how to use adhesives in that product, the company moved into such areas as Scotch masking tape, then into magnetic tape.

Under then CEO 'Desi' DeSimone, the company's 3P Program saved or made over $800 million between 1975 and 1996. Strikingly, too, the company voluntarily announced it would drop the use of the active ingredient in its *Scotchguard* fabric and carpet coatings, which it still believed to be safe, because it had been found to persist in the human body and environment for years.[70]

- *Collins and Aikman Floorings.* Similar to Interface (see below), but smaller and seen by some to be rather more impressive in their on-the-ground delivery. Ralph Earle, who has worked closely with the company, describes them as "a Caterpillar, perhaps even a Butterfly."

- *Dow Jones Sustainability Group.* By linking with the Dow Jones people, Zurich-based Sustainable Asset Management (SAM) not only formed the Dow Jones Sustainability Group, but also sent a wake-up call to chief financial officers (CFOs) and investor relations people across the business world. SAM would normally go in the Butterfly category, but the Dow Jones group has hardly had an inspiring TBL track record to date.

- *Interface.* Although it has had its ups and downs, carpet-maker Interface has a long-standing ambition to become the world's first genuinely restorative company. CEO Ray Anderson is profiled in Chapter 6. One striking feature of his company's UK operations is a total reliance on renewable electricity,[71] but he would be the first to accept that the company's metamorphosis still ahs a long way to go.

- *Johnson Matthey.* As a precious metals processor, the company is linked with massive environmental impacts caused by the mining industry. However, its product lines include catalyst technology which has played a vital role in cleaning up auto exhaust emissions and, potentially, will help the 21st century do the seemingly impossible by turning hydrogen fuels and oxygen into electrical power and water vapor, via the sort of fuels cells now being developed by companies like Canada's Ballard Power Systems and Europe's ZeTek Power.

Ask most Corporate Caterpillars to consider the business case for SD, however, and they would usually only profess an interest insofar as there are real, near-term prospects for shifting to more sustainable forms of value creation. The business case thinking outlined in Figure 10.2 (page 202) might well be of interest, but would need a fair amount of pre-digestion to make it accessible. Many of these companies and business leaders believe they are on the right side of the Values Barrier, which can undermine their capacity to make the necessary jump to the next stage.

REGENERATION

Butterflies are lovely to look at, but are often fragile, at the mercy of the elements. Unlike caterpillars, which live to eat, butterflies seem to exist on air. They are useful pollinators and great indicators of ecosystem health. The same is true of Corporate Butterflies, which are the wrong side of the Value Barrier (page 66). When it comes to economic heavy-lifting, Corporate Honeybees are a better bet. Increasingly, they are on the right side of both the Values and Value Barriers. To date, however, they remain precariously rare.

	Low impact	Traits
Regenerative (increasing returns)	Butterfly 	• Sustainable business model • Strong commitment to CSR/SD • High visibility, loud voice • May publicly attack locusts • Widely networked • Commercial lightweight

Figure 5.4 The Corporate Butterfly: low positive impact. © SustainAbility.

You know them. These are high-profile companies, moving broadly in the right direction, and only too happy to tell the world about it – and to attack those they see as headed in the wrong direction. These businesses are good at communicating symbolically. Like butterflies sporting massive eye-spot patterns on their wings, they often seem to be much larger and more powerful than they are.

Like the caterpillar, the butterfly has come to symbolize transformation and metamorphosis. Its life cycle provides a perfect analogy both for immortality and for sustainable, closed-loop economies: life (the crawling caterpillar), death (the dark chrysalis) and rebirth (the butterfly, or soul, fluttering free).[72] Butterflies have long symbolized both the soul (indeed, the word *psyche*, meaning soul, was once synonymous with butterfly) and immortality.

The butterfly is also renowned for its light, airy grace, and abstemious eating habits. An economic system fit for Corporate Butterflies would almost certainly be a world well down the track towards sustainability. All of which make it a powerful symbol for eco-efficiency, long-term thinking and wider sustainability.

Some butterflies can also perform extraordinary feats of endurance. The migration and winter gatherings of the monarch butterfly are among the most spectacular of all natural phenomena.[73] Up to 30 million monarchs overwinter in little more than 12 acres in Mexico's Sierra Madre. One biologist called it "the greatest aggregation of a living organism – and its deceased kin – anywhere in the world."[74] They arrive and roost there in such numbers that they can literally cause cypress trees to bend over. No wonder Julia 'Butterfly' Hill considered calling herself Julia 'Monarch' Hill instead (panel 4, page 68). The new style of eco-activist can sometimes have the same effect on major corporations. And it is interesting that one of the things that helped to bring Monsanto to its knees during the recent GM foods furore was, yes, the monarch butterfly.

But note that some people in the field, most notably Paul Hawken of the US Natural Capitalism Institute, argue that even if every company in the world was to model itself on such companies our economies would still not be sustainable. For that, we will need to develop and call upon the hive strengths of the Corporate Honeybee. Even so, Corporate Butterflies have a crucial role to play in evolving what we might call Chrysalis Capitalism. Among other things, they model new forms of sustainable wealth creation for the Honeybees to mimic and – most significantly – scale up.

Spotting Corporate Butterflies

Most Corporate Butterflies are easy to spot. By their very nature, they are often highly conspicuous, and in recent years have been abundantly covered in the media. Some of the more striking characteristics of the Corporate Butterfly include:

- A reasonably sustainable business model, although this may become less sustainable as success drives growth, expansion and increasing reliance on financial markets and large corporate partners.
- Potentially, a capacity to trigger quite disproportionate changes in consumer priorities and, as a result, in the wider economic system.
- A strong commitment to the CSR and SD agendas.
- Often defines its position by reference to Locusts and Caterpillars.
- A wide network, although not typically among Locusts or Honeybees.
- Increasingly, involvement in symbiotic relationships, just as some species of blue butterflies have developed close, mutually supportive relationships with colonies of ants.[75]
- Persistent links to degenerative activities.
- A useful, if limited, cross-pollination effect.
- High visibility and a disproportionately powerful voice for such an economic lightweight.

Possible candidates for Corporate Butterfly status include:

- *Ben & Jerry's.* The iconoclastic, socially committed ice-cream maker founded by Ben Cohen and Jerry Greenfield would once have appeared on any self-respecting list of Corporate Butterflies. Its status is less clear now that it is part of Unilever (Box 9, page 89).
- *The Body Shop International.* Love her or hate her, Body Shop founder Anita Roddick not only triggers strong emotions but has consistently been one of the most effective champions of Corporate Butterfly values and business models (Chapter 5). But the company has been buffeted financially in recent years.
- *Guenguel Company.* An example of a developing world butterfly, Guenguel plans to move the Mazquiarán family business from the production of wool from sheep (a major contributor to desertification in the Patagonia region of Argentina) to the production of fiber from guanacos. These are a native wild species, relates to llamas, and much better suited to the ecosystem than the imported sheep. An added advantage is that guanaco wool is far better than sheep wool, better even than cashmere, so enjoying an upscale, higher value market.[76]
- *Novo Nordisk.* This Danish healthcare-to-enzymes group has been a consistent pioneer in corporate social responsibility and SD (see, for example, page 47).

But it is still something of a corporate David in relation to some of the corporate Goliaths operating in its sector.

- *Ocean Desert Enterprises (ODE).* Faced with the growing scarcity of fresh water and arable land, coupled with the ongoing salinization of groundwater and soils, ODE and Saline Seed Mexico have come up with an innovative potential solution: saline agriculture and forestry. If done well, this approach – based on the use of salt-tolerant crop plants – could provide new sources of food, fodder, fiber and biochemicals, while cutting erosion, creating carbon dioxide sinks, and boosting biodiversity and local communities.

- *Patagonia.* This California-based company is a privately-held supplier of high-quality outdoor equipment and clothing.[77] Founded by Yves Chouinard, Patagonia's vision is based on a model of society that is restorative of, rather than damaging to, the environment. In one catalogue, Patagonia went on record as saying that "everything we do pollutes." But the company has done more than most to redress the balance.

  Among other things, Patagonia has adopted a management philosophy to "do no harm". It operates a self-imposed 'Earth Tax', which provides either 1 percent of sales revenue or 10 percent of pre-tax profits (whichever is higher) to environmental activism. It was the first Californian company to commit to using 100 percent wind energy for in-state facilities. And, in an extraordinary internship program, it also pays employees to work up to two months for the non-profit environmental group of their choice. But the company has its critics. One usually well-informed reviewer of this chapter queried the appropriateness of senior management changes.

- *Rohner Textil.* This small Swiss textile firm has turned around its ailing business by 'going green' and inventing a biodegradable and compostable upholstery fabric.[78] Faced with growing competition from the developing world, managing director Albin Kälin decided to make environmental and social responsibility his key selling point. The revolutionary fabric, Climatex Lifecycle,[79] is made of a mix of wool from "free range and humanely sheared" New Zealand sheep and ramie, a fiber used by the Egyptians 4000 years ago and now grown organically in the Philippines.

- *SustainAbility.* Yes, I know it's inviting charges of egotism, but this small company which I co-founded in 1987, when few people had heard the S-word in its current sense, is generally acknowledged to have had a quite disproportionate impact on the SD debate. Among agendas it has helped to develop and promote: green consumerism, environmental auditing, corporate environmental (and now sustainability) reporting, the triple bottom line, the business case for SD, TBL-focused global corporate governance, and transparency in corporate lobbying. In the process, it has worked with Corporate Locusts (albeit refusing to work with the nuclear and tobacco industries), Caterpillars, Butterflies and companies displaying at least some Honeybee tendencies. The five stepping stones of the Learning Flywheel distil this experience.

Like their natural counterparts, Corporate Butterflies tend to occur in 'pulses'. After rain, for example, a desert can suddenly come alive with butterflies.[80] In very much the same way, pulses of Corporate Butterflies were a marked feature of the Sixties, when we saw a boom in alternative publishing, wholefood and renewable energy technology businesses, and again in the Nineties, when sectors like eco-tourism, organic food, SD consulting and socially responsible investing (SRI) began to go mainstream.

To begin with, such businesses escape the attention of larger companies, but once they begin to mutate into a potential competitive threat, the reflexes of the big corporates change. It's all a bit like what happens when a blue butterfly emerges from its chrysalis inside an ant nest: the ants no longer see it as benign, even desirable, and the blue must make a dash for the nest entrance or risk being devoured.[81]

Ask the typical Corporate Butterfly to consider the business case for SD, and it may well be dismissive, at least to start with. Because such companies tend to operate from a strong values base, the business case outlined in Figure 10.2 (page 202) may seem overly complex – although executives drawn in from the outside might well be quicker to see the light.

Box 9: Blips on the screen

Ben & Jerry's

A thousand butterflies must have flapped their wings somewhere. I had just disembarked from a boat onto a small island off Georgia, knowing that Hurricane Floyd was roaring up the East Coast, when a state of emergency was declared. I had flown in from Amsterdam to take part in a Ben & Jerry's board meeting, hoping to get an insight into one of the world's best-known Corporate Butterflies.

But I hadn't expected to do it in the middle of a hurricane.

Now we were all scurrying down to the jetty to catch a boat back to the mainland. Elements of the board meeting happened as we raced the oncoming storm back to harbor – and the conversations continued as Ben & Jerry's director Pierre Ferrari and I joined over a million Americans fleeing the coast and headed inland towards Atlanta.

Ben Cohen and Jerry Greenfield were early, prototypical examples of the 'Citizen CEO' trend. The question now facing them: Should they sell out to a larger company? Even allowing for the darkening clouds, the friction between the value creation and values agendas was creating a heavy static charge among the folk on the boat.

If a sale were to prove inevitable, as seemed increasingly likely, the next question was: Which potential buyer? If a sale was inevitable, I suggested, Unilever was more attractive than the other short-listed buyers. But I also argued that Ben & Jerry's should impose some ethical conditions in the contract of sale. After a series of late-night conference calls with US lawyers, these went into the contract.

Not surprisingly, fans of the Ben & Jerry's philosophy regretted its loss of independence. A group of social investors tried to buy the company out from under the nose of rivals like Dreyer and Unilever, but failed.[82] The sale went to Unilever, which agreed to continue donating 7.5 percent of Ben & Jerry's profits to good works. Subsequent events suggested that Unilever had its own game-plan, not totally to the taste of either Ben or Jerry. Indeed, Ben Cohen had an emergency bypass operation soon after the take-over, suggesting that the stress was getting to him. But the way the game was played to that point suggested another route by which counter-cultural business 'memes' (see pages ix and 231) can cross-infect mainstream corporations.

	High Impact	Traits
Regenerative (increasing returns)	Honeybee 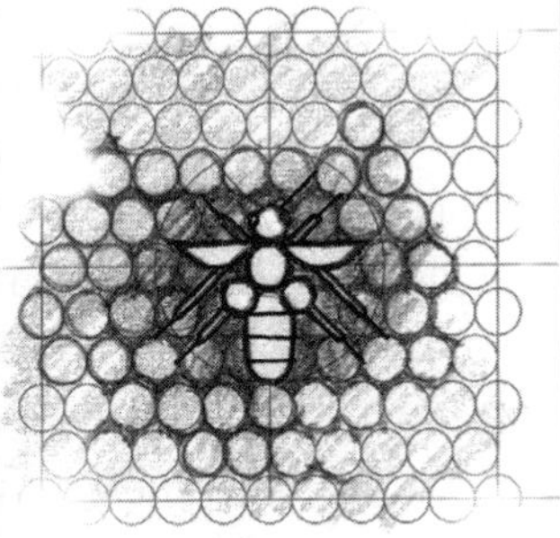	• Sustainable business model • Strong business ethics • Constant innovation, cross-pollination • Capacity for heavy-lifting • Strategic use of natural capital and other resources • Sophisticated technology • Multiple capital formation

Figure 5.5 The Corporate Honeybee: potentially high positive impact. © SustainAbility.

Look it up in the relevant dictionaries, and you will find that the bee – and its honey – enjoys a special place in symbolism. Among the qualities attributed to bees are diligence, organizational and technical skills, sociability, purity, chastity, cleanliness, spirituality, wisdom, abstinence, selflessness and creativity.[83] They are the collaborative go-getters of the insect world.[84] Like the butterfly, the bee is also a symbol of resurrection – and therefore naturally finds a place in the regenerative line of the MetaMatrix.

The bee's numbers, organization, unwearying toil and extraordinary discipline make it seem very much like an ant. A pound of honey on your breakfast table has involved bees flying a distance roughly equivalent to three complete orbits around the planet. But the fact that it distils honey from the nectar of flowers has always given the bee and its buzzing hive a strong, mysterious allure. Watch a hive in action and you see bees guarding, scouting, foraging, transporting, processing, tending, repairing.

But what escapes many observers is just how extraordinary the technology evolved by bees actually is. For example, a comb made with 40 grams of wax and measuring 37 by 22.5 cm can hold almost two kilograms of honey. The thickness of the cell walls is 0.073 millimeters, with a tolerance of no more than 0.002 millimeters. "Astounding precision!" as Nobel Prize-winning scientist and bee biologist Karl von Frisch put it.[85]

Indeed, given the materials available, it's almost impossible to conceive of a more efficient technology for the purpose. The 'fuel consumption' of a bee works out at something like 3 million kilometers per liter of honey – or 7 million miles to the gallon.[86] In addition to using the Earth's magnetic field to lay out combs, bees display eco-efficiency and climate control to a quite remarkable degree. Their 'market intelligence' is also world class. The 'waggle' and 'round' dances of the scouts direct the swarm to the closest, best sources of nectar and other resources.

Bees can alter the temperature of the hive to make it easier to perform certain tasks, including molding wax or propolis. When things become too hot, bees use their wings to fan the hive, or bring in water to set up an evaporative cooling process. When things start to cool down, all non-useful gaps in the hive are plugged with propolis and the swarm forms into a steadily rotating ball to conserve heat. Anyone who has studied a hive closely knows that the combs are not simply used for storing honey. The same sort of comb cells used to store honey, which we might see as a symbol of the Corporate Honeybee's profits, are also used to store pollen (renewable raw materials) and develop bee larvae (future generations of talent).

A sustainable global economy would hum with the activities of Corporate Honeybees and the economic versions of beehives. Although bees may periodically swarm like locusts, their impact is not only sustainable but also strongly regenerative. Corporate Honeybees are on the right side of both the Values Barrier and also, unlike the Corporate Butterfly, of the Value Barrier.

Spotting Corporate Honeybees

Ethical investors, whose funds have grown rapidly in recent years, aim to avoid all Corporate Locusts. Some funds, however, make exceptions for those that they consider are making meaningful progress towards butterfly and honeybee behaviors and business models. Most such funds look for and invest in present and future Corporate Honeybees, in Corporate Butterflies (particularly those with a real chance of shifting to honeybee forms of value creation), and selected Corporate Caterpillars – generally those with a strong chance of making it into the regenerative line. However, when using tools like the MetaMatrix, their analysts would probably change the 'Low/High Impact' labels to 'Low/High Long Term Profits'.

The key characteristics of the Corporate Honeybee include:

- A sustainable business model, albeit based on constant innovation.
- A clear – and appropriate – set of ethics-based business principles.
- Strategic, sustainable management of natural capital and other resources.
- A capacity for sustained heavy-lifting.
- Sociability and the evolution of powerful, symbiotic partnerships.
- The sustainable production of natural, human, social, institutional and cultural capital.
- And a capacity to moderate the impacts of Corporate Caterpillars in its supply chain, to learn from the mistakes of Corporate Locusts and, in certain circumstances, to boost the efforts of Corporate Butterflies.

To date, candidates for Corporate Honeybee status are precariously rare. Among companies that are probably getting close are those that meet vital human needs like healthcare, in was consistent with the TBL agenda. One example is Johnson & Johnson, which explains its commitment to a clean environment by pointing out that "any threat to human health cuts to the very essence of what we stand for."[87] Meanwhile, for want of large numbers of Corporate Honeybees, let's look at some emerging characteristics that such businesses will need to develop – and which we are beginning to see at the level of individual business units:

- *Hyper-connection.* A sustainable world of 10 billion will be a highly connected world. Among the companies whose work in wiring the planet we look at is Hewlett-Packard (page 182). Instead of simply giving away hardware and software, the idea here is to introduce new technology in ways that help people build more sustainable businesses.
- *Environmental and community regeneration.* One of the most extraordinary regeneration projects currently under consideration focuses on Ford's sprawling Rouge industrial site. Spurred by architect Bill McDonough, the company's chairman, Bill Ford, aims to create a model of sustainable capitalism in the same way that, in the days of his great-grandfather Henry Ford, the Rouge complex was a model of production line capitalism (page 116). Other companies that have been working with McDonough's firm to green their factories (if not yet their entire value webs) include Gap and Nike.[88]
- *Nature-friendly materials.* The emerging science of 'biomimetics' will be central in 21st century innovation. Increasingly, we will model materials and techologies on nature's time-tested models. Consider Cargill Dow Polymers.

Its parents (agricultural and chemicals giants Cargill and Dow Chemical) may have spotty track records, but Cargill Dow Polymers has attracted much interest from the sustainability community.[89] Under the trademark *NatureWorks*, it plans a $1 billion business within ten years based on plastics that are simultaneously biodegradable, recyclable and use renewable raw materials. The company claims that its products will represent a "giant step towards sustainability" in all three dimensions of the triple bottom line. Corporate Butterflies like The Body Shop and Patagonia have been queuing up for its products, although genetic modification has been a potential issue with the corn stocks used in the core fermentation processes.

- *Rating and ranking.* Few things spur competition to improve more than the ranking and rating of companies. Ethical investment and index-producing firms have used this fact to commercial advantage, while the World Economic Forum's Environmental Sustainability Index (page 206) may eventually do the same thing for countries. SustainAbility has used the same approach since 1993 with its benchmark surveys of corporate environmental and sustainability reporting (page 176).

- *Skunk works.* The process of innovation often needs research groups to be protected from the day-to-day pressures of mainstream business. Lockheed's original Skunk Works (page 211) has served as a model for many other companies, while the Rocky Mountain Institute (page 212) suggests how eco-efficient technologies might be incubated – and Deka Research & Development (page 212) how new breeds of innovators may even outflank governments in this area. Open competitions, like that sponsored by the Sustainability Institute (page 213), are another way forward.

- *Socially responsible investment (SRI).* Often seen as something that challenges mainstream business rather than being done by major corporations, in-company SRI could involve the screening of pension fund investments and the setting of internal investment hurdle rates in relation to, for example, greenhouse emissions.

- *Stakeholder governance.* If the 1990s were the decade of stakeholder dialogue, the 'Zeroes' are likely to be the decade during which the stakeholder governance agenda takes off. This will involve companies not simply getting stakeholders in to tell them what they have done, are doing or planning to do. Instead, selected stakeholders will increasingly be engaged in basic processes of corporate governance. Among companies that have gone furthest in this aspect of stakeholder engagement are BP, Novo Nordisk and Shell.

- *Stewardship.* The sustainable management of natural resources will require the active stewardship of value webs. Among pioneers in this area is Unilever, which has responded to the catastrophic problems facing many of the world's fisheries (page 17) by developing its cutting edge Marine Stewardship Council partnership with WWF.

- *TBL processes and systems.* Many of the companies spotlighted in Chapters 8-11 are working in this area, with initiatives like the Global Reporting Initiative (GRI), the Global Compact and Project SIGMA (all covered in Chapter 8) pulling a wide range of partners into values setting, standard definition and piloting.
- *Ultra-clean technology.* People will continue to need energy and transport services in a sustainable economy, so we will need technologies that are highly efficient, clean and increasingly renewable. Examples include solar and wind energy (companies like BP Solar, Shell Renewables and Vestas) and fuel cell technology (Ballard Power Systems, ZeTek Power), which could be a key to the hydrogen economy. But even such emerging technologies have a long way to go before they actively *regenerate* natural capital.
- *Values audits.* Honeybee value creation models will reflect – and respond to – a range of values associated with the corporate social responsibility and sustainable development agendas. Values audits will become increasingly common. Among companies that have pioneered in this area are Johnson & Johnson, Royal Dutch/Shell and Vancouver's pioneering city savings credit union, VanCity. Details of one approach are given in box 4 (page 49).

Ask a Corporate Honeybee business unit or company to consider the business case for SD and it will likely show a good deal of interest. The chances are that it will already be using at least an embryonic form of the sort of analysis outlined in Figure 10.2 (page 202). Perhaps it's no accident that SustainAbility's 100-cell Sustainable Business Value Matrix looks like nothing so much as a honeycomb. This is the domain over which the Corporate Honeybees of the future will learn to operate – and across which they will create new forms of value.

Still, as we have seen, companies doing all of this are rare birds, if they yet exist at all. But they will. The selective pressures working in favor of sustainable development (and, we should admit, in favor of clever mimicry of Butterfly and Honeybee traits in companies that are still strongly degenerative) can only increase. That said, as already noted, it's not uncommon to find the same corporation displaying some mix of Caterpillar, Locust, Butterfly and Honeybee behaviors simultaneously.

The one thing we should avoid reading into the MetaMatrix is any notion that a Corporate Caterpillar or Locust is fated to remain trapped forever in that form. Not so. As explained in Chapter 6, Monsanto's Bob Shapiro now characterizes what he was trying to do there as shifting from the Locust cell to the Caterpillar cell, in preparation for a jump into the regenerative line. Tough, but despite Monsanto's bruising experience, by no means impossible.

With the right stimulus and leadership, any organization can start the transformative journey from either of the degenerative cells to either of the 'sweet spot' regenerative cells, although it is usually easier to go from Caterpillar to Butterfly than from Locust to Honeybee, and from low positive to high positive impact than from high negative to low negative impact.

The difference between the natural and economic forms of metamorphosis are obvious and hardly need stressing, but one point needs to be made. The process by which a caterpillar turns into a butterfly, or a pupa into a bee, is genetically programmed. The process doesn't quite run on rails, but the chances of failure are relatively small. By contrast, corporate and economic metamorphoses carry significantly higher risks of failure. That's why the willingness of the Citizen CEOs discused in Chapter 6 to share lessons learned is so crucial.

PANEL 5

Views from the moon

If you want to distinguish Corporate Caterpillars and Locusts from actual or potential Butterflies and Honeybees, it helps to look at the world from a different angle. And that's a little easier these days. Where the ancient Egyptians are best remembered for the Pyramids, some folk see the pinnacle of modern civilization as the Saturn V rocket. Longer than a football field – it measured 363 feet from nose to tail – the Saturn was the most powerful rocket ever successfully flown.[90] Over the years, it has given us viewing points that would have been almost unimaginable to our ancestors.

A total of some 400,000 people may have worked on the Moon shots, but the handful of Apollo astronauts who rode the Saturns across the 240,000 mile gulf between Earth and the Moon were at the very tip of perhaps the greatest adventure of the 20th century. And of those, the spotlight really shone on those who walked in Neil Armstrong's lunar footsteps. The experience was, literally, out of this world. The late Alan Shepard, commander of Apollo 14, is said to have wept when he stepped onto the Moon and looked back at Earth. Most astronauts – and presumably many Soviet cosmonauts – came back profoundly moved, if not transformed.

I recently ran into Dave Scott, commander of Apollo 15 in 1971. That was the fourth lunar landing, but the first 'J-mission', involving an extended stay and the use of the electric lunar rover. Driving on the Moon was interesting. "Every time we would hit a rock or bump, we would sail through space," as Scott's crew-mate Jim Irwin later put it. This was ultra-expensive time: every minute on the Moon's surface was costed at $200,000 in late 1990 dollars.

And the environmental impacts were considerable, too. In Russia and Kazakhstan, for example, rocket launches are followed by what locals call "silver rain", made up of unspent fuel and a range of highly toxic chemicals. But, while parts of the space industry are undoubtedly operating in Locust mode, the outside-in images of Earth brought back by the astronauts were priceless. They fueled a central meme: Spaceship Earth.

Indeed, the first thing I did was thank Dave Scott for his role in helping us see our world from the outside in. Like other astronauts, he promptly mused about the psychological impact of being able to blot out distant Earth simply by holding up his thumb. But his environmentalism had taken an interesting tack. We discussed his ambitions to fire nuclear waste into deep space atop Saturn rockets, which struck me as the wrong answer to a crucial question: what to do with Locust wastes that will be deadly for hundreds of thousands of years?

One thing that might just prevent such things happening is an idea that Al Gore (when still US vice-president) came up with a few years back. I hadn't realized that the full-disk image of Earth we see most often dates from the Apollo 17 mission in 1972. This, as things turned out, was the last manned mission that went far enough out to capture the full disk front-lit by the sun. After wondering how to get more of the same, Gore says he woke up one night having dreamed of placing a satellite into the so-called L-1 point, where the gravitational pull of the Earth and that of the sun are exactly equal.

"You put a satellite out there," Gore said, "and it stays there, between the Earth and the sun. And when the Earth goes around the sun, the satellite stays between them. So it is always looking at the Earth, and the Earth is fully lit."[91] Using a TV camera aboard the satellite, the idea is that we could have access to 24-hour, live color pictures of the Earth. They would be available on the Internet, even popping up as screen-savers.

Pessimists will picture a future in which a million planetary screen-savers twirl unnoticed in a world still blinded by materialism, video games and other short-term passions. But Gore was optimistic. "In the same way that the first photo [of Earth from space] created a revolution in thought," he argued, "this will make it easier to focus our collective attention on what the hell's going on here." Let's hope so. The transformation of our economies to more sustainable forms of value creation will depend on our ability to break frame, seeing what we do from the outside in.

CHAPTER 6

The Citizen CEO
Leaders aiming for the triple win

When it comes to value creation, business is our main engine of change. And the chief executive officer (CEO) usually leads the charge. But if we are to steer our companies and economies into regenerative forms of value creation, we will need the extraordinary leadership skills of the Citizen CEO (see Executive Summary, page xiv).[92] Like an acrobat, he or she succeeds by continuously balancing two worlds: the fast-changing world of value creation and the slowly mutating, highly diverse world of human and societal values. The Citizen CEO may still represent an ideal type, rather than an everyday reality, but many business leaders now display at least some characteristics of the breed.

First, though, why all this fuss about CEOs? One reason is that in times of rapid economic change, the spotlight inevitably shifts to leaders and leadership. As a result, some highly-respected folk say our current obsession with CEOs won't last. "This is the third or fourth time in American history when we had all this emphasis on the 'genius CEO'," Peter Drucker has argued. "The last time was in the 1920s, and before that in the 1880s. That always is the sign of a big economic transition. But it isn't going to last, because the transition to the information economy has already happened."[93]

The argument, in short, is that we are obsessed with CEOs simply because the new economy has been shaking the old to its very foundations. Well, maybe. But interest in the Citizen CEO is surfacing at a time when business is playing an increasingly dominant role in world affairs and when more people than ever before have a real, immediate stake in the performance of business and – through their pensions – of stock markets. Globalization, too, is increasing the stakes. And the ball will be kept rolling by other major economic and sociopolitical transitions, driven by new technologies such as biotechnology and nanotechnology, by innovative business models, and by increasing demands for stronger triple bottom line performance.

Meanwhile, there is at least a risk that the ups and downs of high-profile CEOs will distract attention from the underlying trends. We see new leaders taking over long-established companies or new start-ups, and then doing battle with their competitors and with others in their own companies. Consider Durk Jager, the new CEO who preached the need for speed at Procter & Gamble, 163 years old in 2000. Just 17 months after he took over the role, he was out, the shortest CEO tenure in the company's history.

As *Fortune* pointed out at the time, his fate illustrated a growing trend. "In less than six months," it noted, "we've seen CEO Doug Ivester fizzle at Coca-Cola (after just 2 years at the top), Jill Barad dumped from Mattel (after three years), Dale Morrison canned at Campbell Soup (less than three years), and Rick Thoman cashiered at Xerox (less than two years)."[94] *Business Week* talked of the 'CEO Trap', arguing that the constant quest for CEO superheroes to deliver sky-high growth pretty much guarantees disappointment. Remarkably, it noted, two-thirds of all major companies, worldwide, have replaced their CEOs at least once since 1995.[95]

"The mythologizing of the CEO began in earnest about 20 years ago," *Business Week* recalled, "as a wave of Herculean corporate restructurings gave rise to a brash new breed of corporate miracle worker." People like Lee Iacocca and, later, Bill Gates, Cisco's John Chambers, and Dell Computer's Michael Dell. We look at some Herculean Labors facing the Citizen CEO in panel 6 (page 120).

Whoever they are, wherever they work and whatever their views on the matter, CEOs – and their boards – increasingly must operate in a global goldfish bowl. Figure 6.1, however, makes the point that the companies we hear about are only the tip of an international corporate iceberg. Prepared by the Prince of Wales

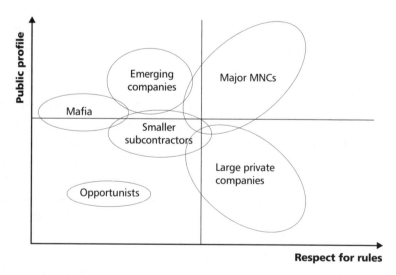

Figure 6.1 Business actors in sustainable development.
Source: The Prince of Wales Business Leaders Forum.[96]

Business Leaders Forum (now the International Business Leaders Forum) to illustrate the role business plays in relation to conflict prevention and resolution, the diagram works equally well in relation to sustainable development.

Meanwhile, whether or not the lives of high profile business leaders should rank as public entertainment, their successes and failures are increasingly visible. All of that said, and however transparent their boardrooms may be, many board directors remain skeptical about claims that a new breed of Citizen CEOs is emerging. Some of the more challenging responses I have heard are summarized below under the following seven headings:

- They're retired!
- They're philanthropists!
- They're mutants, niche players!
- They're in the public sector!
- They're mainstream, but they're failures!
- They're statistical anomalies!
- They can't be serious!

THEY'RE RETIRED!

It's true. Sadly, many business leaders only start to speak up for corporate citizenship or sustainability once they have stood down, or been sacked, from high corporate office. Given the pressures they face in the boardroom, and from the financial markets, this is hardly surprising. But, ask yourself, does that disqualify them from speaking their piece? Surely not. Apart from anything else, who better to start thinking of the legacy – the world – their grandchildren will inherit?

At the same time, major corporations are now ousting their CEOs so fast that the world at the top is becoming a bit of a blur. In the month when I was writing this chapter, and in the USA alone, the CEOs of 129 companies, small and large, left office – up from 60 the year before.[97] Getting such people to think long-term is always hard, but never harder than when the pressure is on for results today, with the threat of very early retirement tomorrow.

So let's zero in on one of the most thoughtful CEO-retirees, Dee Hock, founder and CEO Emeritus of VISA international. "We are living on the knife edge of one of those rare and momentous turning points in human history," Hock has argued. "Livable lives for our grandchildren, their children, and their children's children hang in the balance."[98] The world as it is, he insisted, is simply not sustainable. The Industrial Age, hierarchical, command-and-control institutions that still dominate our lives are increasingly irrelevant. But, he warned, Corporate Locusts and Caterpillars are not so much collapsing, as Communism did, but continue to expand "as they devour resources, decimate the earth, and demean humanity."

It is still rare for someone who has had such an impact on the business world to issue such dire warnings. But Dee Hock's stature as the founder of VISA International, sometimes claimed to be the largest commercial enterprise on earth, deserves our attention. So here are the bare bones of Hock's side of the VISA story. In 1968, when many baby boomers were out in the streets, or otherwise immersed in the counter-culture, Hock was busily developing his concept of a global system for the exchange of value. He had a radically new business model in mind. That part of the story began in 1970, when he founded a company that later evolved into VISA.

In 1992, interestingly, the year the world's attention was focused on the Earth Summit in Rio de Janeiro, Hock was being celebrated as one of eight individuals who had most changed the way people live in the previous quarter century. So what was Hock saying as the 21st century dawned? A linked pair of questions, he suggested, cuts to the core of our current problems. First, as our economic, social and environmental problems build, "will the result be chaos and even more repression and dictatorial regimes so often arising from chaotic conditions? Or, second, will we emerge from the eggshell of our Industrial Age institutions into a new world of profound, constructive organizational change?"

The answer to both questions, he argued, lies in the very *concept* of organization and in the beliefs and values of individuals. In contrast to today's organizations, he said, "the organization of the future will be the embodiment of *community* based on *shared purpose* calling to the *higher aspirations of people*". But what does all this mean in practice? Hock argued that we are on the verge of what he dubbed the "Chaordic Age". *Chaord* is a word he coined by combining *chaos* and *order*. It describes any "self-organizing, self-governing, adaptive, nonlinear, complex organism, organization, community or system, whether physical, biological or social, the behavior of which harmoniously blends characteristics of both chaos and order".

VISA, Hock noted, eventually evolved into one of the most striking examples of chaordic organization. By the time he wrote his book *Birth of the Chaordic Age*, Visa was owned by 22,000 member banks, which both competed with each other for 750 million customers and cooperated by honoring one another's $1.25 trillion in transactions annually, across borders and currencies. Interestingly, however, Hock did not commend VISA as a model to emulate. Indeed, he was often highly critical of the organization he had helped found. In the end, after fourteen years, he left VISA to dedicate himself to environmental regeneration.

In the end, the phrase that stuck in my mind after reading *Birth of the Chaordic*

Age is this: "Things are too far gone for pessimism." Rather than subsiding into deep depression, however, Hock once again plunged into the fray, founding The Chaordic Alliance. This is a non-profit group dedicated to the formation of practical, innovative organizations that "blend competition and collaboration to address critical societal issues."[99] Retired? Yes, but we need more such retirees.

THEY'RE PHILANTHROPISTS!

Again, often true. Many CEOs and other business leaders contribute to society as a parallel activity to – or an offset against – their mainstream business activities. In some cases, like John D. Rockefeller, Sr., or some would say William H. (Bill) Gates III, the philanthropy is used to offset reputational problems caused by those mainstream business activities. The world is now dotted with foundations dedicated to the memory of industrialists or to companies they founded. Examples include the Rockefeller Foundation, Carnegie Foundation, Ford Foundation, Packard Foundation (set up by one of the founders of Hewlett-Packard), the complex web of charitable and part-charitable trusts set up by Ingvar Kamprad of IKEA, and so on and on.

This is one way of funding 'good works', no question. Often, too, there are useful multiplier effects. A rare case, perhaps, of Locusts spawning Butterflies. But some business leaders are now taking a different approach. They are trying to develop their businesses so that there is a direct connection between the products and services they sell, on the one hand, and the causes they espouse on the other. Later, we will take a closer look at Carly Fiorina of Hewlett-Packard (page 182).

First, though, Bill Gates of Microsoft. So great is the interest in Gates and his company, that *Wired* ran an extraordinary article on the two over no less than 50 pages (with no interrupting ads).[100] Like Ron Chernow's brilliant book *Titan: The Life of John D. Rockefeller, Sr.*, the article noted the uncanny similarities between the careers of Big Oil's Rockefeller and Big Software's Gates.[101] But *Wired* also noted an "eerily similar trajectory" in the histories of both Microsoft and its arch-rival IBM. Just as IBM had been forced to abandon its earlier strategy and embrace the PC, so Microsoft was now being forced to stop looking at the future through the PC lens and embrace the internet.

Intel's Andy Grove found the parallel with IBM intriguing. "For a long time in the 1980s, IBM was everything to Intel," he told *Wired*. "We thought about them constantly, lived and died by their whim. Then around 1990, I woke up one day and it wasn't so anymore. It wasn't some momentous event. And now it was Microsoft who we thought about all the time. Maybe this is happening again – only this time, instead of Microsoft being replaced by another company, it's being replaced by the Internet, by a whole bunch of things happening at once."

There's no question that the $21 billion charitable foundation Gates founded is making him something of a hero in the world of corporate philanthropy – and making valuable contributions to international health. But after his entanglement with the US Justice Department, in the *United States v. Microsoft* court case, he has been seen as increasingly flawed. All this despite the fact that he had launched a company that helped create an industry, and then led that industry as it transformed first the US and then the global economy.

"For a long time," *Wired* noted, "Gates represented everything that was inspiring about this protean phenomenon taking shape in our midst – its freshness and its ambition, its sense of possibility and its connection to the future. But like a figure lifted from classical tragedy, Gates sowed the seeds of his own undoing. He created a company that reflected his image and fostered a culture that fed his sense of omnipotence. He mastered a business that rewarded farsightedness, but failed to develop his peripheral vision."

Where Rockefeller found comfort in the belief that he would be vindicated both by history and in heaven, Gates appears to hope that he will be vindicated much sooner, and here on Earth. The problem is that Microsoft's take on business ethics, like Rockefeller's and Standard Oil's, got out of synch with wider values. President George W. Bush may recall the legal hounds, but there are those even inside Microsoft who doubt whether even $21 billion will be enough to repair the reputational damage caused by the court case.

THEY'RE MUTANTS, NICHE-PLAYERS!

Mutant, for some people, is a term of abuse. But for many innovators, and all Corporate Chrysalids, it's no bad thing to be a mutant. Today's niche, they would argue, could well be tomorrow's megamarket. Whether or not we call them mutants, no-one would deny that Body Shop founder Anita Roddick, Ben Cohen and Jerry Greenfield of Ben & Jerry's (now part of Unilever), or Izaac Van Melle of the Dutch candy producer Van Melle (now part of Italy's Perfetti), have been mavericks in the world of business. And the difference between their thinking and that of a Bill Gates could hardly be more stark.

Where Gates sees corporate citizenship in terms of philanthropy, the likes of Cohen, Greenfield and Roddick have tried to incorporate ethical principles into their basic business models, into the very DNA of their businesses. Precious few CEOs were in the streets protesting against the World Trade Organization (WTO) in

November 1999, certainly not Bill Gates whose hometown Seattle is. But Roddick arrived determined to be "sleepless in Seattle". What worries her more than almost anything else, she says, is the "new nomadic capital" that "never sets down roots, never builds communities. It leaves behind toxic wastes, embittered workers and indigenous communities driven out of existence."

Passion glows through every line of her book, *Business as Unusual.*[102] And this prototypical Citizen CEO doesn't pull her punches. "If you look at the way some businesses are behaving in many corners of the world," she says, "the places most business leaders never visit, you can see them alienating humanity in so many ways. I have seen, and still see, corporate crimes in abundance. Industry after industry seems perfectly happy to use sweatshops and the globe is quickly becoming a playground for those who move capital and projects quickly from place to place. When business can roam from country to country with few restrictions in its search for the lowest wages, the loosest environmental regulations and the most docile and desperate workers, then the destruction of livelihoods, cultures and environments can be enormous."

So we know what she is against. And given that her every move with the Body Shop has been chronicled for years, it is hardly necessary to ask what she means by 'Business as Unusual'? But why did she write the book? It is, she says, "more than a chronicle of a decade at The Body Shop, more than a condensed manual for the wannabe business radical." Indeed it is – and one of the most telling bits is an entry from her 1996 diary. "This is driving me nuts," she had scribbled. "The legal department says we can't use the word 'activist' in the (Body Shop) Foundation annual report because of its association with TERRORISM! This really is too Pythonesque for me – I'm going to use it wherever I can. In fact, I'll name a fragrance after it."

Vintage Roddick, as is the sequence that opens the book. The year: 1987. The Body Shop is still in its "protoplasmic period" and the Confederation of British Industry (CBI) has picked it as Company of the Year. Roddick had arrived to pick up the award. "There they sat, the captains of industry, the bankers, the analysts, the journalists, just about the entire British financial establishment, all lined up and holding their collective breath as I mounted the podium." The line in her speech that the media jumped on referred to her audience as "dinosaurs in pin-striped suits".

Half-way through her speech, she recalls, media tycoon Robert Maxwell walked out. "For all I know he had another appointment," she says, "but still I felt a surge of pride." Maxwell would soon come dramatically and fatally unstuck, but the following decade would also see the Body Shop story get "a lot more complex – richer, but darker too." This was life in a minefield, with one of the worst periods being when new management blood was brought in to revamp and grow the business. She quotes consultant Ichak Adizes, who had built a reputation with his 'lifecycle' theory for companies, as saying that the company was "metamorphosizing" from the "Go–Go" phase to "Adolescence".

Adizes may have had an impeccable track record in helping other companies metamorphose, she notes, but "I realized nowhere in our conversations with him was there ever any mention of values or of what was sacrosanct to the company." The tension between those who wanted to focus on values and those who wanted to focus on value creation intensified. A new structure developed, which Roddick dubbed "the Lego set from Hell".

In the end, Adizes went. The process had cost £2 million and the structures he had put in place were soon dismantled. But the original problems that had led the board to call in outside help had not gone away: "We were shocked to find that we had lost around a million customers in about three years," Roddick admits. The news early in 2001 that the company's make-over, partly designed to make the shops "less green", had been something of a flop raised further question-marks over the Body Shop's mainstreaming strategy.[103] But, Roddick believes: "What doesn't kill you makes you stronger."

THEY'RE IN THE PUBLIC SECTOR!

OK, because they are transparent and publicly accountable, perhaps we should expect public sector companies and institutions to be led by Citizen CEOs. But given that many state-owned businesses around the world operate in Locust mode, maybe we should be more welcoming of public sector leaders who push social responsibility and sustainability agendas.

My own experience with the electricity and water industries suggests that some of the most engaged companies tend to be those on the verge of privatization – or those that have only recently come into the private sector. For example, and for a number of years, I have been a member of Anglian Water's board environment (and now sustainability) committee. So I asked Anglian Water Group CEO Chris Mellor and Sustainability Director Paul Woodcock how all this came about?

"The evolution from a 'local authority' to a fully commercial way of life has focused our attention on the demands of customers," they replied. "It is our belief (backed up by market research) that alongside competitive pricing our customers require safe and reliable services taking account of the environment and the impact on communities. Environment and public health are core AWG values. Our traditional role as a regional water services provider places us at the heart of the community, through employment, purchase of supplies, and investment in local economies. Sustainability, you might say, comes naturally to us."

So how was SD sold to the AWG board? "Via a business case," was the reply. "AWG has a 10-target approach to SD. The Board has adopted this on the basis of clear 'bottom line' benefits. But the Board also recognised that there would be additional benefits in our service contracting business if we were seen to be an SD leader. AWG will be competing for a range of asset creation and management contracts across sectors and globally. Municipalities seeking service provision will look for AWG to provide services in away that promotes and enhances the local environment and social infrastructure, alongside competitive pricing. For such customers, SD will increasingly become a guiding philosophy."

Another organization that I have been able to track as it adopted TBL performance and accountability principles is Canada's BC Hydro. This is a commercial Crown corporation, owned by the province of British Columbia. According to CEO Michael Costello, the corporation is "beginning to integrate the three bottom lines into our business decision."[104] The reason: "We know that integrating social, environmental, and financial bottom lines is fundamental to making sound, sustainable business decisions."

Where electricity consumers once asked 'What is cheapest?', BC Hydro's experience is that they increasingly also want to know 'What is most sustainable?' But there are a number of problems. "The difficulty is, no one knows exactly what sustainability means," the corporation notes. There are global dimensions to the sustainability equation, but others are more local. "To define it in terms of BC Hydro and British Columbia," Costello said, "we must first understand how our values are aligned with those of the public we serve. We know our customers want continued reliability and low rates; we are also aware of increasing public advocacy on behalf of BC Hydro becoming a socially responsible energy company."

THEY'RE MAINSTREAM, BUT THEY'RE FAILURES!

Schadenfreude is a uniquely German word, but not uniquely a German emotion. It means taking pleasure from the problems of others. Given that a number of early corporate champions of SD have come horribly unstuck, we might assume that a good deal of pleasure has been taken by those who didn't believe in the idea from the start. Worse, perhaps, many people have also used such early mishaps to persuade themselves that progress in this area is impossible. So, to dig deeper into the debate, I decided to interview the CEOs of two companies that had made high-profile commitments to SD, before stalling in mid-air: Bob Shapiro of Monsanto and Ray Anderson of Interface (page 220).

Before starting with Bob Shapiro, I should declare an interest. Shapiro was spotlighted in *Cannibals With Forks* as an interesting, early example of the CEO of a major corporation embracing the SD agenda. "We believe that pursuing sustainable development is about more than merely surviving, or simply reducing the harmful effects of what we do," the company had said in its first sustainability report.[105] "The more we consider it, the more we conclude that there is a great opportunity to create VALUE for our customers, suppliers, shareholders, ourselves and the world at large."

SD, Shapiro had argued in an earlier interview in the *Harvard Business Review*, "involves the laws of nature – physics, chemistry and biology – and the recognition that the world is a closed system. What we thought was boundless has limits, and we're beginning to hit them. That's going to change a lot of today's fundamental economics, it's going to change prices, and it's going to change what's socially acceptable."[106]

I still believe that many of the things Shapiro tried to do were very much in line with the emerging Citizen CEO agenda. Indeed, for nearly two years, SustainAbility worked for Monsanto, before unilaterally resigning the contract at the beginning of 1998.

Here is the story in headlines. We were hired to help Monsanto get to grips with the emerging stakeholder agenda, particularly in relation to genetically modified (GM) foods. Both the major stakeholder events we later organized had pointed to major roadblocks ahead for Monsanto, particularly in Europe. At the second event, all the external stakeholders (including farmers, food processors, retailers and NGOs) ended up saying pretty much the same thing, while key Monsanto players took a different view. Unhappily, the company's subsequent behavior forced us to conclude that it was, in some very real sense, "constitutionally deaf".

Our resignation itself was a public event, in that it was announced on our web-site. So, even though our worst fears were eventually shown to have been well-founded when Monsanto hit the wall of European public opinion, I was somewhat nervous about asking Shapiro for his views on what had happened. It turned out that he was more than willing to re-engage.

First, then, I asked him to set the Monsanto experience in the context of the MetaMatrix (page 75), his answers were intriguing. "When I was starting at the company in the early 1990s," he began,

> *"Monsanto had probably transitioned from a Locust (which I guess almost every*

company was not so long ago) to a Caterpillar. Dick Mahoney, my predecessor, had taken some dramatic steps, well beyond what was legally required, to reduce Monsanto's ugliest pollution (toxic air emissions). He had committed to a 'Monsanto Pledge' that was quite enlightened.

"My view, as I think you know, was that financial value (as in 'value creation') was ultimately determined by what society wanted. To the extent that society wanted cheap goods more than it wanted clean air, water and soil, 'value' was realized by supplying cheap goods. I assumed that was changing and that sustainable development was going to be wanted – even demanded – as people and politicians increasingly understood what was at stake. Therefore, I didn't see (and don't see) an inevitable conflict between 'value' and SD."

When we began the exchange, Shapiro's first question to me had been why we had felt it necessary to resign? Why, he wondered, hadn't I talked to him before abandoning hope for Monsanto? The answer was that I had indeed flown to the company's St Louis headquarters, but Shapiro had been called away to brief Wall Street analysts on the implications of the just-announced collapse in Monsanto's merger plans with American Home Products. A diary conflict which simply underscored the difficulties even the best-intentioned CEOs find in keeping the SD agenda at the top of their priority list.

Nor was I the only one who had lost faith in Monsanto's transformation process. Paul Hawken, then of the US Natural Step Foundation and now of the Natural Capital Institute (see Chapter 13), was another. "Both you and Paul reached a set of pessimistic conclusions about what 'Monsanto' was, how it thought and what it was likely to do," Shapiro continued.

"Those conclusions, as far as I could tell, were based largely on contact with Monsanto people who were thinking and behaving in ways that were inconsistent with what I had declared to be Monsanto's policy. I know there were a few people like that. There were also a great many others whose hearts and commitments were in the right place.

"The problem, I think, may have been that you and others (including some people within the company) may have assumed (a) that I knew what some of our people were saying and doing and (b) that I must therefore agree with them. What may not have been apparent was that, on this front as on several others, I was trying to create radical change in Monsanto. To do that, I had to get out in

front of the organization to inspire those who were ready to be inspired – and to confront those who preferred the old ways.

"In all these areas, I expected – and got – resistance. But this approach worked pretty well when I was able to get good information as to how things were going. I was often able to change people's behaviors or, when necessary, to change the cast of characters. But when I didn't get good feedback as to resistance or inappropriate behavior, I obviously wasn't in a position to do much about it."

Stepping back from Monsanto for a moment, my own experience of the top floors of the headquarters of most major corporations is that they are often places of hissing silence. It's a bit like it must have been entering the Oracle at Delphi. These are places of power, and top executives, whether they like it or not, are to some degree cocooned from the rest of the world. Whether they intend it or not, they are surrounded either by an 'echo chamber' (in which their beliefs are often fed back to them) or invisible filters (which ensure that they are shielded from bad news their colleagues think they wouldn't want to hear).

That said, no-one denies that transforming long-established corporations and corporate cultures is one of the toughest assignments in business. My colleagues and I, together with some of the change agents inside Monsanto, would often wonder aloud what it would take to wake up top management and the board? When would the company experience its equivalent of Shell's Brent Spar? Well, in the event, the GM food issue turned into a major controversy in Europe – and developed at such a pace, and on such a scale, that Monsanto was virtually run off the road.

The company may yet recover, of course, although following the turmoil it was taken over by Pharmacia Upjohn. Shapiro had spoken of 'Monsanto's Law', a biotechnology version of 'Moore's Law' which has driven the IT industry up a ferociously steep curve of innovation and value creation. So I asked him if he still believed in Monsanto's Law: "Sure," he replied. "The rate of technical progress continues to accelerate along the curve – more researchers, more labs, better bioinformatics and other enabling tools."

So was embracing SD a strategic mistake? "I don't think so," he said.

"The logic is still compelling: one way or another, global demand for more sustainable technologies (e.g. information technology, biotechnology and nanotechnology) must and will translate into economic imperatives. I don't think it was a mistake to try to help develop some of these technologies nor a mistake to say that was what we were up to.

"I will confess, however, that at the time I didn't understand the extent to which a corporation with the audacity to reject the idea that there's a fundamental inconsistency between sustainability and profits would enrage parts of the NGO community. If I had reflected on it more deeply, I might have realized that many NGOs (and not a few captains of industry as well!) were totally committed to the idea that corporations by their very nature must pollute and despoil. Indeed, that belief constitutes the raison d'être for many NGOs: no corporate despoilers, no need for NGOs.

"For some in the NGO community, it was intolerable for a major corporation (as opposed, say, to cute, highly personalized, counterculture enterprises like Ben & Jerry's or The Body Shop) to align our business strategy with the 1992 Earth Summit goals of sustainable development. And it must have been even more infuriating for us to have said, in effect, that all the agitation in the world won't help us get to a more sustainable economy unless we come up with new technologies – and it's the corporations, not the NGOs, who are best suited to make that happen."

But surely there was more to it than that? For what it's worth, my own take on the controversy had been that Monsanto in general, and Bob Shapiro in particular, had made a direct (and potentially misleading) series of connects between a number of different issues. Dematerialization, they had concluded, is central to SD. The shift from atoms to bits, in turn, is critical to dematerialization. The genetic engineering of crop plants to resist pests is a prime example of the shift from atoms (in the form of toxic pesticides) to bits (or bio-bits, in the form of transferred genes). Therefore, the logic ran, GM crops are intrinsically sustainable.

Of course, this is to radically over-simplify a complex sequence of arguments, but that seemed to be the Monsanto worldview. The problem was that many people – including many NGOs that had helped shape the SD agenda – see things rather differently. They want sustainability; they want dematerialization; and they want the shift from problematic atoms to the right sort of bits. But many are far from convinced that the genetic modification of crop plants, animals and food is intrinsically sustainable.

Finally, what lessons would Bob Shapiro want to share with other CEOs, most particularly would-be Citizen CEOs? He was very clear on the point:

"If there was a next time, I'd have much earlier dialogue with a wide range of

interested parties in the scientific, academic, governmental and NGO communities. As you know, Monsanto did tend to assume that if we simply followed the official regulatory processes and provided the required scientific evidence demonstrating safety, and so on, that society at large would respect the decisions arrived at through these processes. In most parts of the world, on most issues, that assumption holds true. But, as events have shown, it's not universally valid.

"Earlier and more thorough dialogue might have helped. It would have taken unusually candid and innovative discussions between ourselves and Greenpeace to create a win/win, but that might not have been impossible."

Bob Shapiro, whether or not you agree with him on every point, is modeling one of the most important traits of the Citizen CEO – a willingness to share insights on what led both to success and to failure.

THEY'RE STATISTICAL ANOMALIES!

Not so. They may have been statistically rare to date, as critics argue, but the appearance of a growing number of Citizen CEOs in such sectors as oil and chemicals is neither an accident nor an anomaly. Such industries have been under pressure for decades, and you don't need to be an evolutionary biologist or psychologist to know that such stresses sometimes lead to breakdowns – and sometimes to breakthroughs.

If you talked to American activists in recent years, one business leader likely to be mentioned early on in the conversation was Robert (Bob) Campbell, who recently stood down as CEO of Sunoco. When he took over the helm of what was then very much a Corporate Locust in 1991, it was against the background of the launch of the International Chamber of Commerce (ICC) Business Charter for Sustainable Development. The Charter was a watered-down version of the CERES Principles, developed by the US Coalition for Environmentally Responsible Economies. During the launch event, one of Sunoco's current board directors – Robert (Bob) Kennedy – made a stirring speech as the-then-CEO of Union Carbide, whose jointly-owned plant had been at the epicentre of the appalling Bhopal disaster in 1984. "Environmental protection," Kennedy concluded, "has become a survival issue for companies."

Campbell decided to act on the health, environment and safety (HES) agenda, but was careful to take his senior colleagues with him. "He was patient and allowed the concept to be thoroughly tested and challenged by his management team – and eventually by the board," recalls one colleague. "Sceptics were encouraged to raise their questions and they were addressed." The result: Sunoco adopted the CERES Principles early in 1993, the first Fortune 500 company to do so.

I asked Bob Campbell how hard he had to 'sell' this approach to the Sunoco board? Not too hard, he replied. "Because a number of our directors had experience in running other manufacturing companies," he explained, "they already bought into the concept that HES excellence is critically important to our business. The only discussion was in regard to how we should achieve our results, for example whether we should go the CERES route or not." Meanwhile, Bob Campbell and Sunoco's COO, John Drosdick, admitted that the company is "at the beginning of our learning curve as we contemplate our future as a more sustainable corporation and start to assess our 'triple bottom line' performance."

Another company I have watched as it worked on its sustainability policy and practices is Lend Lease, the Australia-based international property and real estate company which played a key role in preparing Sydney for the 2000 Olympics (page 163). It has certainly been something of an anomaly in its industry: its business model has emerged from core values recognizing a community of interest between labor and capital. As a result of its long-standing emphasis on teamwork, its strike record has been much better than those of its competitors.

One of Australia's most dynamic companies, Lend Lease was originally the brainchild of Dick Dusseldorp, the son of a Dutch wheat merchant. Dusseldorp, who died recently, was a visionary: "Our goal," he once said, "is the improvement of the human condition, not just that of any specific group, be it shareholders, workers, management or others." As a result, he – and his company – won genuine respect and admiration from government, other business people and, above all, Lend Lease's employees.[107]

When I visited Lend Lease in Sydney before the Olympics, the company was working on a sustainability policy responding to what it sees as a set of interlinked trends. These include: demographic and lifestyle changes; new forms of urbanization; dematerialization; climate change; human wellbeing; knowledge and intellectual capital; stakeholder engagement; and financial markets, with a focus on the impact of the growing social and environmental screening on property values and market capitalization. Increasingly, the Lend Lease people said, sustainability would be an integral part of the company's corporate governance, risk management, and business investment and performance evaluation processes.

More specifically, it was developing a new Sustainability Council to help drive the whole process forward. This was designed to provide a forum in which business unit representatives can openly discuss the issues related to the group's sustainability transition. I was impressed by the plans, and by the people I met, but towards the end of 2000 the company announced remarkable news: its new chairman would be Jill Ker Conway.

An academic and business leader born in Australia but a long-time US resident, Ker Conway is perhaps most widely known through her best-selling auto-biographies.[108] She sits on the boards of some of the world's best-known companies, among them Colgate-Palmolive, Merrill Lynch and Nike.[109] Very few board directors can boast such extraordinary triple bottom line credentials. Among many other things, she is a historian of women and a visiting professor at the Massachusetts Institute of Technology (MIT), where she teaches the history of ideas and attitudes to nature and the environment. A statistical anomaly, yes, but she is working hard to change that. She sees a strong future trend towards more diverse boards, with growing numbers of women involved.

When I met her in London as the final proofs of *The Chrysalis Economy* were being edited, she had been working with a group of 500 fast-track women at Merrill-Lynch, where she was a director. It's currently beyond imagination, but my medium-term dream would be for each corporate board, worldwide, to have at least one director of this caliber.

THEY CAN'T BE SERIOUS!

As the number of Citizen CEOs grows, the final ploy of skeptics is often to say that they will never walk the talk. Time alone will tell, but each of the following four business leaders has broken ranks with their industry. All four companies are Corporate Locusts, but are also Corporate Chrysalids. At various times and in various ways, they have all admitted past problems and spotlighted future issues. They have each pledged their companies to demanding forms of corporate citizenship and SD, leading to raised eyebrows – shading through to outraged disbelief – among their peers and competitors.

All four companies – BP, Shell, DuPont and Ford[110] – have had major problems in other areas, quite apart from the outstanding sustainability-related challenges they still face. But having talked in various circumstances to Sir John Browne, Sir Mark Moody-Stuart, Chad Holliday and Bill Ford, Jr., I am convinced that they have been dead serious in their public pronouncements. Whatever the outcome, they want to ensure that their companies push through the Values and Value Barriers into the domain of the Corporate Honeybee.

First, then, BP chief executive Sir John Browne. His championing of the SD agenda has been particularly valuable, given his track record in value creation. He has transformed BP through a clear and ambitious acquisition policy, taking over companies like Amoco, Arco and Castrol. In 1997, he declared in a speech that global warming may indeed be a real challenge. To the horror of some of his industry peers, he pledged that by 2010, BP would reduce emissions of carbon dioxide by 10% from 1990 levels. Since then, he has also led the charge in relation to a whole range of environmental issues, from cleaner fuels to wastewater disposal.[111]

Asked what his ultimate goal was, he replied that "it's just good business. We know that people are concerned about the environment, that they want to buy products that don't pollute, that governments want to deal with companies that are sensitive to environmental issues, and that people are motivated to work for companies that respect the environment. The big thing is to get the timing right. Our ambition is always to be ahead of the curve, though of course you can get too far ahead of it." The Iceland frozen foods group illustrates what can happen in such circumstances (page 257).

Later, in his 2000 BBC Reith Lecture, Browne went further. "I remain an optimist," he said, "not because I deny the problems – they are real and substantial. Nor because I believe that the existing pattern and structure of development can be sustained – it clearly cannot and should not be. But because I believe that sustainability is built on change, as it always has been." He also stressed the key role of business in all of this. "Business is not in opposition to, but has a fundamental role in delivering sustainable development," he concluded.[112]

Later still, BP decided to re-brand itself, adopting the 'Beyond Petroleum' slogan, alongside a new, more consumer-friendly logo. Critics like Corporate Watch were not impressed: *Beyond Pompous, Beyond Protest, Beyond Preposterous, Beyond Posturing, Beyond Propaganda ... Beyond Belief*, they retorted.[113] Most SD activists and opinion-formers have welcomed such statements and pledges, but have also stressed that BP must now deliver on its promises.

The company's investments in renewable energy are seen to be a positive signal, for example, but recent accidents at the BP Grangemouth refinery complex in Scotland have raised question marks over the company's capacity to do everything at once. It will be fascinating to see how BP's TBL strategy evolves in contrast to hard-nosed competitors like ExxonMobil. And the world will watch with bated breath to see what BP does in Alaska (page 133), particularly with a Republican administration in power in the USA.

Often running neck-and-neck with Sir John has been Sir Mark Moody-Stuart, Chairman of Royal Dutch/Shell until 2001. When I wrote *Cannibals* in 1997, Shell was still struggling to make sense of the Brent Spar and Nigerian controversies that had shaken it so badly in 1995. Towards the end of 1997, SustainAbility began to work with the company, focusing initially on developing a series of annual SD reports, under the *Profits & Principles* banner.

"Far from being a drag on our performance," Moody-Stuart argued in Shell's second SD report, *People, Planet & Profits*, "such a commitment helps us understand the world better and improves our chances of success. Sustainable development is forward-looking, embodies the notion of progress, and encourages liberating new ways of interpreting the world. Our businesses can best thrive by enthusiastically embracing this agenda and providing energy and other products in line with society's expectations for a sustainable future."[114]

Shortly after the company added SD objectives to its long-established business principles, however, it posted its worst annual financial results ever. It was interesting to see how it responded in such circumstances to its SD commitments. Rather than diluting them, to reassure the financial markets that it was focusing right down on immediate priorities, Shell publicly reaffirmed its commitment to SD. There will be other tests, but these early results were reassuring.

This level of commitment has been particularly striking in relation to the positioning of such companies as ExxonMobil, whose absolute priority has been financial performance. Shell's strong emphasis on social responsibility, transparency and accountability, and on the broader SD agenda, were increasingly viewed as potential differentiating factors in the market. "I don't think analysts value those things highly," Sir Mark noted, "but some major shareholders definitely do."[115]

Shell's financial performance has since improved considerably, but your view on whether or not SD could become a strategic differentiator for such companies will very much depend on your sense of what sort of future we are moving towards. That's why Shell, in addition to building internal systems and processes like its Sustainable Development Council and Sustainable Development Management Framework (SDMF), has invested so much effort in its scenarios, including a growing number focusing on the SD outlook (Chapter 12).

The questions that Moody-Stuart's colleagues, among them Rob Walvis (as director, planning, environment and external affairs) and Tom Delfgaauw (as vice president for SD), were asking include: *"What makes SD better than plain old excellent management, as we've always understood it?"* and *"Does the SD approach offer a unique premium – measured in profits, competitive advantage, shareholder value or some other tangible form?"*

Meanwhile, one thing is clear: European companies like BP and Shell are often reaching rather different answers than their US competitors. That said, we have also seen a growing number of major US corporations headed in the SD direction. Let's briefly focus on just two: DuPont and Ford.

So, third, consider Charles 'Chad' Holliday Jr., DuPont's chairman and CEO. His strategy for shifting the giant chemical company's portfolio of businesses in more sustainable directions is illustrated in Figure 11.1 (page 218). In simple terms, it has involved shifting the company's center of gravity from relatively low-value-added, high-environmental-impact activities like oil production to progressively higher-value-added, lower-impact activities.

After taking over the helm of the $29 billion company in 1998, Holliday began to shift its transformation into high gear.[116] His promise to investors: DuPont would transform itself from an old economy supplier of cyclical commodities into a dazzling industrial growth company. Indeed, Holliday has repeatedly spoken in public of his determination to create "sustainable growth". By this, DuPont means "creating shareholder and societal value while reducing our environmental footprint along the value chain." A key dimension of that shift has been growing investment in biotechnology and pharmaceuticals. Indeed, the company's goal has been to generate 30% of its income from life sciences by 2002.

The process of reinvention has involved a reworking of the company's values statement. It now begins: "We, the people of DuPont, dedicate ourselves to the work of improving life on our planet."[117] A major advertising campaign has offered a "To Do List" – and linked solutions – "for the Planet".[118] But, like Monsanto, DuPont's much-vaunted shift has proved to be something of a disappointment. Its failure to secure a pharmaceutical industry alliance left it with a smaller-than-ideal drug operation, while the backlash against genetically modified crops has slowed new product introductions in that area, too.

Many financial analysts have been less than impressed by Holliday's performance. "He has a huge credibility hole to dig out of," said Robert S. Goodof at DuPont investor Loomis Sayles & Co.[119] But Holliday counters that corporate transformations on this scale take a very long time. He still believes strongly in the biotechnology prospect, and is trying to build a dialogue with activists and other agenda-shapers. Meanwhile, underneath the surface, new styles of engagement with customers are evolving.

One example: the new business model adopted by DuPont for the sale of paint to the automotive finishes department of Ford's Oakville assembly plant. To cut the costs of the operation, and reduce the overall environmental impact, DuPont Canada introduced a cost per unit (CPU) program. Instead of being paid for the volume of paint sold, DuPont is now rewarded for the number of automobiles painted. The shift from a model based on gallons of paint sold to area of product painted is said to have triggered a fundamental change in mind-set.[120]

For Ford, costs have fallen by 35–40%, and the volumes of waste have been cut. At the same time, the company's emissions of volatile organic compounds, released during the finishing process, have halved. For DuPont Canada, the lower volumes of paint shipped have been offset by improved efficiencies.

One of the architects of DuPont's 'the goal is zero' campaign is Paul Tebo, the company's vice president for safety, health and environment. Dubbed 'Hero of Zero' when awarded the *Tomorrow* Environmental Leadership Award, Tebo stresses how important the use of the phrase 'sustainable growth' – rather than 'sustainable development' – has been in getting the message across to his colleagues.

"Growth was very important," he says. "I tried sustainability and the business leaders saw it as the status quo. I tried sustainable development and they viewed it as environmental sustainability. I tried sustainable business, but growth is what organizations want – either you're growing or you're not, and not growing is not a very good [situation]."[121] DuPont's long-standing commitment to zero accidents helped enormously. Tebo is good at reducing the business case to headlines: "The quicker we get to zero waste," he says, "the quicker we'll have 100 percent product. The quicker we get to zero downtime, the quicker we'll be at 100 percent uptime." And the next stage will be to drive this approach through what he calls DuPont's "value partnerships", its customers and suppliers.

One key DuPont customer, as we have seen, is the Ford Motor Company. And our fourth and final business leader in this section is Ford Chairman William (Bill) Clay Ford. He broke new ground for the company by publishing a no-holds-barred corporate citizenship report, entitled *Connecting with Society*.[122] The report, which included a four-page interview I did with him on a wide range of subjects, sparked a storm of media comment in the USA. The biggest issue turned out to be Ford's admission that its gas-guzzling sport utility vehicles (SUVs) are unsustainable. Which was a little odd, given that the company was doing little more than owning up to what most people already knew.

Ford summed up his approach in the following words: "We're at the most exciting period in the history of the Ford Motor Company. We're about to be a hundred years old. I wouldn't opt to work in any previous period in our history. We are setting off on a path that will transform us from an old-line industrial company into a model company for the 21st century." One of his major projects is the environmental regeneration plan to "green the Rouge", transforming the dereliction of Ford's sprawling Rouge manufacturing complex into an industrial ecosystem (see page 93).

But hot on the heels of the fuss about the corporate citizenship report, there came something much more serious. This was the massive recall of over six million Firestone tires triggered by a growing number of accidents caused by tire failures on

SUVs, particularly Ford's. Like the problems that rocked the Lloyds insurance market (page 189), the problems first came to light thanks to the efforts of a Texan lawyer, in this case Randy Roberts, who wanted to find out why a high school cheerleader had died in a car accident in 1998.[123] When the family of the victim originally sued the Firestone, the tire supplier, the company had said there had only been one other similar incident. Yet when a judge ordered Firestone to turn over details of all previous complaints and lawsuits, it turned out that there had already been more than 1,100 incidents and 57 lawsuits.

"It is every CEO's worst nightmare," as *Fortune* summed up the growing crisis. "The crisis that strikes from nowhere, jolts customers as well as suppliers and employees, sends the stock reeling, and threatens a company's good name."[124] And then things went from bad to worse. Indeed, as the controversy evolved, this proved to be a double disaster for Ford. Not only would this sort of issue be a headache with any product line, but the Ford Explorer which was implicated in many of the accidents (two-thirds of the tires recalled by Firestone in the first round came from Explorers) had been the automotive equivalent of the goose that lays the golden eggs, providing something like a quarter of Ford's profits.

"We are moving as quickly as possible to replace bad tires with good tires, and to understand what went wrong, so that it never happens again," said Bill Ford when he took the platform at the 2000 Greenpeace Business conference (page 256). "This terrible situation – which goes against everything I stand for – has made us more determined than ever to operate in an open, transparent and accountable manner at all times."

One problem he, and other CEOs, will face in delivering against such promises, however, is the way in which lawyers and legal systems often smother critical information in secrecy. In the Firestone tire case, for example, both companies involved had managed to win protective orders that prevented much of the information generated by early court cases becoming public.[125] Legal reforms that force courts and judges either to make critical information public, or to say why they have decided to hold it secret, are badly needed. One test of a real Citizen CEO will be whether he or she is willing to campaign for such measures.

Whichever way Ford finally jumps on this issue, the company's chairman used the Greenpeace event to make a clear statement of his vision for the new century: "For automobile manufacturers, sustainability is largely an environmental issue," he noted. "I look at it not just as a requirement, but as an incredible opportunity. I want my company to be a leader in driving the transition, and to be in a position to benefit from it. I believe it will be a great way to please my customers and reward my shareholders. Ford once provided the world with mobility by making it affordable. In the 21st century, we want to continue to provide the world with mobility by making it sustainable."

Interestingly, like Shell before it ran into its own mishaps in 1995, Ford had been undergoing a massive internal transformation process. Indeed, one question the business press was soon asking of the Ford top team: were warning signs missed because of the wrenching changes and leadership gaps that this transformation process had created?[126] Whatever the answer, there is no question that once it began, the tire recall issue massively distracted Ford from the corporate citizenship and sustainable mobility agendas as they were beginning to define them.

But taking part in top management sessions with Bill Ford and CEO Jac Nasser, I was consistently struck by their determination to keep the longer-term issues on the agenda. Indeed, just as the tire controversy began to break, we were in the midst of a major stakeholder engagement process in Dearborn, where the company is headquartered. Even so, Bill Ford made sure he got to the event – and engaged the outsiders in a highly effective discussion of the critical issues.

By the end of the session, there were three priorities on the table for Ford: climate change, human rights in the context of the company's operations in emerging markets, and the question of how sustainable mobility could be sold to Wall Street and other financial centers. In retrospect, apart from the fact that safety failed to appear (there were no consumer representatives), one thing that stood out about these priorities was that they neatly straddled the triple bottom line agenda – with an environmental priority (climate change), a social priority (human rights) and an economic priority (Wall Street). Not a bad starting point for any company, although panel 5 lists a wider series of key tasks for Citizen CEOs and other business leaders.

PANEL 5

Five labors

Like Hercules, Citizen CEOs face a number of considerable challenges. As *The Chrysalis Economy* evolved, the Herculean metaphor rode alongside the metamorphosis metaphor for a while, although I struggled to make them work together. Then, on the same day that I first sketched out the MetaMatrix (page 75), with Corporate Caterpillars and Locusts appearing in the 'degenerative' line, I was trawling along the shelves in Foyles, the London bookshop. Among the books I staggered home with was the just-published *Millions of Monarchs, Bunches of Beetles,*[127] by entomology professor emeritus Gilbert Waldbauer.

And on page 160, I stumbled across this eye-popping paragraph (the emphasis is mine): *"The ancient Greeks believed that different gods had domain over different kinds of vermin, and that it was necessary to invoke the help of the appropriate god to prevent or alleviate a pest problem. Zeus, nicknamed the 'flycatcher', held sway over flies; <u>Hercules controlled locusts and caterpillars;</u> and Apollo controlled mice and mildew."*

Here was the missing link, I thought, before I finally decided to squeeze Hercules down into a single panel. So here he is. But whereas Hercules was set 10 Labors and achieved 12, the Citizen CEO faces 'just' five. Linking directly to the stages of our Learning Model, they are to:

1 Clean the stables

Most of us know Hercules had to clean out the Augean Stables. And the Citizen CEOs' first task is usually to tackle past problems, however caused. The process of invasion is described in Chapter 7. Three lessons:

- *Don't shy away from sacred cows, or bulls. The pride and joy of King Augeas were his twelve silvery-white bulls. Unfortunately, they – and all the other animals in the royal flocks and herds – polluted the whole region with manure. Go for the real problem, however painful it may be.*
- *Even if time is pressing, think twice before picking the easy solution. Hercules simply diverted two rivers through the mess of the Augean Stables. The result: the yards, folds and pastures were washed clean within the day allotted. But shifting problems from one environmental medium, or one community to another, is rarely a good idea.*
- *Make sure you get your just rewards. Thinking he had been tricked, Augeas refused to pay Hercules. The sensible Citizen CEO aims to ensure that there is a market reward for improved performance.*

2 Compete in the Olympics

Hercules is said to have refounded the Olympic Games. Whatever the facts, the greening of the present-day Olympics provides useful clues on how companies can build competitive advantage in fast-paced markets (page 163). The second key task for Citizen CEOs involves internalizing all significant 'externalities'. The internalization agenda is outlined in Chapter 8. Three lessons:

- *Be ethical, consistently. Despite rigorous penalties, sadly, some athletes (and a fair number of companies) cheat. For example, the Emperor Nero bribed the Olympic judges in 65 AD. Once the race started, he fell from his chariot. The judges stopped the race so he could remount. Even so, he failed to finish. So the judges declared him a winner, on the basis that he would have won if he had finished. Fight corruption. Remember, in time the truth will out. After Nero's death, his name was removed from the list of winners and the bribes repaid. The CNN World means that such sins will become public knowledge far faster.*
- *Decide which standards to embrace. Key tasks at the early Olympics included working out which standards to require of competitors – and how to ensure they obeyed them.*
- *Remember, the games aren't the world. The greatest prestige in the early Olympics went to athletes winning the short sprint, just as financial markets today focus on quarterly earnings. But when it came to winning battles and saving communities, sometimes only marathon runners could deliver the goods.*

3 Tame the Hydra

Most of us remember Hercules chopping off the heads of the Hydra. This monster haunted a swamp which the self-same Nero is said to have tried to sound – and found bottomless. The Hydra is said to have had eight or nine snaky heads, one immortal. But some credit it with 50, 100 or even 10,000 heads. The Citizen CEO's third task involves taming the multi-headed stakeholder 'Hydra'. It depends for its success on engaging all key stakeholders, both inside and outside the business. The inclusion agenda is covered in Chapter 9. Three lessons:

- *First, learn how to spot many-headed problems early. They are different. The sustainability agenda is complex and increasingly interrelated, with each issue targeted by hundreds – even thousands – of NGOs and other actors worldwide.*
- *Don't expect to touch bottom any time soon. These issues are*

evolving rapidly – and will continue to do so for decades. There are few easy answers. CEOs and their companies should aim to build long-term relationships with all key internal and external stakeholders.

- *Given the second point, and despite the temptation, don't try to hack off Hydra heads. It's tough to do, even if you know how – and for everyone you remove others will sprout. Learn to live – and work – with your critics.*

4 Enlighten the Underworld

Late in his Labors, Hercules descended into the Underworld, to capture its triple-headed watchdog, Cerberus. Given that the color of the Underworld is thought to have been black, it stands as a provocative metaphor for the financial markets. So the fourth task focuses on building real understanding and interest in a company's TBL strategy, targets and performance on Wall Street and in other financial centers. The integration agenda is spotlighted in Chapter 10. Three lessons:

- *Engage the underworld's most important denizens, the financial analysts. Except for a brief honeymoon with loss-making, red-tinted dotcoms, they normally favor companies in the black. Most also focus on a single bottom line, so it's interesting that Cerberus was triple-headed. A potential symbol, perhaps, of the emerging TBL agenda.*
- *Speak to our deepest interests and concerns. Analysts do what they do because ordinary citizens, whether as investors or pension policy-holders, insist on high returns. Work to understand the deep psychological drives and needs shaping investor and consumer behavior before launching new sustainability-focused initiatives.*
- *Don't forget history. Those who drank from the Underworld's River Lethe forgot the past, something few Citizen CEOs can afford to do. But then neither should they be locked in by the past, as Hercules signaled by penetrating the Stygian gloom and then returning to the real world of the present and future.*

5 Reboot the Cornucopia

In the course of his twelfth Labor, some say Hercules made good use of the ever-productive Cornucopia, or Horn of Plenty, filled with golden fruit. So the fifth task, and the most challenging by far, involves harnessing the power of markets to help deliver SD wherever it is needed. The incubation agenda is sketched out in Chapter 11. Three lessons:

- *Remember, most people are switched on by the promise of abundance, not by the threat of scarcity. Hair-shirt approaches are rarely sustainable in the absence of external pressures like war. The Cornucopia has long been the symbol of abundance and happiness.*[128] *So how do we work for a sustainable, livable world of 8–10 billion?*
- *Think truly Cornucopian. How can we develop technologies and business models that produce radically more benefits for radically less cost, right across the triple bottom line? And how do we bring them to market even in poorer world regions?*
- *The fruits of our labors must be widely available. A truly sustainable world is likely to be more equitable than today's. Over the centuries, the Cornucopia became a symbol not only of public prosperity, but also of generosity and hospitality. Given that even the best Citizen CEOs are not specifically rewarded for corporate citizenship, let alone achieving social equity, this remains a massive challenge.*

PART III

STAGE$

Even Citizen CEOs need road-maps.

Cue the LEARNING FLYWHEEL.

Picture not a circle but a spiral process, driven by successive rounds of innovation.

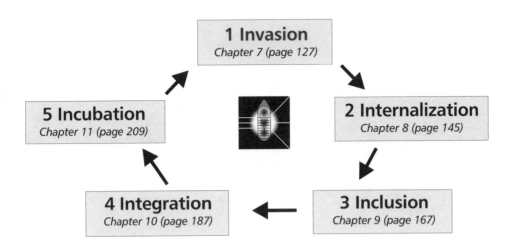

1 Invasion
Chapter 7 (page 127)

2 Internalization
Chapter 8 (page 145)

3 Inclusion
Chapter 9 (page 167)

4 Integration
Chapter 10 (page 187)

5 Incubation
Chapter 11 (page 209)

Invasion

invasion / *n*. **1** the act of invading or the process of being invaded. **2** entry of a hostile army into a country, or of a weed or other species into habitat where it can spread out of control. **3** *process by which technologies, products or business models colonize opportunity spaces, creating economic, social and environmental impacts, positive and negative.*[1]

Look, quick, down there! What are those things? They look like fish, they swim like fish, but they wouldn't fool any self-respecting salmon. The answer: They're fish-shaped robots scientists have been releasing into rivers across the watershed of the mighty Columbia River, in the Pacific Northwest. Each fish is rubber-coated, packed with electronics and designed to mimic the behavior of the millions of young salmon that each year make their way down to the ocean.[2]

But salmon-lovers can relax. No one sees these magnificent, economically vital fish being replaced by robots any time soon. Instead, the fishbots are engineered to make the world a safer place for their natural counterparts. It's an uncomfortable fact of life that nearly a million young salmon die each year after being hit by the sharp turbine blades that help hydroelectric dams turn falling water into electric power. As the tiny sensor fish make their 15-second journeys through the turbines, they each gather and store 96 kilobits of data on such things as water pressure and shear forces. Once through, the researchers plug wires from the tails of the fish-robots into computers and download their experiences.

And the work seems to be paying off. It turns out that young fish often get trapped in the gaps between the spinning turbine blades. When the blades are redesigned to minimize the gaps, the injury rate is cut by 50 percent and survival rates jump 6 percent among the young fish. Interestingly, too, the redesign increases power input by around 4 percent. "It's a double win," said project leader Thomas Carlson.

There are those who see hydropower as less invasive than competing power sources, for example the burning of high-sulfur coal or nuclear energy. But when it comes to doing the TBL analysis on a dam, it's not simply a question of how many fish have to be sliced or bludgeoned to produce a kilowatt of hydroelectricity. There can also be a wide range of human and civil rights issues.

Consider events along the Narmada River in central India, where there have been huge controversies over plans to build 30 major dams. Dams are almost always controversial, but several of these have been particularly so. The World Bank pulled out of the Sardar Sarovar scheme, for example, because of its social and environmental failings. And the country's Supreme Court, after spending four years considering a demand from activists for a comprehensive review, acknowledged that the dam was never given formal environmental clearance.[3]

These dams have been the focus of India's biggest non-violent protest campaign for fifteen years. For a long time, the dams continued to rise, despite the protests, but recently the tide seems to have been turning. In the case of the Sardar Sarovar dam, critical support for the Narmada People's Movement campaign has come from such well-known celebrities as Arundhati Roy, whose novel *The God of Small Things* won the UK Booker Prize in 1997. She stressed the way that the campaign had brought together a huge array of Indians, from *dalit* (untouchable) fishermen and boatmen, tribal peoples, farmers, writers and artists, and even retired admirals.

For many of these people, the concern is practical, immediate: their homes or farmland are being swallowed by the dams. So what drives Roy? "It's a utopian thing," she explained, "a vision of the way things should be. On the one hand, you're fighting for a specific goal, but you're also fighting for a way of seeing." Indeed, from the site of the stalled Sardar Sarovar dam to the streets of Seattle or Prague, what we are seeing is only in part a matter of disputes about particular development proposals. It is also, increasingly, a clash between opposing worldviews. Here, the entire western, industrial worldview is seen as invasive – and on trial.

Not surprisingly, some western companies involved in such projects, among them Germany's Siemens and Sweden's Skanska, have been having second thoughts. Siemens applied to the German government for export credit guarantees to supply turbines for the Sardar Sarovar dam, but subsequently withdrew its application. Skanska pulled out of the bidding for Turkey's controversial Ilisu Dam.

The key point here is that, whether it involves making steam-engines, operating hydroelectric dams or creating genetically engineered crop plants, all economic activity – by its very nature – is invasive. Every company, every business, is an invader. Whether or not it intends to do so, it invades space or territory that 'belongs' to others. This may involve disrupting existing industries or markets, pushing into areas of virgin ecosystem, destabilizing communities, or – in the CNN World – invading our privacy or human rights in various ways.

The diversity of ways in which corporations are seen to be invasive is suggested by the spread of businesses covered in the 2001 'Ten Worst Corporations of the Year' list published by *Multinational Monitor*.[4]

The companies spotlighted this time around were: Aventis (for "contaminating the food supply with genetically engineered crops not approved for human consumption); BAT (for "promoting and facilitating cigarette smuggling on a global scale"); BP/Amoco ("multiple fines and payments for environmental violations"); Doubleclick ("rubbing against the edge of Internet privacy protections"); Ford/ Firestone ("placing the lethal combination of Ford Explorers and Firestone tires on the road, and not removing them after learning of the hazard"); GlaxoWellcome ("blocking efforts to distribute cheap, generic AIDS drugs in poor African countries"); Lockheed Martin ("testing a toxic component of rocket fuel on humans"); Philipps Petroleum ("operating a deadly petrochemical facility in Houston"); Smithfield Foods ("consolidating the meat packing business to the detriment of family farms, and spreading factory farms that are polluting rural America"); and Titan International ("strikebreaking attempt against approximately 1,000 members of the United Steelworkers of America").

No doubt there are other sides to each of these stories. And the effects and impacts of any given economic activity can of course be positive as well as negative. But the diversity of issues raised here usefully illuminates the growing complexity of the business agenda. Many of these issues have the potential to become highly political, derailing even the best-laid corporate plans.

CLEANING THE STABLES

Invasion is often a perfectly natural process. Every time a successful new species, business model or technology evolves, it invades the space of other, less successful, competitors. In the USA alone, for example, there are an estimated non-native 50,000 species that have invaded the continent, mainly with the help of people. Some, like grain crops and livestock, are largely beneficial, providing around 98 percent of the country's food, worth towards $1 trillion a year. On the other hand, less welcome species cause damage estimated at over $130 billion a year.[5] As the invasiveness of modern industrial technologies has grown, however, so the scale of the impacts has gone off the scale.

Indeed, if your company has built up an accumulation of problems, the chances are that you may be near the point where your future license to operate hangs on your willingness – and ability – to clean up past problems. The business impact of such problems obviously depends on what sort of company we are dealing with – and on where it is located. It's a paradox, for example, that many state-owned industries and companies get away with the equivalent of murder when compared to their privately owned competitors.

That's why the first of the five Herculean Labors facing the Citizen CEO means getting on top of – and cleaning up – the mess created by past operations. The nature and scale of the mess will depend on the nature and scale of the enterprise. Most caterpillar companies tend to produce relatively local impacts, although in certain circumstances these can attract wider attention. Locust companies, among them the Big Tobacco firms, tend to be much more invasive and, in the process, much more conspicuous – not least because they are often heavy advertisers.

Nor is it simply an issue of tackling the past. The way some companies operate, they are not only piling up a whole raft of future liabilities but also, potentially, destroying various forms of capital which fall outside their accounting procedures. Some modern business models, like that developed by US retailer Wal-Mart, are purpose-built to be invasive. The 50-year-old company is often described by its competitors as about the scariest thing in retail. With annual sales of some $200 billion, Wall-Mart has operations in eight countries outside America.[6] The company's purchase of UK supermarket chain Asda, as part of its plan to invade the country's retail market, shook UK retailers and triggered a temporary collapse in their share-prices.

Although its UK operations so far appear not to have the infective power of the American counterparts, Wal-Mart's reputation is for merciless competition designed to destroy the businesses of all smaller companies. The economic, social and environmental impacts of what has even been described as a "retail cancer" have been dramatic, particularly since part of the strategy is to force consumers to drive to Wal-Mart supercenters rather than shopping locally. Contrast this approach with that of Lend Lease (page 113), which went out of its way with its Bluewater development in the UK to ensure that local retailers were not driven out of business.

Whether or not businesses like Wal-Mart are sustainable, it's all-too-easy to blame industry for the ills of the world, whether they relate to the environmental, human rights or governance issues raised in Chapter 2. The blame often lies with governments, with the financial markets and, in the end, with each of us. But, whoever is to blame, the sheer range of impacts and issues potentially raised by business activity in the new century is illustrated in Figure 7.1 (page 132), based on the work of two American professors: eco-architect William (Bill) McDonough and Stuart (Stu) Hart, who has done so much to map out the sustainable business agenda.

This TBL framework neatly captures the need to 'raise the bottom', addressing the needs of the poorer parts of the world – an agenda to which we will return in Chapter 11. In the past, capitalism has pushed out from the *economy* tip of the triangle, socialism and communism out from the *social* tip, and environmentalism out from the *environment* tip. The result has been a huge stretch, with governments often left to try to hold things together. Increasingly, however, business will be expected to hold the center, with new business models designed to deliver sustainable growth and development across each of the 'fractals', or sub-triangles.

INVADING CATERPILLARS

One thing is clear: pretty much all businesses want to ensure that they are well into the *profit* fractal. But, in the process, an astounding range of economic activities turn out to leave startlingly large economic, social or environmental footprints across the surface sketched out in the Sustainability Triangle.

Even great works of art have left measurable footprints on natural landscapes. Visit the northern coast of Tuscany, for example, and you will find that marble – a non-renewable form of 'natural capital' – forms the backbone of the Carrara economy.[7] Over 100 enterprises are involved in quarrying and selling the marble, often described as "white gold". While the designation of individual Carrara marble quarries as Caterpillar enterprises is debatable, it's at least possible – because of the extraordinary contribution their product has made to western civilization. But, owing to poor regulation and management in this part of Italy, the local environmental overall effect has been worthy of a small plague of locusts.

Since Roman times, the stone has been carted away in unimaginable quantities to make triumphal arches, cathedral gargoyles, and such masterpieces of western art as Michelangelo's *David* or Gian Lorenzo Bernini's *Apollo and Daphne*. Indeed, Michelangelo himself was a frequent visitor to the quarries, searching for blocks of marble on which to illustrate his notion that sculpting is simply a question of exposing forms that are already within the stone.

Few people who stand in wonder before such sculptures give much thought to where the stone originally came from, let alone to what environmental or social impacts might have been caused. But Italian environmentalists argue that the ongoing working of the quarries is putting the fragile ecosystem of Carrara's mountains at risk. The livid scars left on the mountains, coupled with the streams of waste that run down their flanks, suggest the scale of the damage being caused.

And the pace of extraction has accelerated as new technology has been adopted. The same quantity of stone that would once have been mined over two generations is now extracted in less than a decade. Efficient, maybe, but the sheer speed of extraction raises new issues. In the process, environmentalists say, the

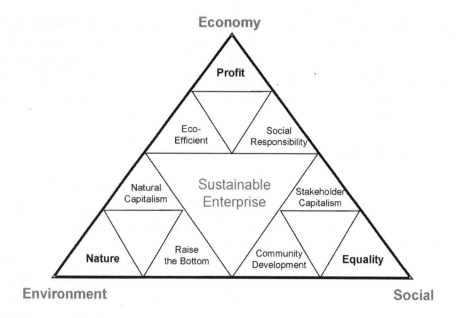

Figure 7.1 The Sustainability Triangle. Adapted by Stuart Hart from McDonough & Partners.

interiors of these mountains are being turned into something very much like Swiss cheese. Stung by the criticisms, the Italian government has now imposed restrictions on new quarries – and forced existing ones to remove much of their waste, rather than letting it cascade down the mountainsides.

The ultimate decision on whether these enterprises have been Caterpillars or small Locusts will inevitably depend on what use is made of the quarries at the end of their lives. Remember the Bamburi cement works in Kenya (page 78). But, while the Italians begin the laborious task of cleaning up past mistakes, the whole sad process of degenerative exploitation is being repeated on a larger scale elsewhere in the world.

INVADING LOCUSTS

Most of us may not have a marble statue to call our own, but the chances are that we do have or use a range of machines that are powered by oil or other forms of energy. Again, when we turn a car's ignition key or switch on a washing machine, most of us give little or no thought to the source of the energy – let alone the materials used to make the machines. But that doesn't mean that someone, somewhere, isn't concerned about the shadows thrown by our machines and lifestyles.

Because of the improvements in technology and eco-efficiency over decades, the environmental and social footprints left by a typical European consumer lifestyle are likely to be significantly smaller than the footprints left, kilowatt for kilowatt or kilo of aluminum for kilo of aluminum, by East European, Russian or Chinese consumer lifestyles.

But, while we may be relatively cleaner and more efficient than many of those emerging from decades of state control, our wasteful western lifestyles are resulting in the invasion of increasing numbers of relatively pristine environments. Up in Alaska, for example, oil giant BP has been wrestling with a hugely political issue. If it gets this one wrong, it could blow its carefully-incubated 'environment-friendly', 'Beyond Petroleum' reputation to pieces.

This is an example where a company might produce oil in an eco-efficient way, minimizing the disturbance of wildlife and other impacts, and yet still fall foul of proponents of natural capitalism. The latter would argue against the exploitation of fossil fuels, not least because of their likely climate change impacts, and in favor of greater use of energy efficiency technologies and renewable energy.

Although all of the so-called Arctic National Wildlife Refuge (ANWR) is protected by law, the coastal plain – widely known by its technical designation as the 1002 (pronounced 'ten-o-two') area, has long had a different legal status.[8] As a result, there has been intense concern that it could be opened up for oil drilling. In the 2000 US presidential election, Republican (and former oilman) George W. Bush was committed to opening ANWR up for drilling, while Democratic vice-president Al Gore said he would protect the Refuge.

In the event, Gore lost and Bush won, promptly appointing a pro-drilling Secretary of the Interior,[9] and raising real concerns about the future of 1002 beyond 2001. But what's really interesting about this story is that it isn't just an environmental saga. BP, or any other company wanting to move into the coastal plain, would have to be acutely sensitive to the economic, social and, above all, political dimensions of oil exploration and production in this vast region.

It's really no surprise that BP wants to look for oil in the Refuge; it's just along the coast from Alaska's Prudhoe Bay, from which the Trans-Alaskan Pipeline has shipped south over 12 billion barrels of oil since 1977. Indeed, for years Prudhoe Bay and the surrounding oilfields have pumped something like 20 percent of US domestic oil production, with BP a major player. But the easily accessible oil has now been extracted, with the result that the productivity of the existing fields has started to fall.

BP obviously wants the revenues and profits new fields would offer. Most American consumers want cheap fuel, while the US government – in addition to its desire to keep consumers happy – is keen to reduce the country's strategic vulnerability to oil prices rises or, worse, embargoes. But there are wild differences in the estimates offered on the likely oil yields. As usual, framing your statistics for maximum impact is half the battle.

Whatever the truth, the ANWR controversy has spotlighted the extraordinary political complexities now associated with such major development proposals. So, while BP had been collaborating with the US branch of the World Wide Fund for Nature (WWF) on a biodiversity strategy, WWF also emerged as one of the leading opponents of oil development in the Refuge. Indeed, the panda-branded NGO has sometimes played hardball, warning BP that if it failed to come out against such development it would not be able to count on WWF endorsing the green strategy the two organizations had been working on together.

Nor is that where the complexity ends. Dip into the community development fractal of the Sustainability Triangle (page 132) and try this for size. WWF has been working with the Gwich'in people – or, more particularly, with the 700 or so members of the Neets'aii clan. For the Gwich'in Indians, the coastal plain is sacred land, where they say their ancestors have hunted caribou for something like 20,000 years. To let BP in, they say, would be a form of sacrilege. Indeed Faith Gemill, an activist on the Gwich'in Steering Committee, which lobbies to protect the Refuge, has stressed that the issue is about a lot more than just oil or caribou meat. "It is a human rights issue," she has argued. "We should not be forced to change for US energy needs. It would be like if I told you when you could sleep or when you could eat."

So all the indigenous people are against oil exploration, right? Well, again, it's a bit more complicated than that. While the environmentalists are lining up with the Indians, it turns out that the oilmen can call on the support of the Inupiat Eskimos. They live in the small community of some 250 people called Kaktovik, on the windswept island of Barter Island. Because they belong to the same borough as other Eskimo villages along the north shore of Alaska, the oil industry has proved to be a welcome cornucopia of royalties, taxes and jobs.

The average income in the Indian Arctic Village has been estimated at $9,661, compared with a dramatically greater $46,250 for the Inupiat people. Because of the way native land settlement deals were done in the early 1970s, the people of Kaktovik own a considerable slice of the 1002 area – so that if drilling were allowed, and were to prove successful, they would benefit massively. For them, this promises to be an invasion of golden locusts. No wonder the Kaktovik people have been keen to support BP's plans!

Nor are such problems confined to the fossil fuels industry or, indeed, to the western world. The highly globalized CNN World effect is tripping up growing numbers of companies around the world, even some that pride themselves on their good practice. The British Museum and the up-market UK furniture store Heals recently found themselves in disarray, for example, in the wake of a two-year investigation by Greenpeace into illegal imports of tropical timbers.[10]

Greenpeace had taken a North Sea repair ship, aircraft and launches along the tributaries of the Amazon. They used electronic tracking devices and fluorescent marker paints to identify logs. And they impersonated customers, entrepreneurs and students in order to penetrate the secretive world of illegal timber traders.

The investigation resulted in what some Brazilians dubbed the "Greenpeace Effect", leading to multi-million-dollar fines being imposed by the Brazilian authorities. Despite protests by loggers, who had been making massive profits at the expense of many of the other fractal interests represented by the Sustainability Triangle, warehouses were raided and some dozens of licences revoked. European companies that had been assured by suppliers that their imports of tropical timber were both legal and sustainable were told by Greenpeace that their research showed otherwise. The group's forestry director, John Sauven, commented that: "All the companies have glowing policies on this, but when it comes to reality they don't know what they are doing."

INVADING BUTTERFLIES AND HONEYBEES

So, is the new economy entirely innocent in all of this? Hardly, although you wouldn't guess it from Ericsson's picture of future trends (Figure 7.2). This IT company clearly believes that mobile telephones and all the other products now streaming out of the e-cornucopia will enable us to grow without any increase in overall negative environmental impacts. We should be careful of such assumptions, whether explicit or implicit.

Most of us, for example, still tend to conjure up old economy images when thinking of the most intrusive forms of economic activity. Our mental images of pollution are based on strip-mining, clear-felling, smoking factory chimneys, freeways bursting at the seams with sport utility vehicles. Meanwhile, if you talk to people who are driving the transition to new economy technologies and business models, they usually argue that their companies and activities represent the transition from yesterday's caterpillar and locust value creation models to the butterfly and honeybee business models, value webs and economies of tomorrow.

In some senses, they may be right. Many of these new technologies have the potential to create more economic value with a dramatically smaller throughput of energy and raw materials. They are, or can be, more eco-efficient than the technologies they replace. But it often seems that for every three steps forward, we take at least two steps back as new uses of a technology explode, ensuring that any improvements in eco-efficiency are more than compensated for by increased economic activity. And even relatively benign technologies can have dramatic consequences.

Consider this: No one who built the first sailing ships, which were largely made out of renewable raw materials and powered by the wind, would have had the vaguest idea that among the consequences would be tens of millions of people dying on other continents from diseases like smallpox. Eco-efficient? Undoubtedly, but the social and cultural impacts were unspeakable. Or, to take a somewhat less dramatic example, remember the case of the silver pollution of San Francisco Bay (page 40).

How many of us think about the ecological impact of having our teeth drilled and filled? And, we discover, the IT and dot-com sectors are themselves far from innocent. In some cases, the issue is how their technologies are used. Remember, for example, our early failure to spot the evolving Antarctic ozone hole. The US Nimbus 7 satellite had been taking pictures of the hole for years, but it wasn't until scientists sent up old-fashioned balloons that we began to get a sense of what was happening up in the stratosphere. Why? The reason seems to have been that the computers analyzing the satellite data back at the Goddard Space Center had been programmed to ignore such extreme results. In effect, we had built our own blind-spots into the hardware and software designed to help us think out of the box.

Inevitably, as the new economy boomed, so media stories about its environmental – and economic – intrusiveness began to surface. Signs of what has been described as a "dotcom backlash" were seen in high-tech hotspots such as Seattle, San Francisco, Austin and Chicago.[11]

As *USA Today* reported: "The industry, which has helped fuel a robust US economy in the past decade, has triggered a construction-and-renovation boom. But it has ushered in a wave of gentrification. Rising rent and escalating 'e-victions' are driving out lower- and middle-income families, artists, non-profit groups and small businesses. And while planners, politicians and developers herald the shimmering new economy as a golden opportunity to upgrade cities, many longtime residents are outraged or resigned."

In Seattle, the 42-story Smith Tower, a well-known historical landmark, once housed a buzzing hive of social activism, including country agencies and non-profits. More recently, however, it had been the subject of a $28 million make-over and had been filling up with internet start-ups. "The new economy is creating disparity between the rich and poor, white and non-white, yuppies and seniors," said John Fox, coordinator of the Seattle Displacement Coalition.

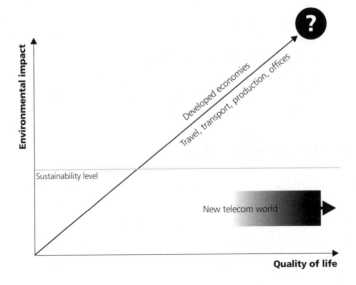

Figure 7.2 A picture of sustainability in the new economy?
Source: Ericsson.

Meanwhile in San Jose, California, protestors were campaigning against networking giant Cisco Systems – which had announced plans to build a $1.3 billion, 20,000-worker campus. The concern was that the development would encourage sprawl, worsen traffic congestion and contribute to deteriorating air quality in the region. Such businesses may produce profits, but their social and environmental impacts are obviously far from insignificant. Yet even these sorts of impacts may turn out to be peanuts in comparison with other unintended effects of the new economy.

What we have been seeing, many believe, is a new wave of 'creative destruction' in the global economy. One real concern is that each time a 'new economy' replaces an 'old economy', we see what have been dubbed "creative destruction depressions".[12] One such, we are told, was the Great Depression of the 1930s. The 'new economy' at the time was built around automobiles, tractors and early electronics. The first two contrived to destroy huge numbers of 'old economy' rural jobs, which had accounted for perhaps a third of all US jobs in the 1920s.

"The elimination of farmers' markets for horses and horse feed by the automobile combined with the mechanization of agriculture to leave millions of rural economy workers without the income necessary to repay their loans or buy New Economy products," says John A. Frisch. "When New Economy inventions slash the income of a third of all workers, you will have a depression every time, regardless of monetary policy."

If, as many believe, the internet is going to bypass the middlemen who clog up old economy distribution systems, we may see a third of all workers facing the same fate as farmers did in the 1920s. Instead of worrying about the wild cycles of investor greed in fear in the much-vaunted new economy, some warn, we should be calculating the risk that a collapse in spending power as millions lose their jobs "will ultimately pull down the New Economy from behind."

CLOSE ENCOUNTERS OF NEW KINDS

Whether or not such fears are well-founded, there are yet other concerns that new economy companies are being asked to address – among them the emergence of the so-called 'digital divide' and of the 'digital underclass'. There are real concerns that the longer-term result could be profound political instability. In this context, it is good news, for example, that CEOs like Carly Fiorina of HP are beginning to address this challenge (page 182), but there is a huge (and growing) gap to be bridged in terms of the 'raising the bottom' fractal in the Sustainability Triangle.

Meanwhile, other commentators are interested in how new economy technologies will impact our sense of identity, our sense of self? You could ask whether the new economy is socially responsible. Or, more starkly, you could ask whether are our young people in danger of turning into aliens? One of the most interesting voices in this area has been that of MIT professor Sherry Turkle. She has studied large numbers of young men and women who spend much of their time in the virtual worlds of cyberspace. She sees strong evidence that they are developing multiple personalities, with the sense of self becoming something of a "distributed system".[13]

As these new technologies and experiences invade our world, the implications could be profound. If, for example, we increasingly operate in a 'windowed' environment where different parts of our experience and thinking are separated from others, what will be the implications for our capacity to grasp and respond to complex agendas such as that posed by the sustainability challenge? The answer is that no one yet knows.

"With the emergence of such technologies as genetic forecasting, body scanning, dust-size cameras, and of course, the Internet, come new questions," argues Tara Lemmey, founder of Project LENS and a past president of the Electronic Frontier Foundation.[14] She asks: "How will we humans think of ourselves and how will others think of us if genetic diagnostics, brain-boosting drugs, and iris-scanning devices truly become a part of everyday life, if we are constantly helped at home by invisible computers, and if designer babies are part of any family's options?" Among the effects, she suggests, will be 'identity lag' and 'culture lag' as new technologies become "capable of whipping us completely out of synch with our own internal sense of self," leaving individuals and even entire cultures struggling to keep up.

And as if that weren't enough, we have Bill Joy, co-founder and chief scientist at software giant Sun Microsystems. In an extraordinary 20,000 word essay in *Wired*, Joy sounded alarm bells that reminded some people of Albert Einstein's 1939 letter to President Franklin D. Roosevelt – alerting Roosevelt to the possibility of an atomic bomb.[15]

The key difference this time, Joy noted, is that the atomic bomb required access to raw materials and resources that – at the time – were very rare. But, he went on, "the twenty-first century technologies – genetics, nanotechnology and robotics – are so powerful that they can spawn whole new classes of accidents and abuses. For the first time, these accidents and abuses are within the reach of individuals or small groups. Knowledge alone will enable the use of them." It is no exaggeration, he concluded, "to say that we are on the cusp of the further perfection of extreme evil, an evil whose possibility spreads well beyond that which weapons of mass destruction bequeathed to the nation-states, on to a surprising and terrible empowerment of extreme individuals."[16]

In the end, Joy concludes that we must stop to consider where our progress is leading – before we end up inadvertently taking the road to extinction. "The only realistic alternative I see is relinquishment," he argues: "to limit development of the technologies that are too dangerous, by limiting our pursuit of certain kinds of knowledge."

His warnings prompted the following comment from Kevin Kelly, *Wired*'s editor at large. "Our society lacks a major feedback loop for controlling technology: a way to gauge intended effects from actual effects. If we can accurately extend our intentions out into the future, then our technology will be more humane. But we have to have a way to compare our initial intentions with actual effects later on." His solution? "We should devise an Intended Effects Impact Report to be issued with each new technology. What do we expect from X in 5 years, 10 years, or one generation? Then measure it in five years, or one generation, and evaluate the results of X. We'll be way off base at first. But if we reward those processes that best anticipated the results and best prepared us, and use them to evaluate other technologies, we'll get much better at it."[17]

The storm of comment whipped up by Joy's warnings suggested that most people working in the new economy area couldn't see this happening any time soon (box 10). Whether or not his fears are exaggerated, however, Bill Joy has done us all a great service by making us think. Whether or not we use tools like the Sustainability Triangle, it is clear that the SD agenda raises new issues – or at least frames old issues in new ways. And that willingness to give ourselves time to analyze and reflect is one of the key dimensions of the internalization challenge, to which we turn in Chapter 8.

Box 10: Blips on the screen

Slowing the Titanic

Bill Joy's apocalyptic warnings about new technologies threatening humanity with extinction, or enslavement by super-intelligent machines, generated a storm of comment in the 'Rants & Raves' section of *Wired*.[18] The responses ranged from the wildly optimistic to the deeply pessimistic. But the debate certainly highlighted one fact: the 21st century is very unlikely to offer a smooth and uninterrupted path to sustainability.

Novell CEO Eric Schmidt argued "that the formulations about the future fail to account for the rise of new economies and the natural positive biases we humans have (i.e., we assume that human behavior will not change in the presence of accurately projected threats)." He suggested an alternative vision. "For example, you can imagine in an increasingly interconnected and educated world, with world population declining by 2050, the very real need for governments to become more peaceful and more people-centered as a natural result of their own self-interests in domestic issues."

Also on the positive side was physicist Freeman Dyson, who stressed that biotechnology is more of a threat than nanotechnology – and that "there is a long and positive history of biologists taking seriously the dangers to which their work is leading. The famous self-imposed 1975–1976 moratorium on DNA research showed biologists behaving far more responsibly than physicists did 30 years earlier." He added that "the problems of regulating technology are human and not technical."

But Roger Frank, a Colorado science teacher, was concerned on precisely this point. Even though he teaches the "brightest of the bright", he said, "it amazes me how when we talk about the issues in the article" his pupils "just don't want to talk about them. Yet they are the ones who will be most affected. They will be the ones that somehow have to control the genie once it's out of the bottle."

Most people believed that banning new technologies would cause more problems than it solved. "Abandonment of broad areas of technology will only push them underground, where development would continue unimpeded by ethics and regulation," said Ray Kurzweil, inventor and author of *The Age of Spiritual Machines*. "In such a situation, it would be the less stable, less responsible practitioners (e.g., the terrorists) who would have all the expertise." That said, Kurzweil supported relinquishment in some areas – to "give us more time to develop the necessary defensive technologies."

But perhaps the most thoughtful contribution came from Stewart Brand, futurist and co-founder of the Global Business Network. "Everyone agrees there's an iceberg," he noted; "the question is, will it hit the ship, miss the ship, or replace the ship? Or maybe – unthinkable! – the ship will slow down and study the iceberg for a while."

PANEL 7

Devil's element

A swirl of butterflies have settled on an abandoned sneaker in the Peruvian jungle. It's a striking picture, by the Dutch photographer Hans Lanting.[19] And the beautiful insects are doing something rather unsavory: they're extracting precious salts from the old sweat. One salt that we excrete both in urine and sweat is phosphate, which is vital to our health, but which is so dangerous in its pure form, phosphorus, that it used to be called 'The Devil's element'.[20]

When my first book, *The Ecology of Tomorrow's World*,[21] appeared in 1980 it included a short profile of Dr Jim Farquhar of the chemical company, Albright & Wilson. Nicknamed 'Dr Doomwatch' after a popular TV program of the time, he oversaw the environmental aspects of the company's operations. When I interviewed him in 1979, he attributed his job to environmental legislation rushed through in the UK seven years earlier.

But, while he was right in saying that "On April 1, 1972, hundreds of companies woke up to find themselves having to take immediate action to stay within the law," the real wake-up call for

A&W had come earlier, in 1968, with the mysterious case of the 'red herrings'.

First made in Hamburg in 1669, phosphorus is one of the most dangerous materials ever discovered. Ironically, it was used in devastating bombing raids on Hamburg in the 1940s, triggering ferocious firestorms in the city. But there had been many earlier problems. Used in making matches in the 19th century, phosphorus was linked to a frightful industrial disease: 'phossy jaw'. The plight of the 'match girls' was a scandal. In the worst cases, patients who had worked in 'lucifer' factories had their jaws literally rot within their skulls. The disease was sometimes called 'matchmaker's leprosy'.

By 1900, Bryant & May (whose employees had suffered terribly) were leaders in trying to relieve such symptoms, but something strange was going on. A nearby factory run by Bell & Co had also been making phosphorus matches since 1832, but with only a single, mild case of phossy jaw. The reason, it emerged, was that Bell & Co mixed the phosphorus compounds on the roof of its building, whereas Bryant & May's process resulted in phosphorus fumes permeating their building.

The plight of the 'match girls' sparked a campaign by the Salvation Army to end health and other human rights abuses in the industry. They even set up a model factory to make 'Social Matches'. Although these matches were more expensive, this early example of ethical commerce exerted real commercial pressure on the industry to clean up. So much so, indeed, that someone flooded the market with fake, cut-price versions, to destroy the ethical competition. The Salvation Army plant was forced to close its doors in 1901.

And the red herrings? They surfaced, literally, when A&W adopted open cycle, flush-away clean-up methods at its Placentia Bay plant, in Newfoundland. This, the world's most modern phosphorus plant at the time, was located in an area of great natural beauty, where fishermen made their living catching herring, cod and lobsters. The plant discharged 10 tons of fluoride, 3 tons of sulfur dioxide, 500 kilos of phosphorus and 40 kilos of cyanide into the bay each day, although at high dilutions. But after many fish-kills, it transpired that phosphorus in seawater can be toxic to fish at incredibly low concentrations. A different form of butterfly effect. The plant closed, only reopening after massive investment by Tenneco, funding new pollution control facilities.

There are two immediate lessons. First, it can be difficult to pick up early, weak signals of surfacing problems. A&W's executives were convinced that phosphorus was innocent of the fish-kills because lobsters held in pots around the plant showed no symptoms. And, second, however hard those playing the Dr Doomwatch role may work, too often they are fighting a rearguard action for business models that are fundamentally unsound. However you ran the calculus, 375 jobs at the Placentia Bay plant could never outweigh literally tens of millions of dead herring, their gills stained red by phosphorus-related disease.

CHAPTER 8

Internalization

internalization / *n*. **1** process of making internal. **2** making (attitudes, behavior, etc.) part of one's nature by learning or unconscious assimilation. **3** *process by which a company or other organization internalizes externalities previously imposed on other economic actors, society or the natural environment.*

Chief Sustainability Officer, or CSO. One thing the ultra-competitive new economy has not been short of is weird job-titles, although I have yet to see a mention of this version of CSO in any of the most popular or weirdest job-title lists. If we are not only to internalize externalities, but to integrate sustainability thinking throughout our companies and organizations, then the CSO role – whatever the job-title actually used may be – will become increasingly central.

If you are a reader of magazines like *Business 2.0*, *Fast Company* or *Forbes ASAP*, you will have seen an almost endless menu of 'job titles of the future', a fascinating, indispensable indicator of the wider agendas pioneering companies are trying to internalize. One job-title I particularly liked, from Palo Alto-based public-relations firm SparkPR, was 'Chief Detonator'.[22] The mission: to help ignite Silicon Valley internet ventures and launch them into orbit. This has been an ultra-fast-paced game. "We run in the same race as startups," explained Chris Holten-Hempel, "only we aim to move faster. In today's environment, companies have a three-month window to make it – or break it." She added: "We find the soul of a company and package it in a compelling way."

It's not hard to see what she meant, but as the pace of New Economy business activity accelerated off the curve, it *was* difficult to work out just where the SD agenda potentially fitted in. Indeed, another job title that caught my eye in the same issue of *Fast Company* was 'Chief Reality Officer', a job Jeff Pundyk held at web-based toolmaker Zwirl.com. The problem for any CRO, let alone the rest of us, is which reality – or realities – to take seriously and engage with? With the end of the dotcom boom, for example, should CROs and CSOs now instead be focusing their companies' energies on the implications of the Chrysalis Economy?

Probably. So a third job title is suggestive: The Truth.[23] Justin Stimson holds that title at myplay Inc. Asked whether the truth hurts, he replies: "Sometimes there are truths that people don't want to hear, but an important part of my job is to tell it like it is." Fine, but there are those who argue that current corporate governance structures, coupled with financial market pressures, make it virtually impossible for corporations to be socially responsible.[24]

Speaking at the 2000 Triple Bottom Line Performance conference in Rotterdam, social investor Steven Viederman noted that Wall Street analysts had recently criticized Timken, a high quality manufacturer of roller bearings in Canton, Ohio, for maintaining high quality and for its 100-year commitment to its hometown.[26] His explanation: "The successful company, according to basic rules of economics, externalizes its costs." And growth is essential. "Like a shark that must keep moving to stay alive," Viederman argued, "so too must a company, it would appear, keep growing. Nike was applauded by *Fortune* some years ago for creating a want for something no one knew they needed."

As Chapter 7 argued, most of us are having to get used to morphing between different realities, each with its own set of stakeholders. For business people, but most particularly Citizen CEOs, the challenge increasingly is to move back and forth between these multiple realities in short order. From Silicon Valley to the World Economic Forum's annual summit meetings, from Capitol Hill and meetings with key financial analysts through to the offices of tiny NGOs – which in today's world may have the power to bring corporate giants to their knees.

The job titles you find in the CSR and SD fields may not yet be quite so exciting, but among those covered in these pages are Chief Responsibility Officer (Chiquita Brands International), Special Counsel to the Chairman on Human Rights (Freeport McMoRan) and Vice President for Sustainable Development (Shell International). These titles symbolize the powerful evolutionary processes now at work in the world of business.

Nor is it simply a question of the job titles we sport these days. You can often tell a great deal about what people are really thinking by listening carefully to the language they use – and how they use it. (Yes, and there's a great deal to be learned from the language they painstakingly avoid.) On the positive side, companies considering the sustainable business agenda often talk in terms of a 'journey' towards sustainability, of 'crossroads', 'milestones' and 'road maps'.[27] A framework for producing a TBL road-map can be found in Figure 10.3 (page 204).

COMPETING IN THE OLYMPICS

Some business people, it has to be said, talk of the journey as a means of putting off the evil day when they have to set out on the hard road, but others embrace the challenge – and are eager to be off. Most do so in response to changes in the outside world and its priorities. They recognize that, just as certain standards have to be met if you are going to compete in the Olympic Games, including new environmental standards (panel 8, page 163), so certain TBL standards are now necessary conditions for – but no guarantee of – business success.

As a result, if you look inside most companies it is like seeing a cross-section of any complex organism. In Chapter 13, we use the analogy of the amoeba, but many modern corporations are more akin to entire ecosystems. Indeed, if you know what you are looking for, you can map and view the evidence of successive waves of external pressures – and of the resulting internalization processes. When we worked recently with British Airways, for example, we were handed the organizational chart shown in Figure 8.1.

The environmentalist eye quite naturally tends to fixate on the bottom right-hand box, with its mention of some 300 environmental champions now operating in different parts of the airline. This represents an extraordinary investment of money, time and effort – and reflects the environmental pressures the airlines industry has been under for decades.

Next, if you're like me, the eye drifts up the right-hand side, picking up the other boxes where smaller groups of environmental champions operate at increasingly rarified altitudes. But the spot we really need to focus on is the middle column. Not on the director responsible for safety, security and environment, for all that is an important role, but on the CEO and the board.[28] As Chapter 13 explains, this is the level at which the triple bottom line agenda is increasingly playing out.

If you could rewind the history represented by such organization charts and then fast forward them, you would see such roles and responsibilities pulsing in from the outside world, sending shock-waves through corporate structures – and progressively driving the agenda towards board level.

In the process, you would see early waves of 'pioneers' struggling to wake up the company to the new agendas. These people are more sensitive to new threats to business than most of their colleagues. Next, many of the pioneers are then superceded – and often dislodged – by a new wave of 'settlers', who start to build management systems and communication channels.

After a while, things would often settle down into more predictable patterns, and you would see the 'professionals' working to ensure that their strategies are

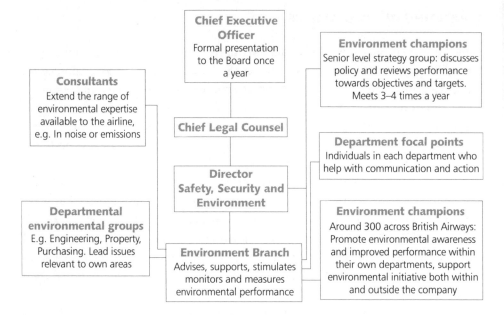

Figure 8.1   Eco-internalization at British Airways.
Source: BA.

state-of-the-art and attending conferences on the subject around the world. Stakeholder engagement (Chapter 9) and corporate strategies and integration (Chapter 10) would be key priorities. Next, and by no means finally if the company is to have any hope of surviving well into the 21st century, you would hope to see the emergence of a new breed of 'entrepreneurs', proposing radically new sustainable business models. This phase, which for must companies has hardly even begun, is tackled in Chapter 11.

WAVES OF CHANGE

So what's driving all of this? One answer is successive waves of social and political change. During the mid-1990s, my colleagues and I plotted two big waves of environmental pressure on industry, peaking in 1969–73 and 1988–91, followed by two great downwaves (the first running from 1974 to 1987, while the second had started in 1992 and, we predicted, would end around 1998 or 1999). We believed a third wave would begin around the turn of the century, but had no way of gauging exactly when – and cautioned that it would be nothing like the previous two.[29] One reason: this time the focus would be on the triple bottom line of sustainable business.

We expected the drivers of the third wave to be somewhat different, too, with the social and economic fallout from globalization likely to be more powerful than climate change, at least in the near-term. Climate change, we suggested, would be far harder for ordinary citizens to respond to than ozone depletion was in the last wave. Simply stated, it's harder to give up the family SUV than it was to switch to a different aerosol in the near-panic of the ozone depletion crisis. That said, the evidence does suggest that the third wave began to roll through 1999 and 2000, in part fuelled by the millennial transition, with the travails of companies such as Shell, Nike and Monsanto through the 1990s suggesting that the implications are likely to be on a different scale than those of previous waves.

Parallel waves of change have been seen in such areas as information technology, total quality management, reengineering, intellectual capital, knowledge management, and so on. As all of this change surges through the economic system, corporate internalization happens at very different levels and in very different ways, depending on what sort of business you happen to be in.

To make things even more complicated, as the new century got under way, those in the know had got used to distinguishing between companies on the basis of whether they were part of the old or new economies. And as it became increasingly clear – what a relief! – that the sustainability debate was going to be just as relevant to the new as to the old, some of us also spotted an odd inside-out symmetry. Whereas new economy analysts are concerned about a company's internal 'burn rate', that is, the speed at which it consumes capital, sustainability analysts are interested in a company's external burn rate, or the rate at which it consumes scarce natural resources or contributes to global problems like climate change.

I mention this because the best book on the first type of burn rate was the eponymous *Burn Rate*, by Michael Wolff.[30] And a column he wrote subsequently for *Forbes ASAP* struck a real chord with me. The title of the piece: "Got it?"[31] His critique of the new economy inner circle, it struck me, could just as well have been directed at the worst excesses of the social responsibility (CSR) and sustainable development (SD) communities. A key distinction in the new economy, he noted, had been that between those who "got it" and those who, well, "didn't get it".

"'Getting it' was an accurate way to describe this inner circle of under-standing," he said, "because it was like getting a joke. It was a riff: That is, there was no real knowledge that you had to possess, no scientific truth to be known. Getting it was closer to a religious truth or cultural thing. It was an insider's thing. It was more about attitude and affect and lingo. Were you hip enough?" It was also, he added, about knowing the right people. And – "with getting it the prize of '90s" – a key dividing line was between those who read *Forbes ASAP*, *Fast Company* or *Wired* and those who, well, couldn't say they did.

As a long-time reader of such magazines, I obviously have nothing against them, but at the same time I wasn't alone in feeling somewhat uncomfortable about the neatly drawn divide between "those who could talk the talk and walk the walk and those who were hopelessly flat-footed." For those on the right side of the divide, as Wolff put it, "it was a little bit like how it must have felt in the '30s to be an agitated student first hearing Marxist philosophy. Here was a new point of view that seemed to explain everything. It was the big picture. Comprehensive. Global. Here was a coherent theory of modern life." It was a binary thing. Your switch was on or it was off. "You were either the future or the ash heap."

If the truth be known, it has often seemed to be the same for those of us trying to work out which companies and CEOs to work with in the CSR and SD fields. Younger colleagues would often ask how I knew whether a company or executive team was worth working with. I would reply that it was some mix of weak signals and intuition, but in retrospect the nature of the game was very much a new economy thing. Some companies and CEOs 'got' sustainability, or showed real signs of wanting to get it, while others didn't. Increasingly, though, getting to see the CEO was a key test of whether a particular company was worth working on.

Those of us leading the charge were often amazed by the extent to which some business leaders would seem to hang on our every word. Wolff remembers even more dramatic dynamics when he sat in on meetings between Time Warner and new economy folk ahead of the merger with AOL. "On the one side of the table sat the Time Inc.-ers," he recalls, "who were like supplicants, novices, even mendicants, in their willingness to get it. On the other side of the table sat the blasé, profoundly arrogant technologists and technology salesmen who got it."

Well, I don't remember any meetings quite like that, but by the late 1990s the balance of power had shifted in a remarkable way in relation to the SD agenda. And there were all sorts of reasons why. In fact, the older I get the more I realize that culture change often moves on a generational time-scale, much more slowly than I had expected in the late 1960s. But then as the time-scales extend and the changes finally begin to happen, the transition can happen extraordinarily fast – as when a chemical solution (like hyper-saturated copper sulfate) undergoes a so-called 'phase change'.

High profile companies had been under pressure of one sort or another for decades. Many of the folk who didn't get it, arguing that all of this was fad that would soon blow away on the winds, were themselves blown away – being claimed by one or other of what I came to see as two of our greatest long-term allies, retirement or death. New blood was sucked in from the outside world, bringing with it new DNA. New perspectives, new priorities and, most importantly, new values.

Those of the old guard who survived had by now seen one major company after another turned inside out by major controversies. Indeed, if any single year marked the watershed, it was 1995. That was the year when Shell was both pummeled by European public opinion over its plans to sink the Brent Spar oil installation out in the ocean and pilloried for its environmental and human rights records in Nigeria. After that nothing could be quite the same again.

But the fundamental reason why many companies really began to switch on to the sustainability agenda was that the world seemed to be getting a lot more complex – and business people sensed that these sustainability folk might have some useful ideas on how to manage at least some of that complexity. Indeed, in retrospect, I think a key part of what we have been trying to do in our probing of potential corporate partners and clients has been to assess, at however basic a level, that capacity for managing complexity.

THREE STEPS TO SUSTAINABILITY

So what, in the economist's world, are externalities? The first thing to recognize is that they can be both positive and negative. Positive externalities include the ways in which new technologies and industries create new market niches and new opportunities for enterprise, employment and tax revenues. In the network economy, for example, so-called 'network externalities' are responsible for the 'increasing returns' that turned companies like Microsoft and Cisco Systems into money-machines.

That said, economic activity very often also creates a range of negative impacts – and, here again, we may see multiplier effects at work. As Julia Butterfly Hill explained her determination to stop the felling of the giant redwood a.k.a. Luna (page 68), "it's all about cumulative impact."[32] To use the jargon, externalities are those consequences for welfare or opportunity costs that are not fully accounted for in the price or in other ways by market systems.[33]

A manufacturing plant, for example, may create pollution and traffic congestion without having to account – or pay – for the related reductions in the welfare of other people. Those adversely affected can include other companies. Many years ago, I recall visiting a warehouse operated by Kodak, where it had been found that the stored film kept developing – because the previous occupier had stored radioactive, luminous watches in the same space. The effect was never intended, but in this case the watchmaker had imposed external costs on a particularly sensitive target, Kodak.

The extent to which an entrepreneur or company can externalize such costs can obviously have major effects in terms of profitability. Investors and accountants, for example, love to calculate the internal rate of return for a project or business. This is the discount rate at which the net present value of a project is zero. Why would you want that information? Basically, to decide whether or not to invest – or, in the accountant's case, to test what a business might be worth. If the internal rate of return (based on capital costs, net revenues per year and expected project life) turns out to be higher than the interest, the investor, entrepreneur or company would have to pay on borrowed money.

Of course, there are many other ways of trying to get similar results, including net present value, but the central point here is that if you can squeeze down your capital costs and boost your net revenues, the profits are more likely to flow. So, in the case of Pacific/Maxxam, the name of the game was to cut as many trees as fast as possible, regardless of the long-term sustainability of its operations or the exploited ecosystem, and to minimize the operating and capital costs it would have to incur in preventing such externalities as land-slides and loss of biodiversity. Indeed, the evidence suggests that many such companies have calculated that it is cheaper to pay fines for their misdemeanors than it would be to ensure they don't happen in the first place.

Such externalities can be internalized either voluntarily or as a result of varying degrees of coercion. So, for example, change can come as a consequence of campaigns, new standards, new laws, more effective policing and enforcement, ecological or social taxes, and adjusted pricing systems. While growing numbers of companies have chosen the voluntary route, aiming to move "beyond compliance", for most of the world's business people this whole agenda is still fundamentally a question of legal compliance. And even for the volunteers, the name of the game is to win enough credit to win a place at the table when the discussions on new legislation and regulations get under way.

So let's start there, before moving on to such 'softer' drivers for internalization of externalities as standards and values.

LONG ARMS OF THE LAW

It's easiest to see the waves when you focus on environmentalism, particularly if you are an environmentalist. But as someone trained both in economics and sociology, I am well aware that there have been similar waves in the areas of economic and social accountability. Indeed, these last two came together most powerfully in the rapid spread – and then spectacular collapse – of various forms of communism and hard-left socialism through the 20th century. And because environmental concerns had been brushed under the carpet, the ex-communist world now faces staggering ecological debts.

Sometimes you have to be an economic historian to spot the cycles, but the interesting thing now is that some of the great cycles of change appear to be converging in new ways. The implications are still far from clear, but one thing is already certain: the economic, social and environmental changes of the 21st century are going to be at least as dramatic as those of the century we have just left behind.

Environmentalism, in retrospect, was one of the – if not the – most powerful social movements of the second half of the 20th century. As already argued, the first environmental wave, which peaked in 1969–73, was followed by a fairly deep downwave that ran from 1974 to 1987. Paradoxically, perhaps, although the political controversies were at their most intense in the 1969–73 period, the peak of new law-making happened during the period of the first downwave.

Figure 8.2 shows the accelerating total of international environmental treaties from 1921 to 1999. In the USA alone, the number of federal, state and local environmental regulations soared from 2,000 in 1970 to 100,000 by the end of the 1990s.[34]

The natural conclusion is that it takes some time to jump-start our government and governance systems when complex new agendas like this erupt into the political landscape. The 1970s saw the formation of the first of hundreds of national environmental protection agencies, departments and ministries. When the Organisation for Economic Co-operation and Development (OECD) published its first state of the environment report in 1979, it included a listing of the new laws passed during the decade. The figures showed that the trend really took off in 1972, the year of the first UN environment conference, held in Stockholm, with the period through to 1976 representing peak years of law-making.

The election of the Republicans in the US in 1979, and the more or less parallel influence of the Conservatives in the UK, heralded a period of retrenchment. Right-wing politicians tried to rein in the regulators, weaken enforcement and switch the focus to market mechanisms. They were generally supported in this counter-reformation by business interests.

Paradoxically, however, their limited successes – and the political controversies caused in the process – led to growing interest in new ways of controlling what companies do. As with the onset of green consumerism in the late 1980s, a trend I had a hand in shaping with our best-selling book *The Green Consumer Guide*,[35] the result

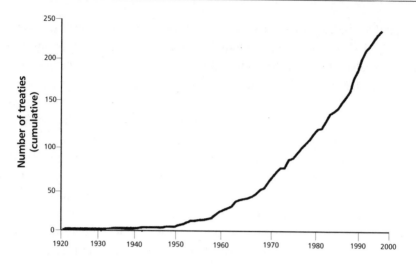

Figure 8.2   International environmental treaties, 1921–1999.
Source: United Nations Environment Programme.

was often new forms of pressure that industry found it much harder to manage than the old regulatory processes.

Faced with such external pressures and demands, companies typically run through the gamut of human reactions. They deny the problems, point the finger at others, lobby to slow new laws, complain that the economics of their industry won't let them do the right thing, and – in extreme cases – threaten to move (or actually move) their operations to less demanding parts of the world.

At this stage of the game, you tend to find companies field considerable numbers of lawyers and government affairs people. Typically, they are on the defensive, wanting to slow things down to a "manageable" pace. But the heat is being turned up considerably. The European Commission, for example, has been considering product liability legislation along US lines.[36] One possible target: mobile phones. Among other possibilities: the introduction of class actions and market-share liability, the latter dividing damages between corporate defendants when it's unclear whose product caused the injury.

SETTING STANDARDS

The second great wave of environmentalism reached full gale force in the late 1980s, picking up through 1987 and peaking between 1988 and 1990. Its greatest spur was the discovery of the Antarctic ozone hole, increasingly seen as conclusive proof of the global damage caused as the undoubted benefits brought by Adam Smith's "invisible hand" of markets began to be seriously offset by the impact of those same markets' "invisible elbow". And consumer pressures were in the forefront of change.

Caught off-balance, many leading international companies found that they were being challenged in areas of their business they knew little about. They were being asked about the impact of cocoa-farming on tropical forest cover, about the links between tuna-fishing and dolphin deaths, or about the stratospheric effects of products they had previously viewed as little more than shelf-fillers. As a result, the pioneers started to carry out embryonic forms of environmental auditing, processes which before long would be extended to cover a range of social, ethical and fair-trade issues, too.

SustainAbility was one of the pioneers in the environmental auditing field, at least in Europe. In publishing such reports as *The Environmental Audit*,[37] we helped to set de facto standards in such areas. Next, working alongside a range of partners, most notably the United Nations Environment Programme (UNEP), we started doing the same thing in the embryonic field of corporate environmental reporting. This is a subject to which we will return, briefly, in Chapter 9. But the key point here was that companies were being driven into new territory, often without maps and with no real sense of what would be expected of them a few years down the track.

By the time the second downwave started in 1990, the commercial opportunity for mainstream standard-setting bodies was clear. In the environmental area, the British Standards Institution (BSI) launched BS7570 as its environmental management standard, an initiative which spurred the International Standards Institution (ISO) to push forward with its ISO 14000 series of standards.

Many leading companies lobbied long and hard to slow down and dilute such initiatives, with US corporations particularly effective in removing the reporting requirements from early drafts of the ISO standards. But 'Comply or we don't buy' pressures forced growing numbers of companies to adopt ISO 14000, just as they had previously taken on board the quality standard ISO 9000.

It's important to note that not everyone believes that such standards are an unqualified success. Indeed, some argue that far from being good for business, the ISO standards are based on bad theory and, as a result, make things worse.[38] They argue that ISO 9000's focus on specification and control overrides understanding and improvement, which are at the heart of real quality. As companies have focused on systems and procedures, they have tended to create excessive bureaucracy rather than better quality.

And there have been any number of cases where self-policing and voluntary auditing processes have failed. *Business Week*, for example, described Wal-Mart's self-policing of a Chinese sweatshop as a "disaster",[39] while even some of the independent consultants hired to vet labor and other human rights performance by suppliers have come under heavy fire. One review of monitoring methods used by PricewaterhouseCoopers (PwC) claimed to have found "major labor practice issues," including hazardous chemical use, barriers to freedom of association and collective bargaining, and violations of overtime and wage laws. A key problem, the independent reviewer concluded, was that PwC auditors talked to managers at sites they visited, rather than to the workers direct.[40]

None of that has stopped the standards bandwagon from building up a phenomenal head of steam. Indeed, new standard-makers have entered the fray, launching a succession of novel standards in the hope that they would drive further change. A selection of emerging standards in the CSR and SD areas is spotlighted in box 11 (page 157). One recent entrant is Project SIGMA, designed as the first TBL management standard.

Indeed, while writing this chapter, I took part in a panel discussion on an early project SIGMA draft at London Zoo. The Zoo, in retrospect, was the perfect venue. Zoos today are allowed to exist largely because of their role in conserving diversity – and here were 70 or 80 people busily beavering away to create more diversity. But it was soon clear that the business people present were worried. At a time when they are increasingly bombarded with new management standards, and when middle managers are already punch-drunk with new initiatives, this event was designed to boost diversity not by rescuing some endangered species but by adding yet another standard to the already-squirming heap.

You can probably tell I am not a management standards fetishist. Of course, no one depending daily on consumer safety and quality standards would deny they have helped improve our quality of life. Where would we be without the MSDOS embedded in our computers? How long before we all insist on the new Bluetooth standard for all the consumer electronics we buy? And who would argue against performance standards for public service providers, like railway companies and airlines?

But I am surely not the only one worried that management standards can encourage a 'tick box' mentality, rather than encouraging people to think outside the box. The number of boxes to be ticked has exploded. In the field of SD, business faces an avalanche of new standards. They cover everything from employee rights and environmental management systems through to corporate sustainability reporting and stakeholder engagement. AA 1000, EMAS, FSC, GRI, ISO 14000, MSC, SA 8000: these are acronyms for just some of the new standards. And all this in the wake of research showing that the end-results of applying mainstream standards, as we have seen, have often been disappointing.

Given my aversion to standard-setting processes, it is ironic that I get involved in so many. The ones I can remember include: an attempt to evolve the European Commission's environmental management and audit standard (EMAS) into a sustainability management standard; the early testing of the British Standard Institution (BSI)'s BS 7750 standard, which later mutated into ISO 14000; the Global Reporting Initiative (GRI); AccountAbility 1000 (AA 1000); the would-be mother of all sustainability standards, Project SIGMA; and the UN's Global Compact.

Odd, yes, but standard setting is where the sustainability community has been investing a growing proportion of its resources in recent years. And, while there has to be a major shake-out among all these competing standards before long, I have learned that some of the most useful outcomes flow from the standard-setting processes, rather than the standards themselves. The necessity to debate what a standard is for, and how it should be developed, applied and verified, spurs engagement between a wide range of business, government, NGO and other stakeholders.

One interesting thing about such standards is that they are driven more by markets than by governments. Once again, that can make them much tougher to deal with than laws. The predictability factor can drop through the floor. Customer industries can decide, more or less at the drop of a hat, or on the basis of an out-of-the-blue media campaign, to require all suppliers to meet particular standards. As long as there are plenty of suppliers to go around, who's to stop them?

Box 11: Blips on the screen

Swarming standards

If a group of lions is known as a 'pride' and a gaggle of crows as a 'murder', what is the collective noun for a swarm of standards? Whatever it may be, the competition between different CSR and SD standards is increasingly important. Which standard should your company back and adopt? It may not be quite as binary as the battle between video standards Betamax and VHS, but the outcome will powerfully shape the 21st century business agenda. So here are 21 of the standards currently competing for corporate and CEO attention:[41]

1. **AccountAbility 1000 (AA1000),** issued by the Institute of Social and Ethical Accountability (ISEA) in 1999, focuses on stakeholder engagement. A good start, but perhaps a little

over-complicated. Something of a standard-maker's standard. Further details: www.accountability.org.uk/B.htm

2. **APEC Business Code of Conduct**, issued by Asia Pacific Economic Cooperation (APEC) in draft in 1999, draws fairly heavily on other standards, including the OECD Principles of Corporate Governance, and Caux Principles (see below) and the ICC Business Charter for Sustainable Development (see below). Further details: www.apecsec.org.sg

3. **Caux Principles for Business**, issued by the Caux Round-table of senior business leaders from Europe, Japan and North America in 1994, are offered as "a foundation for dialogue and action by business and leaders worldwide". Most credible with the business community. Further details: www.cauxroundtable.org/prin4.htm

4. **CERES Principles**, originally called the Valdez Principles, were developed by the Coalition for Environmentally Responsible Economies (CERES) in the wake of the 1989 *Exxon Valdez* oil spill disaster. A tough choice for companies, but as a result potentially offering high credibility. Further details: www.ceres.org/about/principles.html

5. **Clean Clothes Campaign**, started in the Netherlands in 1990, issued the Codes of Labor Practices for the Apparel Industry including Footwear and designed to improve working conditions in the garment and footwear industry. Further details: www.cleanclothes.org

6. **Eco-Management & Audit Scheme (EMAS)**, issued by the Euro-pean Commission in 1993. A better standard than the original ISO 14000 standard (see below), because it encourages companies to report their performance. A hit in Germany, but unexpectedly low penetration elsewhere – largely because many companies prefer the weaker (and higher profile) ISO 14000 standard series. Further details: www.quality.co.uk/ emas.htm

7. **FairTrade Labeling Organization International (FLO)**, founded in 1997 when national Fair Trade labeling initiatives (including Fair Trade Foundation, Max Havelaar, and TransFair) united, awards a consumer label to products that meet

internationally recognized standards of fair trade. Further details: www.fairtrade.net

8. **Forest Stewardship Council (FSC)** founded in 1993, has developed procedures and standards that are used to accredit certification companies, that in turn evaluate forests aiming for certification according to the FSC Principles and Criteria for Forest Stewardship. Further details: www.fscoax.org/principal.htm

9. **Global Compact**, developed by the United Nations (UN) and announced by secretary-general Kofi Annan at the World Economic Forum in Davos, Switzerland, in 1999. Business is encouraged to embrace a set of nine principles in their own operations and support complementary public policy initiatives. Many corporations have been playing a wait-and-see game. Most are nervous of the labor provisions introduced by the International Labor Organization (ILO). But if it achieves critical mass this one could be a real heavyweight. Further details: www.unglobalcompact.org

10. **Global Reporting Initiative (GRI)**, initiated by the Coalition for Environmentally Responsible Economies (CERES; see number 4 above), the GRI has attracted wide support for its sustainability reporting guidelines. Now the *de facto* global standard for corporate sustainability reporting. Further details: www.globalreporting.org/

11. **Global Sullivan Principles**, developed by a consortium led by the Rev. Leon Sullivan, include eight directives on ethics, environmental and labor practices. The original Sullivan Principles focused on apartheid in South Africa. The Global Principles are aimed at multinational companies and their business partners. A main competitor to the UN Global Compact (see above 9). Key criticisms: the process of developing the Principles was not transparent – and they are weaker than the Global Compact. Further details: http://globalsullivanprinciples.org/

12. **goodcorporation.com**, under development by a new company, GoodCorporation, in association with the UK Institute of Business Ethics, is based on a charter committing signatory companies to incorporate social responsibility. The

simple, one-page charter aims to cover all key stakeholder relationships, including those with employees, customers, suppliers, shareholders, the environment and the community. A separate accreditation body, with services provided by KPMG, will oversee the process of certification. The fact that this has been a commercial initiative from the outset may raise question marks in some people's minds. Further details: www. goodcorporation.com

13. **ICC Business Charter on Sustainable Development**, developed by the International Chamber of Commerce (ICC) and launched in 1991, was partly a business community attempt to outflank the CERES-launched Valdez (now CERES) Principles (see above). Following a strong start, the standard has tended to be diluted over time, as the ICC focused more on recruiting new corporate signatories, rather than on paying enough attention to whether or not companies were putting the Charter principles into practice. Further details: www.iccwbo.org/home/environment/charter.asp

14. **ISO 14000**, a family of environmental management and reporting standards developed by the International Standards Organization (ISO), was launched in 1996. As Saddam Hussein might say, the "mother" of all environmental management standards.[42] By 1999, more than 8,000 organizations in 72 countries had formal certification under ISO 14001, most of them in Europe and Japan. By mid-2000, more than 850 organizations had been certified in the US.[43] An early weakness in the area of reporting has been addressed with ISO 14031. But will ISO 14000 follow ISO 9000, now attacked for its contribution to excess bureaucracy rather than improved quality? Further details: www.iso14000.com

15. **Marine Stewardship Council (MSC)**, developed by the World Wide Fund for Nature (WWF) and Unilever and launched in 1996, now operates as an independent organization. It has developed a set of MSC Principles and Criteria that are used to certify sustainable fisheries. Further details: www.msc.org

16. **Natural Step**, originally developed by the Swedish Natural Step Foundation and launched in 1989, has since gone international. To date, the key ecological standard for business.

There are four 'system conditions', three environ- mental, one social. Further details: www.naturalstep.org

17. **OECD Guidelines for Multinational Enterprises**, revised by the Organisation for Economic Co-operation and Development (OECD) and re-launched in 2000, are voluntary. The latest version includes new requirements on the environmental and human rights fronts. The OECD is a heavyweight, so these should be a priority for any multinational corporation. Further details: www.oecd.org/daf/investment/guidelines

18. **Principles for Global Corporate Responsibility** were revised and re-launched in 1998 by the US Interfaith Center for Corporate Responsibility (ICCR), Canada's Taskforce on the Churches and Corporate Responsibility (TCCR) and the UK Ecumenical Council for Corporate Responsibility (ECCR). The nearly 60 principles were shaped by a wide range of environmental, human rights, labor and religious organizations, together with companies. Aimed to help stakeholders assess corporate codes of conduct, policies and practices. Further details: www.web.net/~tccr/

19. **Project Sigma** is designed to be the first TBL management standard. Among those driving the process are the British Standards Institution (BSI), Forum for the Future, and the Institute for Social and Ethical Accountability (ISEA), with backing from two UK government departments. The approach is based on a five capitals model. Further details: www.projectsigma.com

20. **Social Accountability 8000 (SA8000)**, developed by Social Accountability International, itself founded in 1997 as the Council on Economic Priorities' Accreditation Agency (CEPAA), this is a voluntary, factory-based monitoring and certification standard for assessing labor conditions in global manufacturing operations. A pioneering social standard aimed at mitigating the impacts of globalization. More popular with NGOs and smaller companies than with big corporations, but can bring market credibility. Further details: www.cepaa.org/sa8000.htm

21. **Universal Declaration of Human Rights**, adopted by the General Assembly of the United Nations in 1948, sets a common standard of achievement for all peoples and all nations. A foundation stone for other standards, including the UN Global Compact (see 9, above). Further details: www. un.org/Overview/rights.html

A QUESTION OF VALUES

And the third wave? Like the first wave did through the 1960s, there is no question that the third wave of societal pressure on business has been building for a while. And it's different from the previous two, again no question. One key reason is that the drivers and issues are complexed in new ways. They stretch right across the environmental, human rights and governance agendas, as discussed in Chapter 2. But the really interesting thing about this latest set of pressures, and about the internalization challenges created as a result, is that values are at the very heart of the debate.

As I argued in *Cannibals with Forks*, we are seeing a profound values shift in countries around the world. One key dimension of this trend is the way in which what would once have been seen as 'soft' values (such as business ethics or concern for future generations) are now coming in alongside – and sometimes even overriding – traditional 'hard' values (such as the paramount importance of the financial bottom line).

For the most part, this shift is not something that is being regulated or driven by governments; instead, it is happening as a natural outgrowth of people's evolving awareness and concerns. And the problem with dealing with such shifts by means of a compliance-led or even standard-focused approach is that events can so easily overtake you. That's the reason why, in the CNN World, companies are finding that their values – and their employees' values – are being tested both publicly and in radically new ways.

One contributory factor to values-based internalization, oddly, has been the downsizing trend. As companies have opted for flatter hierarchies, bosses have found themselves unable to look – or have someone look – over their employees' shoulders to the same degree. As a result, more employees have been taking decisions that would once have been passed up the hierarchy. In the process, they will do as they think best. "If you want them to do as the company thinks best too," as *Fortune* put it, "then you must hope that they have an inner gyroscope aligned with the corporate compass."[44]

As companies segue through these three broad phases of response, from legal compliance, through standard-setting and observance, to an explicitly values-driven approach, new issues arise. Growing diversity (across new/old recruits, sex, age, ethnicity or whatever) can open up values chasms even within the same organization, but the problem – or opportunity – can be dramatically greater where companies operate across different cultures. As a result, we are seeing growing numbers of companies carrying out some form of values audit (box 4, page 49).

They are also drafting – or revisiting – core sets of business principles. The experience of companies like BT, Johnson & Johnson and Royal Dutch/Shell shows business principles can evolve in various forms, including corporate policies, mission and values statements, or codes of conduct. The basic goal is to create a corporate culture 'touchstone', with companies referring to their business principles as the 'glue' that holds an organization together, or as a 'moral backbone'. To bring such initiatives to life, they need to be developed with as many of the company's people as possible. Among the potential benefits of the approach are increased employee loyalty, higher productivity, higher customer satisfaction, and improved financial performance.[45]

Interestingly, we may see the order of these three main stepping stones to sustainability reversed in the early decades of the 21st century. Values-driven companies, increasingly, get involved in developing and promoting new voluntary standards. Given enough time, the chances are that the next stage will involve them becoming increasingly concerned about 'free-riders' who fail to sign up, but both enjoy the benefits of other companies' efforts – and threaten to undermine the whole effort by various forms of malpractice. When this happens, the logical next step will be calls from the business community for new legislation and for changes in pricing and tax signals and other incentives. Indeed, we can expect tax regimes to evolve reasonably rapidly to help governments drive the sustainability transition.

PANEL 8

Going for green gold

Given that the second major Labor for the Citizen CEO involves competing successfully in global markets (page 121), the Olympics offer an interesting model. The myth may be that the Games were re-founded by Hercules using the spoils of previous feats, including the cleaning of the Augean Stables, but the reality is that they were re-launched in 1896 by Baron Pierre de Coubertin. And the Millennium Games, held in Sydney in 2000, indicated that this is now a huge business by anyone's standards. The spoils are huge: the Olympics generate over a billion dollars of revenues every four years.

With so much money at stake in each Olympic Games, there will always be those who bewail the death of the 'Olympic Spirit'. And there will also be those who counter-charge by saying that the critics are looking back to a golden age that never existed. The Olympic Spirit, they argue, is continually evolving. But given that the Baron wanted the Games to help promote global peace and to develop 'moral fiber', the Olympic ideal – as with global business ethics generally – is in serious need of a makeover.

Infamously, members of the International Olympic Committee (IOC) were found to have taken bribes from Salt Lake City, which was bidding for the Games.[46] Nor were these isolated incidents. IOC delegates, it turned out, had demanded that bidding cities such as Berlin and Stockholm provide everything from first-class plane tickets to prostitutes.[47] Some of the more egregious sinners found that they were for the high jump: the IOC eventually kicked out 10 of its members following the Salt Lake City scandal.

But what is perhaps more interesting is the way in which the 2000 Games absorbed a good deal of the sustainability agenda, with major implications both for the future of the Olympics movement and for a number of the sponsoring companies.

The 'Green Games' idea originated with Greenpeace. Another small wing-beat that helped to move the world. The group suggested the athlete's village become a showcase for solar technology.[48] Eventually, the Australian property company Bovis Lend Lease won the contract (page 113), following a bidding process that gave a rare "level playing field" for SD, according to Maria Atkinson, the company's environmental manager.

To give the grid-linked solar elements of the scheme an even better chance, the company went into partnership with the New South Wales government's Sustainable Energy Development Authority (SEDA) and NSW energy distributor Pacific Power. And a range of other companies – among them the packaging and recycling company Visy – also used the commercial springboard provided by the Games.

The environment is now the official third pillar for the Games. And the message for future corporate sponsors is *be very, very careful – or be very, very green*. When the Sydney Olympics were first mooted, a central element of the design guidelines was a call for the avoidance of CFC, HFC and HCFC refrigerants and processes. So Greenpeace launched a campaign against major sponsors still using HFC refrigerants – ozone-friendly, but still greenhouse gases.

Coca-Cola was an early target, with a Greenpeace internet site (www.cokespotlight.com) featuring a parody of a Coke campaign.[49] The slogan, executed in the world-famous Coke script, was: *Enjoy Climate Change*. Coca-Cola's new chairman, Doug Daft, quickly announced the company would be out of HFCs by 2004. Foster's Brewing Group and the world's largest ice-cream maker, Unilever, soon followed suit. The only hold-out was McDonald's, despite the fact that two of their plants (in the UK Millennium Dome) used 100 percent HFC-free refrigerants. How long would it be, critics wondered, before the Golden Arches melted?

CHAPTER 9

Inclusion

inclusion / *n*. **1** the act of including something. **2** the condition of being included. **3** *process by which a company or organization takes on board the views and priorities of internal and external stakeholders (e.g. the inclusive company, stakeholder inclusion).*

I sensed the ghosts of business past. Indeed, this was one of the strangest places I had yet journeyed to for a stakeholder dialogue process. We were at The Greenbrier, a genteel summer resort in the mountains of West Virginia. In addition to serving as a Civil War hospital for the Confederate Army, it has been a favorite haunt of well-heeled Southerners for over 200 years.[50] But what made the experience particularly strange was the deep secret that for 30 years only around 100 people knew: this place was the architectural icing on top of the mother of all bunkers.

And we're not talking of golf course bunkers here, despite the fact that The Greenbrier boasts several championship-standard golf courses across its 6,500 acres. Instead, this was America's main east coast Cold War bunker. It was designed to house the US government for up to 60 days in the event of a nuclear showdown with the Soviet Union. To give survivors sheltering from atomic storms some semblance of normality, they even had four interchangeable photographs of Washington's Capitol Hill, taken in spring, summer, autumn and winter.

Although it was President Eisenhower who thought of digging out the bunker beneath his favorite hotel, no fewer than 25 American presidents have stayed at The Greenbrier, along with an A-to-Z of the country's business aristocracy. Among the names in the visitor's book: Astor, DuPont, Forbes, Hearst, Pulitzer, Rockefeller, Vanderbilt.

These were some of the folk whose shades I felt heartily disapproving of what we were doing at The Greenbrier. Interestingly, the bunker's 25-ton blast door is still camouflaged by fake doors marked "Warning: High Voltage." In the same way, earlier generations of presidents and corporate leaders got used to protecting their insider knowledge by claiming national security or commercial confidentiality.

How the walls are tumbling! And not just in Berlin. These days, you can get a $25 guided tour of the Greenbrier bunker. The conference I was speaking at, organized by the Society of Automotive Engineering, featured leading NGOs like the National Resources Defense Council (NRDC) and the World Resources Institute (WRI), alongside eco-architect Bill McDonough. Delegates heard top auto company executives using language – including the S-word, repeatedly – that many of them would have seen as un-American just a few years earlier. The theme of this 50th SAE conference: Sustainability.

But talking the talk, as they say, is different from walking the walk. And the cost and other implications of getting all of this wrong are so huge that companies need to be very sure they are headed in the right direction. That's where stakeholder engagement fits in – representing the third Herculean Labor facing Citizen CEOs.

TAMING THE HYDRA

When the WTO summit in Seattle was stormed late in 1999, we began to hear talk of the "stakeholder hydra", the global web of activists, public interest groups, think-tanks, ethical investors and committed companies that now powerfully shapes both the political and business agendas. Hercules hacked off the Hydra's heads – and, the real trick, learned how to stop them growing back. This isn't an option with the stakeholder hydra. Even a country like India has some 10,000 NGOs, and their numbers are growing pretty much by the day.

None of this is exactly new. Capitalism is a "consequence of buffered opposites," as Ivan Alexander succinctly put it: of "management *versus* labour or employees; owners, shareholders *versus* management; corporation *versus* corporation; large corporations *versus* smaller businesses; rule-making corporations *versus* rule-making government; consumers' interests *versus* producers' interests; high returns for the shareholder *versus* low prices for the consumer; exploitation of resources *versus* conservation; protectionism *versus* free trade," and so on.[51]

Citizen CEOs know that these days we have to take all of these people seriously, understanding what they want, engaging them, discussing priorities. Before diving into a bit more detail about how this is best done, however, perhaps we need to step back a bit and look at a bigger picture? At a time when people already talk about 'stakeholder fatigue', and there are real question-marks over the ability or willingness of some companies to make the sort of changes key stakeholders demand in the sort of time-scales they think appropriate, we probably need to ask the obvious question: Why should business even think of engaging non-traditional external stakeholders?

One answer, again, is that the 'CNN World' is not only an emergent reality, but is helping to define our perception of reality. This helps fuel the accelerating shift from exclusive models of governance, both global and corporate, to increasingly inclusive models and processes. Nor is this something you simply see in Scandinavian countries or California. You begin to see it in places like Russia, too.

Remember the *Kursk*, the nuclear submarine that went to the bottom of the Barents Sea in 2000 with its entire 118-man crew? Once, the Soviet Union might have managed to clamp down, keeping the whole thing out of the news. Now it all happens on CNN. Even a horrifying last message, written in the darkness of the rapidly-filling hull by Lieutenant-Captain Dmitri Kolesnikov, was world-wide news within hours of its discovery in the drowned submariner's pocket.[52]

The knock-on effects of the varying versions of reality are likely to be profound. "The news once again makes us doubt the official information that was handed to us as the tragedy unfolded," said a newscaster on the private sector Russian television channel NTV. "We are forced to think that officials are not searching for the truth behind the tragedy, but trying to hide some state secret."

Such open criticism would have been unthinkable even a few years previously, and the transparency revolution – whatever the forces of reaction may try in terms of closing or gagging particular media – is only just getting into its stride in the once-Communist world.

All sorts of factors are at work, many of which we have already touched upon. Oddly, however, the sheer fact that a particular company is listed on a major stock exchange can boost its commitment to transparency and external engagement. When South African Breweries first listed on the London Stock Exchange, for example, its involvement in the international corporate social responsibility and SD networks ramped up dramatically. The company had obviously concluded that this was part of the game once you operate in international markets.

Companies have internalized different parts of the TBL agenda at different times, in different ways and, often, at different speeds. So, for example, Lise Kingo of Novo Nordisk plotted the state of play in the Danish company a few years back as shown in Figure 9.1. I have shifted the social agenda slightly higher up the curve, and added the economic agenda. For each new agenda, a range of different internal and external stakeholders will need to be engaged.

Clearly, the need for financial performance has been on the agenda for a very long time, so boards are used to dealing with this one – albeit not with wider economic performance issues spotlighted by the TBL agenda. The environmental agenda has been a pressure for several decades – indeed, in the case of Novo Nordisk, one proximate cause of the company's 'greening' strategy from the early 1990s was the pressure that flowed from concerned consumers, particularly in the wake of our best-selling book, *The Green Consumer Guide*.[53] The social and economic agendas are still some way down the curve, but Novo Nordisk – which has become one of the

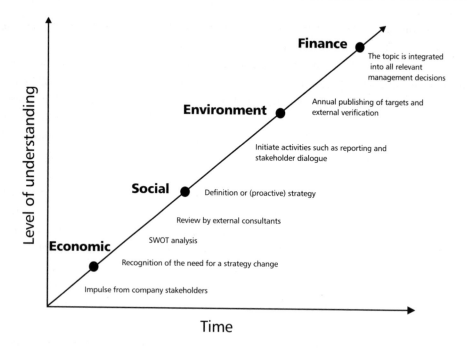

Figure 9.1 Novo Nordisk's view of the stakeholder agenda.
Source: Novo Nordisk, adapted by author.

paradigm examples of the 'engage them, don't try to decapitate them' movement – is now working on these, too.

One of the Hydra's heads was immortal. Environmentalists would say that their voice has to be most important, given that the planet's future is at stake, but the financial world would say that financial performance is the eternal pressure in business. And one place where you can see clearly the evolving nature of the financial agenda for business is in family-owned companies that are also part-listed.

INVESTORS AND CONSUMERS

Take the German pharmaceutical company Merck, a 300-year-old, family-owned concern which separated from its US offspring after the World War I. Descendants of Emanuel Merck II still control over 70 percent of the stock, which lands the company's chairman with the interesting task of keeping 200 or so family members happy.[54] And their lock on the company is pretty strong: they recently agreed to sell their shares only to each other over the next 20 years.

That brings both strengths and weaknesses. "There is a degree of tension between the family partners and (mainstream) investors because their time horizons are very different," explains Merck chairman Bernhard Scheuble. "Institutional investors want to see profits tomorrow – they want us to become a pure pharmaceuticals company, while the family says we have fared well in the past."

Often in such companies, the traditional family-focused management structures lead to a low-risk culture that values continuity over innovation. For executives coming in from the outside, as Scheuble did, there can be real benefits from stock market listing. He sees Merck's listing as a blessing in a number of ways, not least because it has forced the company to become more transparent.

Nor is it simply a question of investors. Companies are finding that they have to open up to their consumers and customers in radically new ways. Companies like Amazon.com and Dell have underscored this trend. And the trend is emerging outside the OECD world, too. Jump from Germany to India, for example, and you find some fascinating rethinking under way at Hindustan Lever. The company, part of the Unilever group, produces annual revenues of around £1.5 billion and has a vast, sprawling supply chain.[55] Its 100 factories make some 110 brands for sale through 7,500 distributors to 3 million retail outlets. And stock worth well over 10 percent of the company's annual turnover is locked up in its supply chain at any given moment.

Although India's telecommunications infrastructure is still woefully inadequate, Hindustan Lever is pursuing a strategy to get radically closer to the consumer. That means the Indian housewife, at whom the company's soaps, shampoos and detergents are largely targeted. And therein lies a real challenge: "We know the Indian housewife," the company's chairman, Manvinder Singh Banga, told the *Financial Times*. "She has lived so close to the bone for so long that, I believe, she is the most astute customer in the world." For Hindustan Lever, at least, the most important head of the stakeholder hydra is the consumer's.

The result of all this is that the Hindustan Lever faces twin challenges, in addition to that of preparing for renewed competition from foreign rivals when tariff barriers go down. The first is to persuade consumers to use more cleaning products, of a higher quality (offering higher margins), more often. This is a low-tech issue, but a key one. In rural India, for example, poverty means that soap is not used with every bath.

The second challenge is rather more high-tech, but it focuses on new levels of stakeholder engagement. It has to do with market connectivity and ways of cutting back on the amount of stock held captive in the supply chain. By using new information technology and business-to-business (B2B) processes, Banga's vision is that the company will be able to connect the supply chain in new ways, to the point where it can begin to operate in real time. So, to take just one example, a villager's purchase of a bar of soap in Assam could be signaled almost instantaneously to suppliers of palm oil and other soap ingredients in Malaysia.

Such real-time information flows would free up resources for use in exploiting other opportunities thrown up by the same new technologies and business models. "Imagine our factories being able to make today what was sold yesterday," says Banga. "It would save working capital throughout my suppliers. That is a paradigm shift."

India clearly has a steep slope to climb here: at the time of writing, less than five million Indians out of more than a billion own a computer, and less than a million subscribe to an internet service. But Hindustan Lever sees the underlying trend and is positioning itself to ride the wave. And initiatives like Hewlett-Packard's e-inclusion program can only accelerate progress in this area (panel 9, page 182).

STEALTH CAN KILL

Jump from India to a European country like Britain, and you find plenty more reasons why greater transparency is also now being demanded of major industries in the developed world. When the inquiry report on the BSE, or 'mad cow', crisis was published, for example, much of the blame was laid upon the civil service machinery of Whitehall. This was found to be riven by inter-departmental rivalries and, even worse, cloaked in unnecessary secrecy. It was characterized not simply by a lack of openness but by the active suppression of information.[56]

Instead of letting the real facts flow through the system, the final inquiry report concluded, the government had tried to protect the beef industry – and to limit the political repercussions – by continuously and vigorously reassuring the public that there was no danger from eating contaminated meat. In addition to highly-publicized stunts like Agriculture Minister John Gummer feeding a hamburger to his young daughter, the government pursued an approach designed to achieve the "sedation" of the public, to use the inquiry's own words.

In the scale of human crimes against humanity we obviously have seen infinitely worse. And we may also now be seeing the beginnings of a backlash against the whole 'victim culture', where people sue companies for sums of money which often seem totally disconnected from the scale of the damage caused – or, in some cases, from those most directly affected. In his book *The Holocaust Industry*, Norman Finkelstein even challenges what he describes as the financial exploitation of Jewish suffering during World War II.[57] His provocative tack was illustrated by the title of the book's first section: "Capitalizing the Holocaust". Unpleasant though they may sometimes be, such counter-challenges have to be seen as part of the process of maintaining a healthy, open society.

But, whatever the facts in the BSE case, there were real victims. By the time the inquiry report was published over four million cows had been destroyed and some 85 known victims of the linked Creutzfeldt–Jakob disease (CJD), of whom at least 75 had already died. These may be the tip of an iceberg of disease which will build in future years, though no one really knows. These may be small numbers when compared to the millions who died in concentration camps, perhaps, but almost every one of those CJD deaths could have been avoided if Britain had evolved a more transparent form of governance.

The same government failures also turned up within weeks when the UK's whole rail system went into spasm, following four deaths caused by a derailed train. This proved to be the tip of an iceberg, with subsequent work uncovering huge numbers of worn-out rails needing to be replaced. Indeed, once the news broke there were even leaked letters showing how a few months earlier the responsible company, Railtrack, had dismissed pressure from the regulator to deal with the problem as little more than a distraction.

The real question at issue, though, is not just who should have been responsible and can therefore be blamed for such tragedies. It has to do with governance systems, not just lines of accountability. As Will Hutton put it: "The issue is not that (Britain now possesses) a blame culture which fosters an impossible demand for risk-free travel or risk-free-eating, but the gut reaction of some, especially on the Right, which allows them to conclude that the system of governance can be excused its manifest shortcomings. For them, the problem is, instead, people."[58]

If developments in Britain are anything to go by, European countries will see growing demands for freedom of information legislation, along the lines long practiced in the United States. Where markets evolve under their own steam, it may be harder to point the finger and allocate blame, but where industries have been privatized relatively recently – as in the case with the British rail system – it is much easier. Privatized or not, however, the markets and industries of the 21st century will require and offer radically higher levels of transparency, information and accountability. Most business models that fail in this respect will fail. Period.

If companies need to think out of the box even to survive these days, shouldn't more of them be trying to raise their sights a little? Instead of simply seeing stakeholder dialogue and engagement as a means to ensure outsiders understand all the positive stuff that the media didn't pick up from the press releases, maybe we should be thinking of all of this as strategic? Thinking about what sort of company or organization we want to evolve into? What sort of partnerships we will need? And how we can get some of these people engaged in strategic conversations before our competitors get there first?

TOWARDS ULTRA-TRANSPARENCY

Even those CEOs who have made the effort to climb out of the bunker, to embrace the transparency revolution and early elements of the stakeholder governance agenda, can still be caught out. Partly this is a result of things moving too fast, but partly, too, it can be because they ignored early, weak signals.

And the speed issue can only get worse. Sky News front-man Jeremy Thompson still remembers the days when news was recorded on film and tape, then flown back to base. Increasingly, however, news-gatherers 'go live' from wherever they happen to be. "As the digital technology improves," says Thompson, "so too does the TV news broadcaster's mobility and ability to reach the stories deemed off the beaten track. On 24-hour rolling news channels live, breaking stories are the priorities. Get there first, tell the story live, stay with the drama."[59] One interesting side-effect: "There's precious little time, to stop, think and prepare."

So that's today's reality. But there are those who already see this level of transparency and immediacy as positively Stone Age. "During the next 50 years," says Peter Schwartz, chairman of the Global Business Network (GBN), "machines will get a billion times smaller, a billion times faster, and a billion times cheaper."[60] He invites us to try to contemplate the likelihood that "consequences too large to imagine may develop from devices too small to be seen."

Ultra-transparency is on its way (page 55). And the language is changing in response. Venture capitalist Jennifer Fonstad is not the only one talking in terms of "zero latency", and the prospect that before long we will all be immersed in real-time information.[61] Some of us will drown in data, while others will work out how to do old things in new ways, or how to do completely new things.

And we can count on the stakeholder hydra continuing to make unexpected uses of state-of-the-art technology. "It's ironic that we use the Internet," as protester Chelsea Mozen put it to the *Wall Street Journal* during the Prague demonstrations against the World Bank and IMF, because the internet is a globalizing force in its own right.[62]

Without designated leaders, new networks have coalesced to bring pressure to bear on those they see as driving or unduly benefiting from globalization. The net result is that a good deal of power is flowing away from businesses and government. Big companies and the institutions of global governance alike have become very much more vulnerable to globally networked protesters.

So, where next? Listen to John Gray, Professor of European Thought at the London School of Economics. "Business," he says, "has a vital interest in under-standing the values and goals of the critics of globalization for two reasons." First, he notes, the power of pressure groups to articulate and shape the public mind is often greater than that of any political party. And they can exert a leverage on events that is greater than that available to most governments. Second, though, he also points out that the power available to protesters "is to a large extent the power of veto." They can sometimes prevent things happening, but they have many fewer opportunities for more constructive interaction.

And that's where stakeholder processes fit in. Companies that can successfully compete for the attention and positive – if still challenging – engagement of those shaping the agenda potentially have a strategic advantage. They have new forms of market intelligence. They can test out new concepts or business models for potential problems, before investing to the point where they are virtually locked in. And they can build strategic alliances with some NGOs and other partners to begin shaping political agendas and markets in such a way that they support and reward companies investing in more sustainable technologies, products and services.

An interesting example of this trend was described to me by Alan Young of Mining Watch when I chaired the UN's first stakeholder consultation of the Global Compact (page 159), in Nairobi. "In British Columbia," he said, "a region known for its battles over forestry and mining, we have seen an excellent example of the co-operative development of solutions by environmental and corporate interests. The mining industry was worried about duplication conflict among provincial regulations covering such areas as waste management and mine reclamation. Rather than lobbying in the traditional way, the industry joined a small committee with government and environmental representatives. The result: better integration of the different Acts, the maintenance of key safeguards, and real progess towards more effective regulation."

COMPETING FOR MIND SHARE

The emerging economy really is different. We see growing displays of so-called 'weak power', in which activists, citizens or consumers turn the old order on its head – often as much to their own surprise as to that of their victims.[63] Governments are losing control of their citizens, and companies are losing control of their customers and consumers. No one is arguing that rioters should be given immediate access to corporate boardrooms, but their evolving agendas should be monitored carefully and continuously.

As Kevin Kelly put it in his book *New Rules for the New Economy*, "the only thing becoming scarce in a world of abundance is human attention."[64] This is a new game for most companies, often requiring new attention-grabbing and communication skills. But progress is being made on many fronts. Growing numbers of companies are diving in, many of them producing corporate environmental, social and even so-called sustainability reports.

Indeed, while researching *The Chrysalis Economy*, my colleagues and I were carrying out the first-ever survey of corporate sustainability reporting, worldwide. The work was done for the United Nations, against the backdrop of an emerging reporting standard (the Global Reporting Initiative), and focused both on printed reports and web-based reporting. The results are headlined in box 12 (below).

Ultimately, we have learned to pursue what my friend and colleague Geoff Lye has called the 'Hierarchy of Engagement' (Figure 9.2). Many companies still operate at the basic levels of communication, such as advertising, lobbying and surveying. At best, such activities build awareness, but they rarely promote real understanding and commitment, let alone significant changes in behavior.

To ensure that we move through these higher levels of engagement, we need to learn how to consult, co-operate and collaborate across agendas and across cultures. The best way to do this is through shared learning and shared projects. We expect to see growing numbers of companies moving in this direction, but in the process they will need to pay much greater attention to the integration of their own thinking, strategies and initiatives.

Box 12: Blips on the screen

The global reporters

When SustainAbility carried out the first-ever international survey of corporate sustainability reporting, the results showed striking developments in the field.[65] From the perspective of the 1980s, even the 1990s, dramatic progress had been made. But a huge – and growing – challenge remains. Among the key conclusions:

- The initial focus on corporate environmental reporting is opening out to embrace the economic, social and environmental dimensions of business performance
- European companies are leading the charge in terms of voluntary triple bottom line reporting
- Among the Top 50 reporting companies, a third (32 percent) mentioned sustainability, the triple bottom line or corporate citizenship on their front page
- Of the three dimensions of corporate performance, environmental performance is covered most comprehensively, while

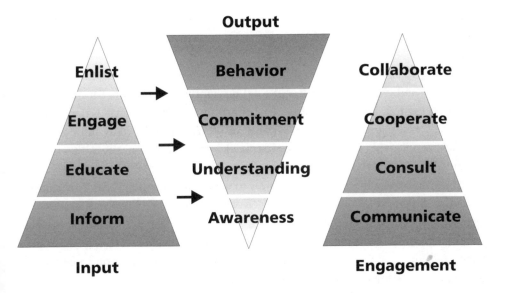

Figure 9.2 The Hierarchy of Engagement.
Source: SustainAbility.

    the lowest scores in the benchmarking process were received for coverage of economic, and social and ethical performance
- That said, reports still frequently leave out some of the most important sustainability impacts associated with companies' activities – and nearly all of them fail to systematically address companies' activities and impact upon the developing world
- Reporting companies still represent a small fraction of the tens of thousands of major multinational corporations doing business around the world, let alone of the millions of medium and small-sized enterprises.

But the uncomfortable fact remains that companies get a lot more media attention when they slip up than when they launch a new sustainability report. So, for example, at the same time that one team at Nike was working on the company's first-ever sustainability report, another had used the Sydney Olympics to launch a new advertising campaign – featuring a woman being pursued by a man with a chain-saw.[66] The ad, apparently intended as a spoof on slasher movie *The Texas Chain-Saw Massacre*, was seen by many viewers as playing on women's fears. The US TV network NBC, which had exclusive rights to screen the Olympics, banned the commercial.

The business challenge is not simply to get attention, but to get the attention you need – and then to sustain it. Nike did brilliantly on that score for many years. Indeed, some folk are now turning all of this into a science. "Getting the attention you need" was the title of a recent paper in the *Harvard Business Review*.[67] With business people and consumers alike barraged with information, the authors noted, we are all "on the verge of an acute attention deficit disorder."

All sorts of advice are given on how to handle the "disorder". So, for example: "Manage attention knowing that it's a zero-sum game. There's only so much to go around." We are told to focus down on a single critical topic, to send the message through multiple media channels, to use narrative and storytelling to engage people's emotions, and so on. But what happens when the messages are meant to be coming the other way, from the outside world into the company?

Since the mid-1980s, I have worked on a series of stakeholder engagement projects for clients such as BP, Procter & Gamble, Novo Nordisk, ICI, Shell, Cargill Dow, Ford and Nike. I also recently co-chaired a stakeholder session for the French waste company SITA, in Paris. With 60,000 employees, the company operates no less than 76 incinerators, 224 landfills and 117 sorting plants in 23 countries.[68] The session went well, which is more than can be said for a subsequent event, in London.

Apparently, the invitation for this London event read: "Is SITA sustainable?" What was later described as a "four-hour lunch," offered four courses at the Dorchester Hotel, with just 15 minutes allowed for questions. Groups like Friends of the Earth were kept at arm's length. Not surprising, perhaps, given that Greenpeace was in the second day of its occupation of SITA's flagship UK facility, the Edmonton incinerator. Scaling the smokestack, they managed to shut the plant for a week, draping it with a large banner proclaiming "London Cancer Factory".

When I later asked SITA CEO Jacques Pètry whether the company fell between the Locust and Caterpillar categories, he accepted the classification. "Values have not been strongly related to value creation in the waste sector," he admitted, leading to poor environmental performance. A key problem for companies trying to adopt higher standards has been that the barriers to entry are very low. But he stressed that SITA was firmly committed to the sustainability agenda. "We plan to walk the talk," he stressed.

Recalling an earlier debate within SITA about whether to use the term corporate social responsibility or sustainable development, I asked whether the company planned to adopt the CSR or SD lexicon. "Given that translations of both terms into French are unsatisfactory," he said, "we may end up using the triple bottom line!"

But what about that last stakeholder session in London? "We have a potential difficulty with integrating the more 'terrorist' stakeholders into the process of stakeholder engagement," he replied. Allowing for the perils of French–English translation, Pètry's reply still underscores the different attitudes between the most effective corporate stakeholder engagers and the somewhat less effective. The best companies, in my experience, view it as a real coup if they can get groups like Friends of the Earth or Greenpeace around the table.

So what do external stakeholders look for when considering whether to engage a company? My own take on this approach is summarized below and in box 13. Experience suggests that most change agents work off something fairly similar, although often with a different spin reflecting their interests and priorities.

STAKEHOLDER FATIGUE

As corporate interest in engaging the NGO world has grown, however, so the risk of stakeholder fatigue has increased. Some NGOs have even begun to ask themselves whether some companies are viewing stakeholder dialogue sessions simply as a cheap form of consultancy, of finding what is going on in the outside world?[69] "We are now much more choosy about the stakeholder dialogues we get involved in," explains Fiona King, international advocacy coordinator at Save the Children. "There is a slight sense of it all being a one-way flow (of information and expertise), with all the flow going into companies, which are already very well resourced."

So here are some basic principles that we find make for successful engagement, even with some of the world's most demanding stakeholders:

- First, make sure you *invite in at least some difficult voices*, not just the easy ones. Anyone can build an echo chamber, but the result may be a dangerous cocooning, or insulation from reality. Feel able to provide some information under conditions of confidentiality, but accept that this side of the process is rather more one-way than you might like: you have to ensure your people do not breach confidentiality, but you can almost guarantee that one or more of the visitors, intentionally or not, will fail to observe the confidentiality rules once back in their own world.

- Second, *ensure that your engagement is not just a one-off*, with a single mega-meeting followed by silence. The best engagement often flows from ongoing, low-key discussions, focused on real issues, in the context of mutually agreed principles for engagement.

- Third, *don't be afraid to ask stakeholders to co-evolve the process* and to agree shared priorities. Their time is limited, too, and most will also want to cut to the chase.

- Fourth, *field your very best people*. If your chair, CEO or president isn't going to be able to make the key meetings, at least for some of the time, ask whether the process is really going to change anything inside your organization? Equally, make sure you get some of your young, committed people into the process, too, and give them air time.

- Fifth, *co-evolve and embrace standards*. These provide a vital framework for discussions and negotiations. Among emergent standards in this area, as we saw in box 11 (page 157) are: CEP's SA8000; the Global Reporting Initiative (GRI), launched by CERES; and AA1000, the accountability standard developed by the Institute for Social and Ethical Accountability (ISEA).

- Sixth, *go interactive*. Study what leading companies have done to set up interactive processes and web-sites. Shell's Camisea project in Peru didn't come to fruition, for example, but the web-site is a model of how to handle the virtual side of stakeholder engagement.

- Seventh, *be prepared to make real changes in your project, company or business model*. If you are not prepared to make such changes, don't waste your scarce resources of money, time and effort – nor those of your stakeholders. Once lead them up the garden path, and it's going to be very much next time around.

 Box 13: Blips on the screen

Do they *really* get it?

As competition for scarce stakeholder attention and time grows, business people need to know how stakeholders judge the trustworthiness and interest of companies wanting to engage them. Indeed, young colleagues have often asked me how I decide whether we should work with a particular company, CEO or management team. Here's what I tell them.

First, different people use different ways of assessing companies, corporate cultures and the quality of leadership. Most are valid – and we all tend to rely on other people's assessments to test our own conclusions. My own style, though, is fairly intuitive.

Sometimes it hasn't worked out as expected, as when we ended up resigning a major contract with Monsanto (page 108). Not that such reverses are absolute failures – above all, this is a learning process and we must all be willing to take risks, push the envelope, experiment. And to report back on progress.

Second, my intuitions are probably based on more inputs than the previous paragraph might suggest. So here are some of the things that feed into the equation:

- To begin with, a critical question: *Is this a company, industry or value web that potentially has real leverage (for good or ill) in terms of the sustainability agenda? If not, should we even be thinking of engaging with them?*
- If the answer is "yes", it triggers a series of other questions. For example: *Does this company or organization have a champion, or champions, for some or all of the triple bottom line agenda?*
- And this question would rapidly be followed by others: *What are these people like as individuals? How much passion and energy do they bring to their work? How genuine do they seem in their willingness to engage both inside and outside their organizations? Would it be interesting – fun – to work with them?*
- Then there would be top team questions: *Is the top management team in or out of the bunker? How soon can we meet them? Who has ultimate responsibility in this area? How do they see their accountability?*
- If you are kicking off with members of the top team, as is increasingly usual, you will want to know: *Do these people have a grasp of the Big Picture? Do they have a real feel for complexity? And is there any humor in the meeting?* (Used in the right way, humor can signal not a lack of seriousness about real problems so much as a willingness to engage and play with creative ideas and innovative solutions.)
- You will want to ask: *What is your strategy? How do triple bottom line issues fit in? What management systems and frameworks have you developed? What standards have you adopted?*

- And: *What sort of toolbox are you using? Impact assessments? Audits? Life-cycle assessments? Eco-efficiency tools? Scenarios?*
- And: *How innovative are you in the areas of new product development and supply-chain management? What new business models are you exploring?*
- And: *How much of this do you report publicly? Is your reporting verified, available on the internet, or even online and in real-time?*
- And: *How are you defining and engaging your key stakeholders? What sort of priorities have emerged from these processes? How do you give feedback? What are you doing to engage Wall Street and the other major financial centers?*

Like it or not, outline answers to such questions can flash into the brain in seconds. And companies often unwittingly give you key pieces of the jigsaw. One major company in the process of committing itself to sustainability, and asking for our help, told us how their president had encouraged the retail industry in the relevant sector to consider taking competitors' products off their shelves. They weren't aware until later of the switches that had flipped to 'off' in our brains.

PANEL 9

$1 billion bet

"We're at the beginning of a second Renaissance," said Carly Fiorina, as chairman, president and CEO of Hewlett-Packard (HP). This, she argued, will be the Digital Renaissance. The focus will be on helping individuals unlock "their richest core asset, a great idea, a great invention." The internet and related technologies, she said, "hold the promise of rapid, sustainable economic growth that directly benefits everyone on the planet." Not so, counter some critics, arguing that these new technologies are aggravating the 'have/have not' divide, worldwide. Increasingly, they believe, we will face an unbridgeable 'digital divide', with enormous social and political implications.

Whatever, no one would accuse Fiorina of being blind to the challenge. "The same forces," she accepted, "could also exacerbate social and economic disparities. How much of each the world will see depends to some degree on how companies like HP approach sustainability and the deployment of technology across markets, cultures and continents." She noted that we are all now "in a single global ecosystem, wired, connected, overlapping and bumping into one another, benefiting from each others' successes, and suffering each others' failures." Massively exposed, in short, to the Butterfly Effect.

"Complexity theory tells us that the imbalance and asymmetry will resolve itself in time," she noted. "either through negative resolutions like war, or disease, or economic breakdown, or through positive solutions, like the breaking down of barriers, the opening up of systems, the movement of wealth and knowledge and personal opportunity, and fulfillment, to a more balanced geographic distribution."

To nudge things along, HP has launched a new strategy, dubbed 'World e-Inclusion', extending HP's business focus to include traditionally excluded markets. The emphasis will be on "sustainable business ventures" designed to improve the livelihoods of the roughly four billion people on low incomes in Africa, Asia, Central and Eastern Europe, and Latin America.

Speaking (by video-link) at the World Resource Institute (WRI)'s 'Digital Dividends' conference in Seattle, Fiorina said that in the following year alone HP would target $1 billion of HP and partner products and services to be sold, leased or donated through special programs. The extraordinarily ambitious plan also includes enlisting the help of one million partners for the program, which is designed to provide benefits to at least 1,000 villages.

So what will all of this mean on the ground? Fiorina instanced one Peruvian village where a computer, big screen monitor and satellite dish were recently installed, with the result that the leader's hut now doubles as a tribal cyber café and the villagers have used the Net to sell organically grown oranges in Lima, 250 miles to the east. "Sustainable solutions and models," Fiorina concluded, "respect social and cultural mores – and idiosyncrasies." What differentiates HP's approach to bridging the digital divide," explained Debra Dunn, VP for strategy and corporate operations, "is that we're focused on people, not technology. We are working with a broad range of partners who share our vision and values to provide solutions that are economically sustainable, culturally sensitive, and environmentally friendly."

In Costa Rica, working with the Foundation for Sustainable Development – itself led by former President José María Figueres Olsen – HP is helping develop telecenters for remote villages. Housed in recycled shipping containers, they are equipped with solar-powered computers and high-speed internet connections. Among the other benefits potentially on the menu: telemedicine, education, information-based jobs, environmental monitoring, and access to markets and to microcredit and other financial services.

But how did HP get involved in all of this? Having heard Fiorina in Seattle, I flew on to Toronto, where I bumped into Jim Sheats, responsible for 'technology for sustainability' at HP. It turned out that in 1997 he was part of an HP 'skunk-works', charged with investigating sustainability. He attended a session organized by Joe Laur and Sara Schley of SEED Systems, which in turn sparked networking between a number of companies involved in evolving sustainability strategies. Eventually, some of this stuff was written into one of Fiorina's speeches. And the rest, as they say, is history.

Interestingly, however, the WRI conference was closed by Microsoft's Bill Gates. And he had a very different view on what the world's poorest people need. "The world's poorest two billion people desperately need healthcare, not laptops," he said. "Computers are amazing in what they can do," he noted, "but they have to be put in the context of human values." He recalled that when he had started giving away his fortune six years earlier, he had been "naïve, very naïve."

At the time, Gates recalled, he had expected computers and information technology to make up the bulk of his donations. But something like two-thirds of his $21 billion Bill and Melinda Gates Foundation's assets would now be targeted on Third World healthcare, including the development and distribution of vaccines.

No one denies that a mother with a dying child is hardly going to welcome a computer, nor that much high-tech equipment parachuted to date into developing countries has gone to waste. But some of Gates' competitors felt that he had missed the point. "After listening to three days of serious analysis and work, and then to have Gates rather flippantly say, 'You've got to have clean water and food' – that wasn't exactly the point of the entire meeting," retorted John Gage, chief research officer at Sun Microsystems. So where's Gage coming from? Well, he heads Netday, a charity that aims to wire the world's classrooms to the Net.

And a last word from Fiorina? "Sustainable solutions create their own momentum," she insisted. Let's hope so. As *The Chrysalis Economy* went to press, HP was once again in trouble with Wall Street over its failure to meet Fiorina's ambitious targets. It remains to be seen whether she can once again make HP the management icon it once was, for six decades.[70]

CHAPTER 10

Integration

integration / n. **1** the act or an instance of integrating. **2** the intermixing of person or things previously segregated. **3** *the process of reconfiguring a business, organization or market system to ensure sound, consistent performance against the triple bottom line.*

His name was Clarence. He was married, tired and dying. But, tired or not, when asbestos worker Clarence Borel walked into the offices of a legal firm in a small Texan town to ask for help, he unwittingly tipped over the first in a long line of financial dominoes that would eventually rock the world's best-known insurance market to its foundations.[71] Indeed, this single act triggered one of the most spectacular avalanches of industrial injury litigation the world has yet seen. Hundreds of people would lose millions of dollars each as a result, many committing suicide as a direct consequence.

The year: 1969. And the $79,000 compensation awarded to Borel's widow – his lungs were badly damaged and he died shortly after starting the legal process – would have been little more than a blip on the insurance industry's radar screen. But thirty-one years after Borel's visit it would be described as "the beat of a butterfly wing that was eventually to power a typhoon at the other side of the world."[72]

Risk – specifically the management of risk – has always been central to business. And the insurance industry has been one of the most spectacularly successful means by which the capitalist system has buffered risk, allowing ordinary citizens, entrepreneurs and companies alike to cope with the vagaries of life. The modern world simply could not function without insurance. But what happened to Lloyd's of London, the world's leading insurance center, spotlights the ways in which the financial sustainability of even such mighty institutions can be called into question by new risks linked to such issues as long-term health impacts or climate change.

The implications for many CEOs and their organizations are profound. As the sustainability agenda morphs the risks and opportunities they face, so they must learn how to engage the financial markets – and not just the insurers – in new ways. This is the fourth Herculean Labor. It involves bringing light to the benighted denizens of those modern Underworlds, Wall Street, London's City, and other major financial centers around the world.

ILLUMINATING THE UNDERWORLD

There has been a great deal of talk about corporate integration. You don't have to tell most business leaders that they need to reconfigure and rewire their organizations. They know they must pull people out of their silos, integrating not just internal policies, strategies and management systems, but also external – and increasingly complex – supply chains and value webs. In some cases, as with European agriculture in the wake of the "mad cow" and foot-and-mouth disease problems, the challenge is to reconfigure an entire market system.

It's a hopeful sign that growing numbers of CEOs are encouraging their organizations to internalize at least some of the externalities once imposed on society and the environment – although to date the pressures have more to do with compliance than with values. It's reassuring, too, that more are now opening up their organizations with challenging external stakeholder engagement processes. But the next step will be to sell all of this to insurers, lenders (including banks) and, most important of all in today's world, the analysts and institutions of Wall Street and other major financial centers.

This will not be an easy task. You might think that the problems faced by Lloyd's would have woken up the financial markets and institutions to the new risks and opportunities flowing from the environmental, corporate social responsibility and sustainability revolutions. A significant proportion of the liabilities that crippled Lloyd's resulted from ill-advised underwriting of risks related to asbestos, contaminated land, radioactive waste and other forms of pollution. But despite the bankruptcy of so many of the 'Names' who supply capital to Lloyd's (box 14, page 189), and despite the collapse of a fair number of insurance syndicates that had incurred these liabilities, financial markets and institutions also often seem to operate in silos of their own.

To get a sense of the integration challenge facing CEOs and other business leaders, let's consider six waves of change that have already hit the business world, or are in the process of doing so. Each wave started off as a weak, distant signal on corporate radar screens, then built to the point where it turned into something worthy of *The Perfect Storm*, with massive impacts on the business world. Taken individually, each of these waves would have been a challenge, but taken together they have triggered revolutionary corporate changes. In some cases, the financial markets have driven the changes; in others, they have been borne along on the waves, currents and tides.

Box 14: Blips on the screen

Names led into abyss

Hercules went down into the Underworld and brought back its three-headed guardian, Cerberus. He was lucky to get away with it. In recent decades, an extraordinary roll-call of actors, pop singers, sporting celebrities, politicians, business people, a wide range of professionals and minor members of the British royal family have been dragged into a hellish financial abyss as Lloyd's of London threatened to implode.[73]

The people who bankroll Lloyds are the so-called 'Names', of whom there were around 7,000 in the 1970s. The idea is that their wealth is used to underwrite risks. If something goes wrong for a particular insurance syndicate, then the relevant Names are called upon to pay. In good times, this can be a highly lucrative business, and people can be misled into believing that Lloyd's is little more than a money machine for Names. But when things go badly wrong for the insurers, the Names are liable – almost literally down to the shirts on their backs.

I confess that when I first heard how the game was played, I concluded that the problems facing the Names were simply inevitable fall-out from ill-informed greed. Indeed, in the early 1980s, I had challenged some of those carrying out early environmental 'audits' of US businesses for UK insurers – arguing that it seemed naïve to base insurance risk estimates on half-day visits to companies whose managers had every reason to conceal potential problems.

Then the issue came closer to home. Years ago, I was invited to join The Environment Foundation as a trustee. The Foundation, which I was next invited to chair in the mid-1990s, was originally funded by monies raised as a percentage of premiums paid by companies insuring themselves against environmental and health liabilities. The relevant insurance syndicates were massively affected by the asbestos and other environment-related liabilities that came home to roost in recent decades – and a number of my co-trustees were hard hit financially as a consequence.

Over time, I learned to see the whole saga differently. Insurance, I came to understand, is essential to the operation of healthy market economies. But it also became increasingly clear that Lloyd's had not been a healthy system for some time. Indeed a group of dissident Names have argued that the Lloyd's – whose motto *Uberimma Fides* means Utmost Good Faith – had displayed anything but.

They contend that the Lloyd's ruling council, behind a "cocoon of secrecy", not only knew that asbestos and pollution problems had rendered Lloyd's technically insolvent – but that they responded by recruiting enormous numbers of new Names. The indisputable fact is that the original 7,000 Names had jumped to over 32,000 by the late 1980s. There are even allegations that the new money was selectively funneled into the problem syndicates, guaranteeing disaster for Names who had no idea that the odds were totally stacked against them.

The moral of the tale would seem to be that a successful 21st century insurance market will be much more transparent, much more accountable, and very much more alert to the full range of risks generated by the impending sustainability transition. Climate change, for example, has unthinkable implications for some parts of the insurance business. But if it's any comfort to despairing Names, The Environment Foundation now focuses on the triple bottom line agenda – and in 2001 launched a five-year "Values for Sustainability" program.[74]

SIX WAVES OF INTEGRATION

Different companies and industries will have different memories of which waves of change hit them when, in what sequence, and with what results. But few major companies will have been unaffected by most, if not all, of the following transformations outlined below. In each case, even the best companies suffered from some form of 'integration gap'. The six are: environment, health and safety (EHS; also sometimes HSE or SHE), total quality management (TQM), information technology (IT), shareholder value added (SVA), corporate social responsibility

(CSR) and sustainable development (SD). Potentially, at least, sound responses to the first five challenges can help companies lay the foundations for tackling the business end of the sixth.

Integrating EHS

Core message: protect the health of people and planet!
Unless they were in the midst of a disaster, most CEOs and boards have seen the environment, health and safety (EHS) agenda as peripheral. Many persist in that view. But, whether or not we are prepared to pay more, most of us want to be reasonably confident that the products we buy and use have been produced in ways that are safe, healthy and, as far as possible, environment-friendly. The EHS agenda, which hit hardest such sectors as mining, chemicals, oil and gas, nuclear power and tobacco, focused on safety, health and – in due course – the environment.

There may not have been a health and safety revolution as such, although every major industrial disaster drove these issues higher up the political and management agendas. But there most certainly was an Environmental Revolution. Some companies labeled their combined initiatives EHS (for environment, health and safety), others HSE, yet others SHE. We will adopt EHS here, for alphabetical reasons as much as anything else, but – while the acronyms may have differed – the underlying agenda has pretty much been the same.

In terms of immediacy, safety was usually the number one priority, followed by spreading circles of health concerns (from workers, through consumers to others potentially affected by later stages in a product's life-cycle) and then, ultimately, environmental issues. And that 'ultimately' was itself sometimes an issue. Indeed a number of companies, concerned that the immediacy of health and safety concerns could overshadow the environmental agenda, actually split the E out from the HS, as a separate unit, to give the environment a 'bit more oxygen'.

The 1970s and 1980s saw growing numbers of companies adopting their first written policy statements in this area, while the 1990s saw leading companies beginning to stress eco-efficiency[75] and build EHS considerations into their strategies and their merger and acquisition (M&A) activities. Indeed, a business slated for acquisition these days is likely to be subjected to increasingly rigorous due diligence audits by prospective purchasers. And a group company slated for sale, at least by a reputable group, will often be re-configured (in what Shell Chemicals has graphically described as a 'carve out' process) to ensure that EHS management systems are transferred an integral part of the operations sold.

The integration gap here often reflected that the EHS professionals were generally good at the professional and technical aspects of their jobs, such as building management systems, but simply were not trained – or in some cases even suitable – to help top executives integrate these concerns and priorities into corporate strategy and governance systems. Often, too, EHS systems were divorced from other key functions, among them community relations, government affairs and investor relations. In short, EHS professionals were kept in their silos. Consultants talked of a 'green wall'. Not the best way, clearly, to ensure a quality outcome.

Integrating TQM

Core message: boost quality, as defined by your customers!

Quality, on the other hand, has become a board priority in a growing number of companies. Whether or not we spend much time thinking about quality as consumers, most of us appreciate products that do what we expect them to do, and do so reliably. If we buy a car, we don't want rust breaking through its panels after a year or two in use. If we buy a TV, we would prefer it didn't burst into flames. But many products have done just this, or worse. So this second great wave of integration, which in the western world reached its first major peak in the early 1990s, focused on quality.

Many of the pioneers saw themselves as quiet revolutionaries. Their language included such terms as *total quality management* (TQM), *quality circles, continuous improvement* and *zero defects*. The TQM movement first took root in Japan, then spread as western companies tried to work out why their Japanese competitors were wiping the floor with them in one sector after another.

Increasingly, many leading companies came to see their environmental, health and safety activities as a subset of their quality activities. So, for example, some companies began to talk of TQEM, or total quality *environmental* management. This trend was reinforced as quality standard organizations, like the International Standards Organization (ISO), developed and promoted standards covering such non-traditional areas as environmental management.

The TQM movement has brought many benefits. In the sense that TQM helps cut waste – what the Japanese call *muda* – throughout the value web, this is certainly true, but there are many cases where the results have been counter-intuitive. The 'just-in-time' (JIT) aspects of TQM, for example, have resulted in considerable air quality and traffic congestion problems. The reason is that companies have slimmed down their own storage and warehousing facilities, instead relying on JIT deliveries from suppliers, involving endlessly shuttling truck fleets which are often only partly laden.

Like all great waves, the quality surge eventually showed signs of fading. There was growing concern that many TQM initiatives had failed to produce the desired results, for a number of different reasons. Once again, the integration gap was a contributory factor. So-called 'quality councils' were often made up of staff quality professionals, rather than core management team people, with direct profit-and-loss responsibilities. As a result, like many of the EHS programs before them, these initiatives started out – or ended up – stuck out on the periphery.

One powerful response to early TQM failures was the 'Six Sigma' approach, pioneered by Jack Welch at GE and picked up by a number of other leading companies. There are a number of key characteristics of this approach: the lead comes from the very top of the organization; there is a simple, consistently repeated message, coupled with clear stretch targets; direct links are made between progress towards these targets and both business and personal bottom lines (with significant proportions of staff bonuses linked to indicators of progress); 'silo-busting' is seen as critical; and great attention is paid both to tools and to learning and training.[76]

Let's zero in on two aspects of this approach: silo-busting and learning. These are important in tackling all six challenges outlined here.

- So, first, silo-busting. Once the lack of integration was recognized as a key barrier, GE and other Six Sigma companies put silo-busting high on their priority lists. When the focus is on the management and improvement of cross-functional processes, it's hardly surprising that the result tends to be more efficient and effective companies.

- And, second, learning. Rather than just talking about 'learning', some companies have been making major investments in training and other forms of learning. GE's so-called 'Blackbelts', who have led the Six Sigma charge, are given three weeks of training, with follow-up exams and continued learning through conferences and other forums.

Integrating IT

Core message: get wired!

Even more than the TQM revolution, the information technology (IT) revolution has turned the cosy world of corporate boards on its head. Directors have had no choice but to become more IT-literate – or get out.[77]

Like it or not, computers have massively invaded our lives, although the process has still barely begun. Distrust all predictions, but the US Bureau of Labor

Statistics forecast a 117 percent jump in IT positions between 1998 and 2008, making it by far the fastest-growing sector of the economy.[78]

As most people understand it, the IT revolution really started in the 1970s, took off through the 1980s, and exploded in the 1990s. More column inches have been devoted to IT in the world business media in recent years than to almost any other topic. One reason has been the extraordinary pace of development in the underlying technologies, which has often meant that companies have had to write off major investments as they became obsolescent almost overnight. For the most part, we welcome the process, although few of us have escaped the downsides of the IT revolution, including computer errors, crashes and virus attacks.

The early challenges of picking the right hardware and software were hard enough, with the many companies appointing Chief Information Officers (CIOs), or similar. In the process, computers, networks, intranets and the internet all became indispensable parts of the EHS and TQM worlds. And now they are also on the same sort of growth curves in the closely linked fields of shareholder value added (SVA), corporate social responsibility (CSR) and sustainable development (SD), of which more in a moment.

The integration gaps here were many and various, but perhaps the biggest was the failure of many companies – including some employing CIOs – to spot the logical next step. Those who saw IT as simply a way of making business operations more efficient suddenly found a wave of new economy entrants, most notably the dotcoms, carving up established competitors by linking innovative uses of IT to new business models. The case of Hindustan Lever shows that this pressure can be at least as great in the emerging markets and developing world as it is in the developed world (page 172).

But the curve of acceleration shows no sign of abating even in the rich world. "In rapid succession the deregulation of telecommunications, the miniaturization of satellites, and the development of mobile technologies have made connection available to anyone, anytime, anyplace," Stan Davis and Christopher Meyer noted in their book *Blur*.[79] "Now, with the explosive takeoff of the Internet, we've entered the second half of the information economy, which uses the computer less for data crunching and more for connecting people: people to people, machine to machine, product to service, network to network, organization to organization, and all the combinations thereof."

One US company that has embraced e-business with a will is Caterpillar, best known for its earth-moving and construction equipment.[80] So if Caterpillar isn't itself a Corporate Locust, it helps Locusts do what they do. The company has created an internet-based electronic marketplace, using software from i2 Technologies, a leading B2B software house. The goal of the exercise is to drive costs out of Caterpillar's business operations through faster product introduction cycles, better design collaboration with suppliers, improved inventory management, and more cost-effective ordering and fulfillment processes. In the first year of operation, Caterpillar hoped to save $100 million.

But as the connected economy evolves, the implications for manufacturers are likely to be profound. "Today's manufacturers cannot just build a product, ship it and forget about it," says Bob Espey, an e-business consultant with the Computer Sciences Corporation (CSC).[81] "They must think in terms of the whole product life cycle – and gather information to feed back into design improvements."

Digital factories and much more dynamic digital supply chains open up the possibility of existing companies – or, more often, new ones – offering consumers and customers cradle-to-grave (or, even better, cradle-to-cradle) solutions, ensuring that end-of-life products are reclaimed and recycled. And the key market benefit for the producer is that it gets an early warning from the customer when a new product is likely to be needed.

Clearly, the integration of IT systems can help with integrating the EHS, TQM, SVA, CSR and SD agendas also discussed here. So, for example, in the EHS field many multinational corporations are now using integrated internet and web-based technologies to pull together their auditing, permit tracking, emissions monitoring, training and cost assessment activities. Companies like Alcoa, Hewlett-Packard and Seagram have been installing intranets for ISO 14001 systems in plants around the world.[82] Union Carbide uses a networked program to consolidate its 200 different environmental reporting systems into a single system that can be accessed by 4,000 users across 27 sites. And AT&T and Dow Chemical are among those now using internet systems for EHS training.

Integrating SVA

Core message: build shareholder value!

However much some of us may believe in various forms of stakeholder engagement, even 'stakeholder governance', investors and shareholders are the ultimate owners of companies. The shareholder value movement of recent years makes the obvious point that such companies should be run with their interests in mind.[83] Many shareholder value campaigners argue that companies should maximize financial returns, while others believe that the focus should be on maximizing wealth. Whatever, a key task of corporate governance mechanisms is to keep managers focused on shareholder interests, and incentivizing them with shares or share options has become a common way of achieving this.

Anyone who has a pension policy based on shares clearly has a vested interest in the success of the shareholder value revolution. But, while we may assume that companies have always kept investor and shareholder interests in mind, it's simply not true. The spread of public companies through the 19th century led to increasingly bureaucratic forms of capitalism, sometimes dubbed 'managerial capitalism'. By the 1970s, as a result, executives running many major corporations were no longer pursuing shareholder interests; instead, they were treating them pretty much as baronial fiefdoms. The result was that a great deal of their effort went into enhancing their own power, status and remuneration.

Big was seen as beautiful. Companies like Daimler-Benz evolved into a "sprawling empire, spanning automobiles, aerospace, trains, electrical engineering, services and much besides, but, in the process, billions of Deutsche Marks were poured down the drain."[84] German conglomerates included Mannesmann, Preussag, Siemens, Veba and Viag. In Britain, there were BTR, Hanson and BP, the latter embracing everything from mines and nutrition businesses to salmon farms. The shareholder value movement was largely a reaction to this lack of focus – and the consequent destruction of value.

Shareholder value approaches typically concentrate on a limited number of strategies. Among other things, they stress the need to maximize returns on existing capital invested (by cost cutting, improving service or boosting sales), optimizing the use of the capital employed (either by expanding the business if it is earning more than the cost of capital, or shrinking it where it is earning less), minimizing the cost of capital (gearing up the company, reducing risk, or improving communications with the financial markets), and optimizing the business portfolio (for example, acquire when $2 + 2 = 5$, sell when $2 + 2 = 3$).[85]

Again, the integration gaps are many and various. Managers once saw (and some still see) businesses as almost having a divine right to exist and survive, whereas shareholder value campaigners (including the proponents of the shareholder value added model, page 64) have taken a more realistic view. Businesses that are weak should be radically overhauled, spun off or shut down, they argue. Some of the world's most financially successful companies, such as GE, have managed to infuse their entire corporate culture with just this sort of thinking.

Clearly, at least done in the right way, the results can lead to dramatic growth and very much higher returns to shareholders and other investors. Many critics of this approach argue that shareholder value is achieved at the cost of other stakeholders, but excellent companies recognize that they cannot build returns and wealth at the cost of others without putting the whole process at risk.

Integrating CSR

Core message: be socially responsible!

Inevitably, however, the shareholder value revolution has triggered a reaction. The growing focus on corporate social responsibility (CSR), for example, has noted that at least some companies stressing shareholder returns have tended to downplay community, employee, human rights and environmental priorities, among others. CSR advocates see themselves as redressing the balance. To buttress their case, they point out that: of the world's 100 largest economies, 50 are now corporations; the world's largest corporations employ only 0.05 percent of the world's population, but control 25 percent of the world's economic output; and recent EU research has shown that 58 percent of the general public believe that industry and commerce do not pay enough attention to their social responsibilities.[86]

'Stakeholder capitalism' is one phrase that has been used to label this new movement – and, inevitably, it has been seen as a potentially powerful rival to the SVA movement. This approach is based on the idea that shareholders are far from the only people with a legitimate interest in what corporations do. Employees, local communities, customers, suppliers and a whole host of other groups also have a direct or indirect 'stake' in the present and future performance of a given business.

Critics of the stakeholder approach argue that it is too fuzzy, that a company that is accountable to just about everybody ends up being accountable to nobody. Clearly, there are real risks here, but the CSR and SD movements argue that business must acknowledge and embrace new forms of accountability in the 21st century. As we saw in Chapter 8, there is a whole raft of new standards designed to help (or force) companies to move in this direction.

A host of new organizations has evolved to develop and promote the new agenda. In addition to NGOs like Amnesty International, Greenpeace International and Transparency International, there have also been growing numbers of business-led organizations, among them Business for Social Responsibility (BSR), Business in the Community (BitC), Business in the Environment (BiE) and CSR Europe.

Now these organizations and campaigns are beginning to cross-link. While writing this chapter, for example, I took part in a conference featuring what was billed as the first trans-Atlantic satellite link-up between BSR and CSR Europe. The CSR Europe people aim to boost both social cohesion and social innovation. In response to a call by the recent Lisbon European Council Summit for Europe to develop a dynamic knowledge-based economy, capable of sustaining more growth, with more and better jobs, and with greater social cohesion by 2010, a new European

CSR campaign has been launched. Focusing on the world of enterprise, government and civil society, this is due to climax in 2005 with a 'Special European Year on Corporate Social Responsibility'.

The integration gaps for companies seeking to understand and respond to the CSR agenda are many and diverse, reflecting the diversity of the CSR agenda itself. A growing number of corporate social reports discuss how the Values Barrier is best tackled, and the component initiatives best integrated. "One of the most significant outcomes of our 1997 social audit was the decision to develop a corporate-wide ethical policy to keep us true to our values as we respond to changes and challenges in our industry," was the way Greg McDade (Chair) and Dave Mowat (CEO) put it at Vancouver's pioneering city savings credit union, VanCity.[87] And it's no accident that their latest social report was titled *Guided by Values*.

Integrating SD

Core message: perform against the triple bottom line!

SD requires progress in all of the previous five areas of expectation and performance. The much-discussed 'sustainable corporation' may be something of a Holy Grail, but as a minimum it would involve pushing towards zero in many areas: zero defects, zero waste, zero pollution, and, longer term, zero ethical stumbles. As previous chapters have illustrated, the specific risks and opportunities flowing from the SD agenda, and the strategies most likely to succeed, will reflect the particular markets a given business serves.

So, for example, when Monsanto first dived into the sustainability domain, it set up seven working teams. They covered eco-efficiency, full-cost accounting, performance monitoring, new products and business opportunities, water, global hunger, and internal sustainability training and culture change. The number of working groups and the subjects tackled will vary between companies, but the approach remains valid – despite the problems subsequently experienced by Monsanto (page 108).

The benefits of integrating the SD agenda are suggested in Figure 10.1, developed by consultants ADL and Shell International.[88] Done in the right way, SD can maximize the value of four business levers: cost reduction, option creation, customer acquisition and retention, and risk reduction. Simultaneously, it can enhance a company's reputation as organization of first choice with shareholders, employees, customers, business partners and society in general. SustainAbility's mapping of the domains over which SD strategies can dig up such 'buried treasure' is shown in box 15 (page 199).

If markets are to work for sustainability, extraordinary efforts will be demanded from politicians, opinion formers, and business leaders. A key driver of change will be the fear that those who fail in the transition will see economic value migrating to those who succeed. The central challenge for the next few decades will be to make markets work strongly and consistently in support of SD objectives and targets.

Those campaigning for TBL performance need to become 'market makers', bringing business models and technologies that have so far been on the periphery of the modern world directly into the mainstream. However we may wish it otherwise, sustainable corporations and value-webs will rarely evolve spontaneously. Instead, their development will require well-directed governmental intervention and focused market pressures, sustained over decades.

 ## Box 15: Blips on the screen

Buried treasure online

The environmental, CSR and SD communities have long tried to uncover the hidden links between corporate leadership in these areas and business value creation – the 'buried treasure' referred to the title in a recent SustainAbility report for the UN.[89]

Based on our Sustainable Business Value Model™, the aim is to offer a user-friendly map of the state of the evidence linking ten dimensions of SD performance with ten more traditional measures of business case, including financial results, such as shareholder value and financial drivers, such as attractiveness to customers and corporate reputation.

Perhaps it's no accident that the SBV Matrix (Figure 10.2) looks like nothing so much as a 100-cell honeycomb. Companies that learn to create value right across this new domain will be the Corporate Honeybees of the future. Readers wanting to learn more should turn to the SustainAbility web-site: www.sustainability.com/business-case.

JOINING UP THE DOTS

Given the nature and scale of the SD challenge, the integration gaps in the business world are greater than they would be in all five of the previous integration challenges rolled together. So how confident should we be that we will tackle this challenge in

Actions			Benefits		
Build sustainable development issues on core values	Embed sustainable development in decision-making	Maximize value of business levers	Enhances reputation as organization of first choice	Attracts resources	Creates wealth
Natural capital	Management framework	Reduce costs	Shareholders	Capital	Shareholder value
Economic prosperity		Create options	Employees	Talent	Wealth for society
Social capital		Gain customers	Customers		
		Reduce risk	Society		
			Business partners		

Business principles (vertical, left axis) · *Business profits* (vertical, right axis)

Figure 10.1 Shell's view of the business case for SD.
Source: Shell International.

time and in good order? History suggests that we should be seriously worried. Time and again, we have failed to see the future coming, despite repeated warnings. Indeed, there is much we can learn from some of the major military intelligence blunders of the 20th century.

Think of the Russians before Hitler launched Operation Barbarossa in 1941, the Americans at Pearl Harbor in the same year, the British in Singapore in 1942, the Germans before D-Day in 1944, the Americans again just before the Tet Offensive in 1968, the Israelis before the Yom Kippur War in 1973, or the British before the Argentine invasion of the Falkland Islands in 1982.[90]

In each case, the evidence was there, but the dots were not joined up in the right way. So bad have some of these blunders been that it has become a standard joke to say that 'military intelligence' is a contradiction in terms. Unfortunately, we could often say more or less the same things about business intelligence – and perhaps come up with an even longer list of extraordinary blunders.

There are certain similarities between the challenges facing military intelligence experts and those facing their counterparts in the business world. First, you have to have a system for gathering intelligence – and one that is trustworthy. Second, you need processes that enable you to collate the relevant intelligence. Third, you need to be able to work out what it all means. And, fourth, you need to be able to 'Tell the Boss'. And that's often where the best-laid plans start to come unstuck.

There is a huge temptation to tell our leaders what we think they want to hear. Sometimes, the instructions are explicit. In 1916 and 1917, for example, General Haig's intelligence chief told his junior staff not to report bad news or intelligence that contradicted the accepted assessment of the German Army. "We shouldn't upset the Chief with this sort of stuff," he said; "it merely increases his burdens and makes him depressed." In wars, such willful blindness can lead to hundreds of thousands of casualties, in business to the destruction of entire market sectors and long-established companies.

Indeed, one of the key characteristics of the Citizen CEO is not only the readiness to listen, but the ability to hear and understand the significance of what is being said. Nor is this simply a question of individual companies and their CEOs. If the sustainability transition is to happen, change will need to occur at every level in our economic systems – and broadly in the direction of the business models and patterns of economic behavior outlined in Chapter 11. The challenge has been described as akin to changing a biplane into a 777, in flight. But to make things easier, Chapter 13 will summarize the advice of some of those who have helped early Citizen CEOs get into the air.

OK, some people will say, we all know integration is important. But what do we do about it? How do we join up the dotted lines, particularly when there are so many ways to do it? The answer very much depends on where an individual, a department or a business unit sits within an organization.

The challenge facing a CEO, for example, will be very different from that facing an internal champion like Chrys at Amoeba Inc (panel 1, page 19). But SustainAbility's road map for companies planning to embark on the journey is summarized in Figure 10.3.

The process starts with values and ethics, driving the drafting – or redrafting – of the organization's business principles. It evolves through new forms of accountability and engagement, as described in Chapter 9. It will require new forms of impact (and value creation) assessment, exploring such issues as diversity, equity and learning across all three domains of the TBL agenda. It then moves on to the development of strategies designed not only to increase efficiency and innovation, but

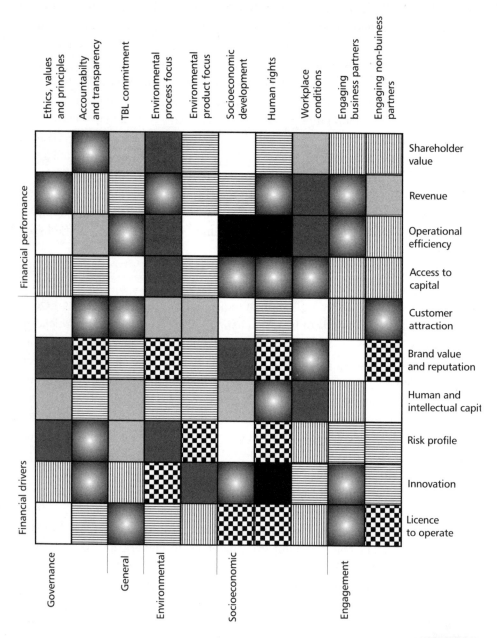

Figure 10.2 Sustainable Business Value Matrix.
Source: SustainAbility (for real data and key, see
www.sustainability.com/business-case).

also to evolve a company's business portfolio. The net result: market-leading TBL performance and, as a direct consequence, sustainable stakeholder value.

A new growth industry is now at work development key performance indicators (KPIs) and metrics to measure progress in all these areas. And, as Figure 10.4 indicates, the degree of consensus on triple bottom line indicators, including integrated performance indicators, is growing all the time.

In the end, the extent to which business helps us all emerge in good order from the Chrysalis Economy will depend on whether business leaders acknowledge – and learn to penetrate – the Values and Value Barriers described in Chapter 4. Increasingly, companies will need to review the capacity of their boards to perform against this new agenda. Growing numbers of companies are evaluating their boards,[92] but very few indeed have done so against the requirements of the triple bottom line. This, as the World Economic Forum is beginning to recognize (panel 10, below), is tomorrow's challenge.

PANEL 10

CEO Mecca gets religion

For global movers and shakers, the annual Davos meeting is a secular Mecca. If you want to consort with the super-wealthy and mega-powerful, with CEOs and board members from top companies, this is the place. You could even see it as the annual board meeting of Planet Earth Inc. Behind intense security, you will find the place humming with an extraordinary mix of Corporate Locusts, Caterpillars, Butterflies and Honeybees. Maggots too.

The event was founded on some of the most exquisite forms of exclusion yet developed by the world's élites. Amongst those invited to what is described by its organizer, the World Economic Forum (WEF), as "the world's global business summit," are 1,000 top business and 250 political leaders, 250 academic experts, including many Nobel Prize winners and some 250 media leaders. In what is described as "a unique club atmosphere," participants are called upon to "address the key economic, political and societal issues in a forward-looking, action-oriented way."

2000, however, marked a watershed for WEF.[93] Indeed, addicts of the so-called 'Davos Spirit' found a new mood. WTO director-general Mike Moore – in a session titled "Can We Take Open Markets for Granted?" – acknowledged Seattle had spurred

SustainAbility's Trimaran action research program focuses on the links between sustainable development, corporate governance, financial markets and board-level decision-making. The basic hypothesis being tested is that companies that effectively integrate TBL thinking will be more competitive and build stronger reputations and relationships. The underlying model is illustrated in Figure 10.3. Further details on: www.sustainability.com/trimaran

a serious rethink. He was quick to stress that "this is not a case of a few wealthy white guys trying to fix the rules for the rest of the world." And the WEF team worked hard to signal real changes afoot. The effort was not entirely in vain: *Time* magazine billed its report on the event as: "Davos Listens to the World."

The theme was "New Beginnings: Making a Difference," in stark contrast with the 1992 focus on "Megacompetition."

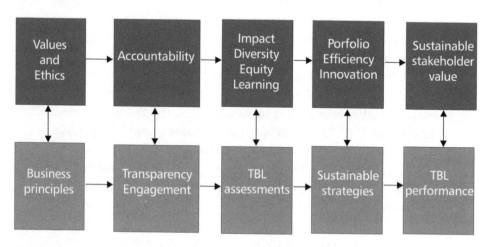

Figure 10.3   SustainAbility's TBL road map. © SustainAbility.

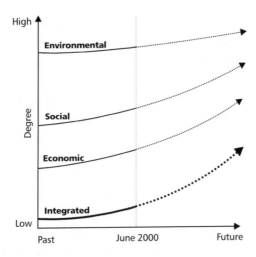

Figure 10.4 Growing consensus on TBL indicators.
Source: Global Reporting Initiative.

Shareholder value was still very much on the menu, but it was now interwoven with sessions on the next generation of information technology, strategic sourcing, and the impacts of large-scale dam construction and climate change. The summit is changing because a widening coalition of environmentalists, trade unions and other critics have forced at least a grudging acknowledgement of the growing demand for transparency, ethics, accountability and – perhaps most seditious of all for an event so exclusive as Davos – growing inclusion.

"Davos was never designed to be transparent," explains Molly Harriss Olson, who directed the US President's Council on Sustainable Development and now runs Australian consultancy Eco Futures. 2000 was her third trip to Davos. "In 1996," she recalled, "the environment and sustainability were just not on the Davos agenda. I felt like a fish out of water. This year, there were over a dozen sessions on various aspects of these subjects. At the opening plenary, climate change was voted the most important issue out of all the issues raised by six speakers, to many people's surprise." Nor was this all. "Bill Clinton argued that the WTO will not be able to succeed unless – and until – the labor, environmental and social NGOs have a legitimate place at the table, to share their views."

WEF founder Kurt Schwab says he has long supported wider participation. Thirty years ago, at the first annual meeting, says WEF, he "irritated many of the business participants by including what we now call civil society: non-governmental organizations and trade unions. Corporate attitudes have changed slowly, but in the wake of a number of highly damaging incidents, perceptive CEOs realize that they need to engage civil society rather than scorn it."

Now that engagement was upfront. Panels brought a number of adversaries face-to-face; for example Greenpeace International executive director Thilo Bode and Monsanto senior vice-president Nick Rosa. In a session dedicated to the future of biotechnology, arch-bio-critic Vandana Shiva confronted DuPont chairman and CEO Charles O. (Chad) Holliday, increasingly betting the future of his company on biotechnology.

"What really interested me was how CEO sentiment on leadership had shifted to a much broader appreciation of the 'softer' aspects of leadership," recalls London Business School professor John Stopford. "The same opening of mental doors was going on for many of the environmental issues." Stopford himself had chaired a packed session on labor issues and was told by a union delegate: "Eight years ago, when I first came to Davos, there would have been 10 people in the room'."

Ken Roth, executive director of US-based Human Rights Watch, recalls finding "a thirst on the part of the corporate leaders present for solutions to some of the much-neglected problems related to globalization. Everyone knew in general terms the problems that Seattle had highlighted, but few understood how to build the global architecture to address these problems, or what responsibilities corporations had to accept for dealing with them."

Davos is not just a talking shop. Despite the *Financial Times'* wry comment that "during the Davos weekend, roughly 70 percent of the world's daily output of self-congratulation is concentrated in one place," concrete triple bottom line solutions are also being rolled out. These include the Environmental Sustainability Index (ESI), launched by the Global Leaders for Tomorrow (GLT) Environ-ment Task Force. "Businesses, as well as societies, need clear indicators on how to make their processes more environmentally sustainable," explained co-chair of the 2000 event, DuPont's Holliday.

An environmental chapter has been developed for the next *Global Competitiveness Report*, while the first full-blown sustainability index was presented at Davos 2001. It measures and ranks economies, based on their success in facilitating economic growth without crossing environmental sustainability barriers. The long-term goal is to find "a single indicator for environmental sustainability in the same way GDP gives a single figure for the economy." The pilot Index incorporated 64 variables, under the following headings: environmental system; environmental stresses and risks; human vulnerability to environmental impacts; social and institutional capacity; and global stewardship.

It may be a candidate for the Butterfly Effect Award of 2010, but the first round of results were a bit odd.[94] Norway came top, followed by Finland, Canada, Iceland, Sweden, Switzerland, Australia, Denmark, the United States and Netherlands in the 'Top 10'. And, among the 'Worst 10', why does Singapore rank down there alongside Algeria? Given the record of some of these countries, including Australia and the USA, in relation to such issues as climate change, expect lively debate!

The key questions, however, now relate to corporate and global governance. As globalizing capitalism moves into something of a governance vacuum in various parts of the world, there are warning signs that the coming years will see major economic discontinuities. These may have less to do with ecological unsustainability than with the sustainability of our financial and social systems. Unless the annual board meeting of Planet Earth Inc gets its act together, the chances are that we will all have cause to regret it.

CHAPTER 11

Incubation

incubation / *n*. **1** the act of incubating an egg, micro-organism or infection. **2** the period between exposure to an infection and the appearance of the first symptoms. **3** *the process by which companies or other business organizations invest in and nurture new SD-focused ventures with the potential, in some cases, to destroy their existing businesses or markets.*

The dinosaurs were perfectly integrated. They were adapted to conditions that had been fairly stable for millennia. The problem was that their environment changed, dramatically. And the same is happening with traditional capitalism. However seductive it may be to work with major corporations, debating mega-issues with CEOs and their colleagues around boardroom tables, often the best we can hope to achieve is to limit the damage they cause. Even if we work through all the four stages outlined to date, the chances are that we would still often be tinkering at the edges. If, instead, we want to put the world's economy on radically new tracks, we can count on one thing: those who benefited most from the old order will rarely lead the process of tearing it down to prepare the ground for the new.

Viewed through this lens, working with major multinational corporations on SD could prove to be like searching for your lost keys under the street-lamp, even though you know you dropped them way over there in the dark. An ability to work in the dark may be one critical skill for those whose aim is to incubate a sustainable future, but those of us doing this for a living should periodically review our partners and clients to ensure that at least some are in the incubation game proper.

Careful, though, incubation can be a dirty word! Or at least it can be if you talk to the thousands of investors who lost money on what were once described in the *Harvard Business Review* as "Hothouses of the New Economy".[95] But we must now learn how to incubate the sustainable business models and technologies of the 21st century – even if they prove to be "the children that eat their parents," in the sense that their very success will undermine the market position and share of their parent companies. We must learn how to create what Generon Consulting has called "generative cocoons" to foster the future. Key skills will include rapid prototyping and feedback, with an increasing premium placed on working alongside lead customers who are determined to achieve radically more sustainable outcomes.[96]

This is a lesson already learned by organizations like Bell Labs and BT, which have been encouraging employees to take company ideas and patents, and to start new companies around them. In some cases, they are doing this in the full knowledge that the result may be a threat to their established product lines.[97] They have no choice. Ever since the publication of Clayton Christensen's *The Innovator's Dilemma*, we have known that even the best companies can fail precisely because they do the right thing.[98] They keep their competitive antennae tuned, listen carefully to customers, invest heavily in new technologies, and yet still the sheer disruptiveness of innovation means that the game goes against them

Even before most internet stocks came crashing back to earth, however, some investors worried that many so-called incubators were sheltering clutches of start-ups that would otherwise have failed to find a perch. Many of the ideas they spawned were 'no-hopers'. Indeed, some skeptical investors see business incubation as rather like forcing caterpillars to go through the chrysalis stage ultra-fast, simply so they can turn into butterflies and be turned loose. Even at the best of times, the death rates are high for recently launched butterflies and business start-ups alike, but they tend to go off the scale when outside conditions are stormy.

Once the dotcom correction got into its stride, flurries of recent incubatees joined the casualty lists. But we should be careful of learning the wrong lessons. It is not so much the concept of business incubation that is at fault, but the practice. Whatever they are called – 'business accelerators', 'B-school hatcheries', 'campuses', 'econets', or 'internet keiretsus' – the basic principle is usually the same. Designed to help business fledglings to find their feet and take wing, literally hundreds of incubators have been formed to provide funding, office space, coaching, IT, accounting and a range of basic services to start-ups.

Some of the more notable early entrants in the incubation stakes were Generics, Hotbank, Internet Capital Group and Idealab!. Before long, however, the stocks of many such companies were trading at dramatic discounts, with several forced to pull their IPOs.[99]

But one interesting question raised by the whole incubation industry has been whether such initiatives are even necessary? Why even bother with start-ups? Why can't mainstream companies do this sort of thing for themselves? The answers to such questions also tell us a good deal about our prospects for incubating more sustainable technologies and business models in the heartland of the old economy. It may well be possible, but experience suggests that it is rarely easy – and more often either very difficult or actually impossible. Even Ray Anderson has found it a real struggle at

Interface, long seen as one of the model companies as far as sustainable business models are concerned – and, incidentally, a company he largely owns (panel 11, page 220).

SKUNK WORKERS

So what pushes people to start the new rather than trying to transform the old? One answer is that they have already tried to transform the old, but found the task unproductive and unrewarding. Another answer is that new ventures generally provide a sense of adventure, of risk, and of potential gain which is lacking in many mainstream companies. Indeed, these were key motives driving many talented people to leave mainstream companies for start-ups in what was dubbed the 'Great Web Migration'.[100]

Well-designed incubators also help maintain a spirit of entrepreneurship. In addition, they work hard to ensure that the incubated ventures are free from undue strategic, bureaucratic or organizational impediments that often slow down or stall risky new enterprises. They don't just cut through red tape, they try not to create it in the first place. And they can provide useful economies of scale, helping incubated ventures get a jump-start on their competitors.

Perhaps most powerfully of all, they ensure that the focus is on the opportunities afforded by new ideas, technologies, and business models. One of the worst examples of what can happen when a company fails to exploit its own innovations was Xerox PARC, which invented many of the most important features of personal computing – but then failed to capitalize on them. By contrast, one of the most spectacular examples of incubation at work has been Lockheed's 'Skunk Works'.[101] The phrase has even gone into the language as a description of a secretive, highly innovative unit designed to break the mould.

The Lockheed company may have become something of a byword for corruption in a scandal that nearly brought down a number of governments, but its Skunk Works potentially has much to teach us. Throughout the long, tense years of the Cold War, this ultra-top-secret facility was high on the hit list for Soviet nuclear forces in the event of war. The reason: it had proved a high-tech cornucopia from which poured a stream of world-beating aircraft. These included the P-80 (America's first jet fighter), the F-104 Starfighter (the first US supersonic attack aircraft), the U-2 spy plane, the SR-71 Blackbird (flying at three the times the speed of sound) and the F-117A stealth fighter that many people first saw on CNN during Operation Desert Storm.

What linked these projects, and all the others developed in the Skunk Works, was that each was initiated at the top levels of government as part of an ongoing effort to tip the balance in the Cold War balance of power. Motivating people to respond to issues like climate change or species loss is a lot harder than waking them up to a clear and present danger like the threat of military invasion, or to the challenge of getting a man on the Moon, but we should look for clues on how to do this stuff wherever we can find them. Only if we can unleash unparalleled levels of innovation will we have any real chance of success.

So how was the Skunk Works built? As Ben Rich, who headed the operation for nearly two decades, put it: "We became the most successful advanced projects company in the world by hiring talented people, paying them top dollar, and motivating them into believing that they could produce a Mach 3 airplane like Blackbird a generation or two ahead of anybody else." But the outfit also was noted for the extraordinary amount of initiative it gave to employees. "We encouraged our people to work imaginatively, to improvise and try unconventional approaches to problem," Rich added, "and then got out of their way."

We would be mistaken, however, if we concluded that future skunk works will necessarily follow the Lockheed pattern. Some will no doubt be hidden away to ensure they are not slowed down by mainstream politics, but others will be out in the open, networked, virtual. Nor will they simply work on sustainability issues, at least not if they are to succeed commercially. Instead, they will need to embrace values enabling them to pursue a range of sustainability objectives profitably. One interesting model already out there is the Rocky Mountain Institute, set up by Amory and Hunter Lovins to work on projects like the 'hypercar'. And, despite the collapse of internet stock prices, there are still an awful lot of relatively young businesspeople around with extraordinary amounts of money that could be invested in the right sort of ventures.

So far, the USA has been the most successful economy in putting the various ingredients together in interesting ways. Look around, and you will find new breeds of innovators who see important, exciting challenges in such areas. One spotlighted by *Wired* was Dean Kamen, of Deka Research & Development.[102] Kamen believes technology and ingenuity can solve all sorts of social ills, among them pollution, limited access to electricity and contaminated water in Third World countries. Whether or not Kamen makes a commercial reality of the fuel-efficient, low-pollution Stirling engine his team has been working on, his can-do attitude is exactly what is needed to make the sustainability transition happen. (Although the media hype that accompanied his announcement that he had an invention that would transform cities, which he coyly named 'It', suggests that New Economy euphoria may well erupt in other areas.[103])

Later, *Wired* also spotlighted the efforts of science fiction writer Bruce Stirling to revolutionize the energy meter industry. He launched the Viridian Movement (www.viridiandesign.org) to fight climate change by reinventing everyday items that guzzle energy. Spurred by a spoof ad written by Stirling for the 'Viridian Electricity Meter', the Vermont-based Sustainability Institute jumped in and sponsored a design competition (www.sustainer.org).[104]

First place went to the Wattbug team, which created the "Tamagotchi of meters". It looks like a toy caterpillar, with a whip-like tail. This flashes green when power use is low, yellow when moderate, and red when high. The bug's face also changes: a smile replaces a frown as power use falls, and at really sustainable levels it actually begins to purr!

Whether they are entrepreneurs or CEOs of big companies in the process of transformation, business leaders need one skill above all others. That skill, as Tim Smit explains, is to make people believe in change. "I have one skill," says Smit, the man mainly responsible for the Eden Project, a long chain of greenhouse-protected biomes that has sprouted in an old china clay quarry in Cornwall. "I'm a facilitator," he says. "I can make other people believe in themselves. If I believe something's going to work, my belief seems to rub off."[105]

It is hard to exaggerate the scale of the Eden Project, which looks like nothing so much as a giant high-tech honeycomb snaking around what used to be a huge hole in the ground. It now ranks as the world's second largest open space after the launch center at Cape Canaveral. Interestingly, Smit came from an unusual background, in popular music, as did Nicholas Abson, the film director who once made some of the first pop videos with Stevie Wonder and Diana Ross, and is now CEO of ZeTek Power, a European start-up company diving into the fuel cell area.[106]

Abson insists he is not a gambler, instead taking calculated risks to develop planet-friendly technology. "It's the Brooklyn philosophy," he explains, referring to his New York childhood. "You had to think on your feet when I was a kid. Assess situations, weigh up the risk, and act. I've always applied that to business." He would dismiss outright the notion that a fully-formed plan on how to do anything would simply drop into your head. And he stresses that the ability to drive change can be learned. "You have to learn to be a businessman," he notes. "You have to learn to be an entrepreneur. You have to learn how to raise funds. You have to learn how to build a corporate structure. You invent it as you go along."

Sometimes such change runs on rails, making it fairly easy to decide and act; at other times, however, it lurches off into areas of extreme uncertainty and unpredictability. The old rules no longer hold. In such uncertain times, as skunk workers have long known, it helps enormously to free up the brain, to feed the imagination. Some years back, in fact, designer Bruce Mau unveiled a seductive 43-point program designed to help organizations cope with such periods of change and to grow creatively.[107] Among the points that caught my attention were these:

- *Ask stupid questions.* Growth is fueled by desire and innocence. Answer the answer, not the question. Imagine learning throughout your life at the rate of an infant.
- *Capture accidents.* The wrong answer is the right answer in search of a different question. Collect wrong answers as part of the process. Ask different questions.
- *Drift.* Allow yourself to wander aimlessly. Explore adjacencies. Lack judgement. Postpone criticism.
- *Make new words.* Expand the lexicon. The new conditions demand a new way of thinking. The thinking demands new forms of expression. The expression generates new conditions.
- *Take field trips.* The bandwidth of the world is greater than that of your TV set, or the internet – or even a totally immersive, interactive, dynamically rendered, object-oriented, real-time, computer-graphic-stimulated environment.
- *Stand on someone's shoulders.* You can travel farther carried on the accomplishments of those who came before you. And the view is so much better.

Thinking of that last point, it's important to find the right shoulders to stand on. One man whose ability to rethink the world had a huge impact on my own thinking was Buckminster Fuller. In fact, his geodesic domes find powerful echoes in Tim Smit's Eden Project. Fuller, who I finally met in Iceland in the late 1970s, was often billed as the man who coined the phrase 'Spaceship Earth', which helpfully links to the fourth of Mau's points above. He played with language constantly: indeed, he was also an early champion of the dematerialization agenda, what he called *ephemeralization.*

It's enough to stand behind or alongside someone like that, let alone stand on his shoulders. Fuller's work underscored the fact that we should all be thinking much more creatively. He was continuously incubating new language, new ideas, new designs, new technologies. And the natural world, he knew, is full of clues.

Shark skin, for example, has recently shown scientists how to design plastic coatings that reduce frictional drag on an object moving through air and water. The tiny scales of a shark's skin seem to smooth out the flow of water over the skin's surface, suppressing turbulence that would otherwise cause drag. A plastic film using the same texture, when fixed to the fuselage of aircraft, can cut friction by around 10 percent.[108] Another example of 'biomimetic' design is Velcro, whose tiny plastic hooks are modeled on those of burred seed pods.

And talking of Bruce Mau's advice on taking field trips, Viagra was the last thing on my mind as I snorkeled across Australia's Great Barrier Reef recently. But a century and a half after its first gold rush, a new breed of prospectors is now criss-crossing the island continent in search of natural sources of future cures for everything from impotence to cancer. The Barrier Reef, with its 1,500 fish species, 400 coral species and 4,000 mollusk species, may provide clues to tomorrow's blockbusting drugs. "This is going to be a multi-billion industry," one expert had recently told *Asiaweek*. "It really is a gold mine."

Well, maybe. Bioprospectors are hunting for natural clues to new pharmaceuticals just as explorers half a millennium ago sailed in search of spices. But the problem is finding the right substance, the right gene. To make things easier, laboratories use robots to prepare hundreds of samples an hour for screening. The substances – from microbes, animals or plants – are tested for activity against a range of disease-causing agents, with the reactions monitored, analyzed and tabulated by computer. Even so, it is like searching for needles in the proverbial haystack. One Australian lab reckons to run 700,000 screens a year, uncovering at most 20 novel, biologically-active molecules.

So why focus on reefs? One reason: competition. Sea creatures are promising sources of anti-cancer compounds because natural selection has forced them to evolve elaborate chemical arsenals. Many are brightly-colored, slow moving and soft-bodied. It is as if they had an "eat me" sign slung around their necks. To cope, they have developed complex toxins – and toxicity is the reason cancer specialists use drugs, hoping to kill cancer cells while leaving healthy cells unscathed. One recent discovery: a potent painkiller extracted from the venom of a reef cone snail.

I was up in Port Douglas to address a conference organized by Australia's Plastics and Chemicals Industries Association (PACIA), focusing on SD. The trip to the reef on the Quicksilver trimaran was courtesy of DuPont Australia, but even if they weren't paying some of the industry guests were clearly uneasy. The reasons surfaced the next day. With increasing global competition, their profits were falling, investment in new plant was negligible and the outlook was bleak. "This is real decision time," warned PACIA CEO Nicole Williams. "Not one penny of the $50 billion to $60 billion in investment in the world chemical industry in the last five years has reached Australia." The industry needs to reinvent itself, DuPont Australia chairman John Foote concluded.

Faced with such pressures, perhaps we should be looking for more than tomorrow's Viagras in the natural world. Indeed, industrial ecologists argue that there will also be clues on how we can reconfigure our industries for the 21st century. Reefs are not just laboratories churning out novel toxins, but also heave with strange specializations, symbioses and other adaptations which could catalyze new visions of the chemical industry's future.

CHANGING THE GAME

I doubt many of the conference delegates made the connection, but as they snorkeled over the reef, answers to their problems may have been literally staring them in the face. That said, many large, long-established companies – and many smaller ones – find it hard to begin the process of change. But, while it may be hard for most companies to mimic the creativity of some of the individuals and outfits discussed earlier, some are experimenting with new ways of sparking innovation. The emerging field of biomimicry, promoted by people like Janine Benyus, promises to be a particularly fertile source of inspiration for sustainability-focused innovation.[109]

At DuPont, as explained in Chapter 6, there has been a sustained effort to shift the center of gravity of the company from chemicals to life sciences (see Figure 11.1). Here there has been an explicit attempt to massively boost the value created per unit of environmental impact or footprint generated. In many other companies, the links between innovation and sustainability are less explicit. But, whether explicit or not, processes designed to catalyze change in the old economy are generally highly desirable. Monsanto's experiences with driving life science technologies into the market should give investors pause when assessing DuPont's chances, but at least the company is thinking in the right sort of framework.

At Shell, meanwhile, GameChanger is a process designed to create an entrepreneurial environment even within a giant company – and help identify new ways of creating value. A key problem for Shell has been that the traditional source of innovation is corporate, with the allocation of research and development funds from top down. This can work well enough when market conditions are predictable and slow moving, but new ways have to be found of stimulating innovation when things become less predictable.[110]

The basic concept behind GameChanger is deceptively simple. Anyone with a bright idea can come forward and present a short outline to the GameChanger board. The board's job is then to sift quickly – within a week – through the ideas and decide whether or not to fund them. The next step is then to produce a business plan – what Shell calls a 'value proposition' – that then goes back to the board for further assessment. About 10 percent of the ideas initially accepted make it over this second hurdle and enter the experimentation phase. If these experiments succeed, then they are switched into the company's mainstream development channels, brought back into the business, or funded through Shell venture capital programs.

You come across similar initiatives in growing numbers of other companies these days. "Businesses are being drawn into a tidal wave of transformation," says Josephine Green. She is director of trends and strategy at Dutch consumer electronics giant Philips. Or, as she told me in a taxi racing back to Toronto airport, and using the joking words of one of her colleagues, "Director of Stress and Tragedy." Joking apart, stress and tragedy are inescapable at the colliding interfaces between the old and new economies. And, as the world's headlines have spooled out long lists of corporate and dotcom wipe-outs, Philips has often seemed to struggle to keep its balance on the speeding wave of change.

So how can such companies learn to surf the speeding tsunami whipped up by globalization, global networking and connectivity? The answer, Green believes, lies not so much in accurately predicting long-term future trends – one of my first questions had been whether she sees herself as a 'futurist'? – but in understanding how the deeper currents in social values will shape tomorrow's world. "The future is not just something that will happen to us," she says, "but to a large extent something that we co-create through a combination of insight, creativity, curiosity and the desire to create a better world."

Sustainability, she argues, is "*the* vision of advanced capitalism." To help Philips to create its own vision for the future, she and her colleagues at Philips Design have evolved the Strategic Futures™ process. "Through our research we have found that customers will be seeking holistic and flexible solutions," she explains, "rather than simply products or technology. The customer has become a stakeholder who not only buys the product but is also buying the values of the company."

Consumers, Philips believes, are moving beyond products to the consumption of information, service and solutions. "The emergence of a 'solutions economy'," Green argues, "means that people are looking as much to the intangible as they are the tangible. At the same time, personal stress and environmental stress are challenging the basic notion of progress and that 'more means better'. In the future, an increasing number of the consumers and citizens will reward those brands that take on the roles and responsibilities of creating a more personally, environmentally and socially sustainable futures."

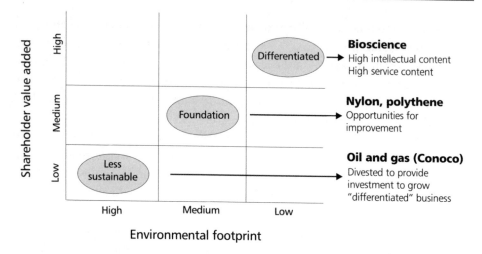

Figure 11.1   DuPont's portfolio matrix. The goal is to grow business value and cut environmental footprint.
Source: DuPont.

The key to pushing the incubation process forward in the right direction is to combine vision, incentives and a fair degree of freedom for the incubators. This is the recipe used at one of the most creative places in the world, Corning Inc.'s Sullivan Park research facility. "Scientists, like any other human beings, perform best when they are driven by inspiration," explains Lina Echeverría, director of glass and glass ceramics at the facility.[111] "It's the same in an artist or a scientist. We depend on their creativity. I tell my guys, If you think something is really important, follow your heart. It energizes you, and you give your best performance. That's how you get scientists on a roll – what for athletes is called 'being in the zone.'" But that doesn't mean that anything goes. "This is not just a green field where you can run in whatever direction you want," she continues. "As a group, our performance is evaluated first and foremost on results."

SILENT REVOLUTIONS

The problem is that the results that companies focus on may not be those that are going to be most valuable to society. The incubation process, even in companies like 3M, Corning Glass, Interface or NatureWorks, often needs a strong push from the three main pressures outlined in Chapter 8: laws, market standards and values. These can link to any or all of the dimensions of the SD agenda, but the process has probably been most dramatic in recent years in the environment field.

Want an idea of where OECD governments will eventually go on environmental standards for business? Take a look at California – or Holland. The Dutch environment ministry VROM is now more than ten years into what it dubs a 'Silent Revolution'. This has influenced the thinking of both national and international government policy-makers, despite the fact that the country's first national environmental policy plan (NEPP1) was something of a paradox.

The plan urged rapid progress towards strict environmental targets, yet relied heavily on voluntary agreements (or 'covenants') negotiated with high-impact industries. The Dutch, it turns out, like to talk their way to solutions. VROM explains that "Dutch environmental policy is strict because it has to be: the Netherlands is a densely populated country with a great deal of industry. But 'strict' does not mean that measures are simply imposed from above. Environmental policy is first and foremost a matter of talking, talking and talking some more. The primary aim is consensus."

Scarcely surprising in a country where even the nursery school day begins with group discussion. But, at a time when the Dutch want to export their model of consensus-based environmental governance, we should ask whether it works and, even if it does, can it deliver results elsewhere? The evidence suggests that the approach is succeeding in Holland, encouraging industries as diverse as chemical, carpet and dairy production to shrink their ecological footprints. But it has a powerful sting in its tail. If an industry fails to deliver, the government warns that it will regulate.

While tough standards will spread, it is less clear that the covenant approach to incubating economic, industrial and technological change is readily exportable even to most other European countries. The European Commission adopted the Dutch model in the early 1990s, in its fifth environmental action plan, "Towards Sustainability". For some seven years through to 2001, I was part of the European Commission's consultative forum on sustainability. Progress was made, but too often it was a case of talking, talking, talking, without the benefit of the Dutch consensus culture to ensure implementation.

Now, as the Commission moves to implement its sixth action plan, we should be concerned that the nineties emphasis on 'shared responsibility' and voluntary initiatives has largely failed to engage across the European Union. One reason: most Europeans don't think and behave like the Dutch. Worse, the Commission may have offered the carrot of consensus, but has been less inclined to use the legal stick. Undaunted, VROM has been hard at work on NEPP4. This time, the focus is on 'intractable problems' like climate change, hormone-disrupting chemicals and genetically modified foods. But visiting VROM recently, I found them wrestling with a deeper problem: an apparent decline in public willingness to support radical environmental action.

You don't have to be Dutch to know what is going wrong yet fail to act. On the flight back, I read *The Knowing–Doing Gap*.[112] Companies talk endlessly about intellectual capital and knowledge management, the authors note, but often fail to convert knowledge into appropriate, effective action. Many act as if talking about a problem was the same as solving it. There are no magic recipes, in business or civil society. But the spread of relevant values and effective leadership will be critical in ensuring incubation happens in the right ways and at the right pace.

The greenhouse gas trading market, although embryonic, is expected to become one of the largest commodity markets in the world,"[113] said one of the leading emissions trading firm. The US Agency for International Development predicts that the market for clean technologies and services in developing countries could grow to £36 billion by 2010. But none of this is going to happen automatically. We need to build the generative cocoons that will drive sustainability-focused innovation. In the process, we will not only need the new laws, standards and values outlined in Chapter 8, but we will also need to invest a great deal more effort in taxing carbon emissions and other undesirable aspects of our environmental, social and economic footprints.

Next, in Section IV, we will look at two factors that will help determine how things turn out over the next generation or two. First, the images of the future that we carry in our heads, and, second, the mental maps and ambitions of some of those who are helping guide the sustainability transition in some of the world's leading companies. Finally, we take a brief look from completely outside the box, raising the question of whether it is even possible to consciously build a sustainable civilization.

PANEL 11

Ray on the carpet

Ray Anderson, founder, Chairman, CEO and majority shareholder of Interface, was looking at me quizzically. We were both speaking at a conference outside Toronto, and had managed to squeeze out half an hour to talk before he flew back to Atlanta. Things had gone well to start with, but then he asked what was really on my mind? Well, I replied, much as I admired Interface's attempts to transform the world's carpet markets towards more sustainable business models, I was genuinely concerned that the company's recent financial problems would damage the confidence of CEOs in the commercial viability of SD.

His face cleared. "I wish we had got to that sooner," he said. He promised to send me a just-finished update on the Interface story, an additional, eighth chapter to his 1998 book *Mid-Course Correction*.[114] A few days after I got back to London, the document arrived.[115] And a few weeks later, back in New York, I heard Ray run through the whole story for the annual Business for Social Responsibility (BSR) conference. In headlines, the story went like this:

"Interface's commitment to environmental sustainability is well known," he began. He had made nearly 500 speeches on the subject since 1994 and, as a result, Interface "became the great corporate hope for environmentalists and socially responsible investors. At last, a $ billion, non-food, manufacturing company had come along that was showing the way, proving companies could change and showing that sustainability could be good business." Unfortunately, after a four-year run of success, Interface hit a wall.

In the first quarter of 1998, Interface's shares (IFSIA) peaked at nearly $23 per share, before going into a decline that lasted fully 10 quarters. When the shares hit bottom, in June 2000, they were valued at just over $3 – a decline, from peak to trough, of 87 percent! "If that's what a company's commitment to sustainability does for its shareholders," as Anderson summarized the reaction of other business people, "who needs it?"

Mid-Course Correction had explained Interface's plans for "creating the prototypical company of the 21st century, metamorphosing, as it were, from a typical company of the 20th century, petrochemically intensive, *taking* natural resources, *making* our short-lived products, and *wasting* through emissions, effluents and scrap in all our production processes." No-one doubted that this was something new, but Anderson admits that the widespread adoption of this new business model "had been significantly impeded by Interface's unsettling stock market performance and financial results."

A key reason for the problems, he says, was the succession plan he had put in place late in 1993. New management took over increasing responsibility – and sales went from $625 million in 1993 to almost $1.3 billion in 1998. But in 1995 something unexpected had happened: Interface suddenly faced new competition from a major competitor (Shaw Industries) and a key supplier (DuPont). Feeling threatened by DuPont's growing investment in the carpet business, Shaw started a major acquisition drive to protect its position. Then the Interface team, also concerned to move towards closed loop recycling and a reverse logistics collection system for old carpet, launched its own $150 million acquisition drive.

All hell broke loose. As Anderson puts it: "We woke up one day to realize that DuPont was, at once, our largest supplier (fiber and yarn), our largest competitor (distribution), and our largest customer (their acquired contractors that were still buying and installing our products)." Some of Interface's own acquisitions performed badly and, as if that wasn't enough, the Y2K compliance issue massively squeezed the carpet market as companies cut back on non-essential costs.

The biggest mistake, Anderson thinks, was "an incomplete commitment to sustainability." Environmental and financial sustainability were part of the plan from the outset, but "the critical missing factor, glaringly exposed during the over-reach stage, was a corresponding, genuine focus on people, i.e. *social sustainability*. An arrogant management team, well-proven and flush with success in carpet tiles, but neophytes" in other key areas of the business, resorted to telling key Interface people: "Do it our way. My way or the highway." As Anderson recalls: "Many of the top performing broadloom sales people replied, 'OK, the highway for me'."

So, he says: "We now realize that social equity begins at home with our own people, and sustainability is not achievable without social equity." Anderson decided to move back into active management of the business – "in short order, six of the top 12 management personnel were removed, including the Chief Operating Officer, his top lieutenant, and the lieutenant's top financial manager."

Recently, Anderson brought together 125 members of the company's top management team to "reach consensus on a set of values to which all could subscribe. I was overjoyed when, after three days, *the core value* of our company emerged clearly to be *sustainability*! The soul of the company had come through the ordeal intact." To put it another way, the central Interface meme was alive and hopefully on its way to renewed health. Just as important, though, Anderson notes that the company's financial results have been rebounding.

"Having stayed the course on environmental sustainability while suffering the harsh learning experience about social equity in our own back yard," he says, "Interface has emerged financially stronger than ever." Whatever the ultimate outcome, the Interface story underscores a basic lesson: in highly competitive markets, CEOs and other business leaders cannot afford to take their eyes off any of sustainability's bottom lines.

PART IV

MIGRATION$

The best-known butterfly? Probably the Monarch.

This is the insect that helped bring Monsanto to its knees.

Strong fliers, Monarchs migrate thousands of miles.

Economies must also migrate.

So, where are we headed?

And who will gain – and who lose?

CHAPTER 12

Future memories
Scenarios and their uses

Stanley Kubrick may be dead, but he's still inside my head. His epic *2001: A Space Odyssey*, which tried to capture the deep future way back in 1968, left me with powerful memories. I first saw the film in the year of its release, a time of profound change. One memory it left was strikingly different from the pre-revolutionary scenes erupting in the streets. The scene is a defining moment in the film: an elegant white Space Clipper moves into a synchronized, rolling orbit prior to docking with a giant space station. Playing in the background, the heavenly strains of the Blue Danube waltz, *An der schönen, blauen Donau*.

But, some predictions in the film have proved to be slightly off. Yes, we have the beginnings of a space station, a $60 billion orbiting symbol of international co-operation due for completion in 2006, but nothing like the revolving ring Kubrick featured.[1] Instead, as I was writing these words, we were being warned that the 130-tonne wreck of the Russian space station *Mir* could crash-land on a city like Sydney.[2] It didn't, but perhaps Wagner's *Götterdämmerung* might have been a more appropriate sound track?

In Kubrick's future, passport control screened travelers by using their unique voiceprints, whereas in today's world this remains a luxury most folk queuing up with their passports can scarcely even dream of.[3] Another oddity was the fact that computing was represented on the spaceship *Discovery* by HAL 9000, with no PCs or laptops in sight. But for me one of the most interesting glitches had to do with Pan Am, the American airline whose logo appears on space shuttles in the film.

The company is long gone, having finally bitten the dust in 1991 – a decade before that celebrated movie docking was predicted to happen. For decades, Pan Am aircraft had provided the backdrop for press photos of arriving presidents, movie actors, Beatles. The sun never set on the airline's far-flung empire. "In four decades of operation," notes the airline's biographer, "Pan Am had been responsible for virtually every innovation in commercial aviation, from the invention of radio navigation by air to the jump-starting of the jet age."[4] But long before the Pan Am

747 Clipper *Maiden of the Skies* was ripped into flaming shreds by a terrorist bomb over Lockerbie, in 1988, the airline was in a deadly downward spiral.

Following a massively unsuccessful take-over and the Gulf War, which had travelers scurrying across to non-American airlines, Pan Am was cannibalized and shuttered. TWA went down not long after. So why do such great companies come so badly unstuck? The reasons are legion. Nor should we expect pioneering companies to live forever. Indeed, the more a particular company was involved in the opening up of a new market, the more vulnerable it is likely to be when market conditions change.

But there were also many other factors at work in the demise of Pan Am, among them the arrogance and obsessive secrecy of the company's founder, Juan Trippe. He had a vision, but in the end it misled him – and the market he helped create overtook his company's capacity to mutate in line with market demand and expectations. It is hard to say at this distance of time what Trippe and his colleagues could have done to guarantee that a Pan Am Space Clipper made that rendezvous in space, but the use of scenarios might have helped.

These days, the pressures for dramatic, continuous change are even more intense. "Never has incumbency been worth less," says Gary Hamel.[5] "Schumpeter's gale of creative destruction has become a hurricane. New winds are battering down the fortifications that once protected the status quo. Economic integration has blown open protected markets. Deregulation has destroyed comfortable monopolies. The Internet has turned bricks and mortar into millstones. And venture capitalists pour millions of dollars into terrorist training camps for industry insurgents."

If, in the middle of all of this, you want to know what CEOs dream about – and what some have nightmares about – try sampling some of the future scenarios they are using to try to get a grip on the future.

AHA!

People have always wanted to get a sense of what the future held, particularly in uncertain times. When the Cold War ended, a reasonably stable world order also ended.[6] In many ways, it had been a mad world, not least because its stability had been maintained through the nuclear doctrine of mutually assured destruction (MAD). Now, a new world order is evolving, creating a highly turbulent, uncertain business environment. Companies trying to grasp the emergent structure of this seemingly chaotic world have increasingly turned to scenarios for help.

So what are they? One of the best descriptions I have yet heard is that scenarios are "memories of tomorrow." Often, they are fairly elaborate, but they don't have to be. When working on a life sciences scenario project recently, I came up with three one-word 'scenarios'. We were trying to work out whether genetically modified (GM) products would be accepted in particular world regions. The three scenarios: *nuclear*, *antibiotic* and *microchip*.

The first (*nuclear*) hints at a world where GM technology starts well, but then hits insuperable barriers. The second (*antibiotic*) points to a world where the early promise of GM products is delivered, but worrying side-effects progressively undermine their utility. And the third (*microchip*) suggests a world where GM products prove so successful that they become indispensable, ubiquitous and, to all intents and purposes, invisible. Such word-pictures provide a form of shorthand for those thinking about the future.

Most scenarios, however, are much more detailed. According to the World Business Council for Sustainable Development (WBCSD), scenarios are

> powerful tools for addressing what is fundamentally significant and profoundly unknowable – the future. Unlike forecasts, which impose patterns extrapolated from the past onto the future, scenarios are plausible, pertinent, alternative stories that are concerned more with strategic thinking than with strategic planning, and more specifically with the quality of thinking. As we enter these alternative stories, we are guided to practice a flexible approach to the future and to alter our mental maps.[7]

Over at the Global Business Network (GBN), in California, they put it this way:

> Within the organization, scenarios provide a common vocabulary and an effective basis for communicating complex – sometimes paradoxical – conditions and options. Good scenarios are plausible and surprising, they have the power to break old stereotypes, and their creators assume ownership and put them to work. By recognizing the warning signs and the drama that is unfolding, one can avoid surprises, adapt and act effectively. Decisions which have been pre-tested against a range of what fate may offer are more likely to stand the test of time, produce robust and resilient strategies, and create distinct competitive advantage.

Ultimately, they say, "the result of scenario planning is not a more accurate picture of tomorrow but better thinking and an ongoing strategic conversation about the future."[8] And anyone reviewing the short history of these strategic conversations rapidly stumbles across the footprints of Shell and of Pierre Wack.[9] Indeed, one of GBN's founders – Peter Schwartz – was also previously part of the Shell scenarios team, and his successors at the giant energy company have helped WBCSD put their own scenarios together. An even earlier architect of Shell's long-standing program in this area, Wack published two seminal papers on the subject in the *Harvard Business Review* in 1985.[10] In them, he outlined "one thing or two learned while developing planning scenarios for Royal Dutch/Shell."

Scenarios, Wack said, deal not only with the hard facts of the "outer space" beyond the organization but also with the softer, fluid perceptual "inner space" of people's minds and emotions. At the time, his ambition was to bridge these two realms in such a way that Shell managers experienced a creative insight that generated a heartfelt "Aha!" as new strategic insights emerged. But the most useful and effective scenarios must now capture what is going on not only in the inner space of the corporate mind but also of the public mind.

Shell later pulled the two articles together to form a slim, blue-covered document called *The Gentle Art of Re-perceiving*. There were three key insights. First, during a time of rapid change, companies differ greatly in their effectiveness and speed in identifying and transforming information of strategic significance into strategic initiatives. And, second, the sheer amount of 'noise', caused by the conflicting signals to which they are exposed, infinitely complicates the task. Locked into the past, governments and companies alike can suffer strategic failure.

The third insight seeks to address these two problems. It stems from the fact that the human brain is much better at discriminating significant trends from the noise when it is listening (or watching) for something – or for one of several things. Hence the value of scenarios sketching out several possible emerging realities.

Any company has – or should have – a central business model, or 'Business Idea'. Once you have a plausible, exciting and above all divergent set of scenarios, says Kees van der Heijden in his book on the 'art of strategic conversation', "the analytical task is to 'walk' the Business Idea mentally through the various scenarios" to test whether they continue to create value in each. If they do not, the company may need to change its core competencies. And, in any event, uncertain times mean that any organization cannot afford to become locked into any particular strategy: it must develop and maintain an ongoing "strategic conversation".[11]

"Scenarios do not claim to be, and are not, value free," explained Ged Davis, the Shell scenarios expert who directed the WBCSD Global Scenarios Project.[12] "They recognise that we are prisoners of our own mindsets and language, and that understanding can be furthered with a new word or image, and especially a new story. We know our successors will have a richer language to discuss sustainability, and our task is to shine a light in their direction." The challenge, he concluded, is that we "want it all: human dignity; prosperity; and care for the planet."

THE LONG BOOMERS

So let's ask the obvious question: can we have it all? In the early years of the Environmental Revolution, forecasting exercises – most notably the Club of Rome's *Limits to Growth* study[13] – suggested that the world was racing towards a brick wall. Rising pollution and shrinking natural resources, we were warned, would undermine any prospects for a sustainable future. As we saw in Chapter 2, there are still very real grounds for concern. More recently, however, some scenario teams have begun to suggest that a degree of optimism may be more appropriate.

By their own admission, they are attempting a global confidence trick. Every so often, an entrepreneur plants a new idea or desire in people's brains. Think of Henry Ford's Model T, helping put America (then the world) on wheels, or Apple with its start-up claim that personal computers would provide "wheels for the brain". Evolutionary biologists like Richard Dawkins see such ideas as 'memes', the cultural equivalent of genes. They infect our brains, mutate, spread. And, every so often, they revolutionize what had once seemed to be the natural order of things.

So how about releasing the idea that the world is set for a 'Long Boom', running from 1980 through 2020? You can hear the protests from the economists, not just from hard-core environmentalists. Ridiculous! Incredible! Indeed, anyone who knows economic history knows that economic booms are aberrations, resulting from unusual combinations of contributory factors. Most economic historians would also argue the bigger the boom, the greater the ensuing bust.

But the very first line in *The Long Boom*, by Peter Schwartz, Peter Leyden and Joel Hyatt, explained: "The Long Boom is a positive meme about a better future." The hope was that the idea will prove contagious, spreading and influencing what people do. The internet was seen as providing fertile conditions for infecting perhaps 200 million people, then – as the print media pick up the story – a billion or two more.[15]

I have long been a believer in long-wave theories of economic expansion and contraction, so all of this reeked of heresy to me. But Schwartz has a strong track record. He worked for Shell's scenarios team, then co-founded GBN. So what persuades him that the Long Boom is, if not guaranteed, at least a real possibility? New technology, for one. While most of us tend to focus on how IT and the internet will transform our worlds, Schwartz and his colleagues argue that three other technology clusters will drive further revolutionary changes. They are biotechnology, the development of fuel cells and other new energy technologies, and nanotechnology – the process of manufacturing one atom at a time.

The only real barriers to the Long Boom, we are told, are political. So no problem there, then? Well, in the wake of what happened to Monsanto, after *The Long Boom* went to press, and then to the World Trade Organization (WTO) in Seattle, many people would see the prospect of a Long Boom as deeply unappealing. Even more so if it required further globalization and, speak it softly, further Americanization. So consider what the book dubs the "Politics of the Long Boom".

The three biggest constraints on economic growth, it concludes, have been: political conflicts resulting from clashes between interests or ideologies; social stresses arising from economic gaps producing misery amidst wealth; and, "finally and increasingly", ecological problems. All true, but who really sees politicians embracing this agenda? Well, Schwartz, Leyden and Hyatt, for three. They ended their book with an e-mail to the US President-elect, dated 15 January 2001, offering hints on how to turn the New Economy into the Long Boom.

Having been in the US as the extraordinary events around the 2000 presidential election unfolded, I know that George Bush and Al Gore had other things on their minds at the time, among them the "Butterfly Ballot", the dotcom crash and the deteriorating state of the US economy. But one thing is clear: whether or not we are in for elements of a Long Boom, the social, ecological and economic dimensions of future growth and wealth can only become more urgent. And some of the biggest breakthroughs, as box 16 suggests, may well come not only from rank outsiders but also from those we now see as "total losers".

 Box 16

Imagining the unimaginable

The fundamental trick with scenarios, says Ulrich Goluke, who helped direct the scenarios work at the World Business Council for Sustainable Development (WBCSD), "is to imagine the unimaginable, say the unspeakable and explore the painful." No wonder that so many of these scenarios remain secret! Perhaps there's another reason, too. When the Society for Organizational Learning (SoL) recently came up with four new economy scenarios, they noted: "There is nothing as boring as someone else's scenario of the future."[16]

Well, maybe, but WBCSD has produced several rounds of scenarios that have helped open out the sustainability debate. So, I ask Goluke, how do CEOs and other business leaders respond to challenging scenarios? "Overwhelmingly with denial," he replies.

"But that's normal and to be expected. As long as no one takes quality seriously, for example, we can all enjoy decent profit margins with shoddy products. Breaking away from the pack is usually not highly regarded. That's why I am more and more convinced that business leaders are the wrong pool for innovation. More likely, innovation will come from business losers (just as the Germans and Japanese came roaring back after WWII) or from new entrants."

That said, Goluke believes that scenarios can powerfully assist any company trying to undergo metamorphosis. "Scenarios are nothing new," he suggests. "It's the same technique we use to help our children develop ever more nuanced and discriminating frames through which to make sense of their world. We start them off with pure black and white, good and bad, do's and don'ts, and then introduce shades of gray, even color. Scenarios can – and do – fulfil the same function with Corporate Caterpillars or Locusts thinking of transforming themselves into Corporate Butterflies or Honeybees."

The transformation process, Goluke notes, is usually driven by charismatic leaders – "our heroes". But, he stresses, "once the tasks filter down to mere mortals in companies, who then need to perform heroic deeds, scenarios provide 'safe spaces' in which to explore the worlds to come."

FORTRESSES, FROGS AND JAZZ

The GBN team took a range of environment- and sustainability-related issues into account, but their scenarios were not primarily sustainability-focused. By contrast, the sets produced by the World Resources Institute (WRI) and, separately, by WBCSD were. The WRI scenarios are summarized in panel 12 (page 237). But, briefly stated, there is a pessimistic scenario (*Fortress World*), a halfway house (*Market World*), and an optimistic variant (*Transformed World*).

Both the WRI and WBCSD sets of scenarios reach out to the year 2050, and both have one negative scenario and two rather more positive variants. Both are fascinating, but the WBCSD scenarios are perhaps more relevant here because of the involvement of over 140 CEOs in that organization's governance and programs. They are all based on the same, pre-determined elements: the 'new', the 'many', and the 'connected'.

The *new* factors include the impact of technology (e.g. biotechnology, IT, nanotechnology), new business models (e.g. the dot-coms, Interface, the Grameen Bank in Bangladesh), the emerging global trading regime, and new forms of partnership between business, governments and NGOs. The *many* are the planet's growing world population, set to jump from just over 6 billion today to 9–11 billion by 2050 (see Chapter 2). The resulting demands for natural resources and for space will impose huge new stresses on global ecosystems. And the *connected* captures effects both of globalization and the evolving 'technosphere'. Our growing interconnectedness brings dramatically greater levels of interdependence.

Since they were first developed by WBCSD, the following three scenarios (*FROG!, GEOPolity* and *Jazz*) have been widely used. I have been involved in projects using these scenarios which focused on the implications for the life sciences sector and for global governance, for example, and with Denmark's Sophie's World Foundation, which focuses on young people around the world, on the implications for youth. While a fair number of scenarios have been developed and published since these three were launched, my sense is that this trio have most influenced the CEO class to date, at least in terms of their thinking on SD.[17]

The world of FROG! is comfortingly familiar, at least to begin with. Like WRI's *Fortress World* scenario, this is the least attractive of the three. Many countries experience a fair degree of economic success. Indeed, economic growth is a primary concern with most of them – and with most political parties. But as time passes the environmental and social costs are increasingly obvious. The problem is that when there are calls for higher environmental and social standards, the developing and emerging economies respond by saying 'First Raise Our Growth!' People value SD in this scenario, but don't give it high priority.

Corporate Caterpillars and Locusts are given a fairly flexible license to operate. The focus is mainly on profitability and short-term growth. There are signals of impending disaster, but they are misread or ignored. Technology does evolve, but too slowly. Business does launch significant SD initiatives, but they are typically too few, too little and too late. Local improvements in environmental quality lead to a perception that all significant environmental problems are being effectively tackled.

People here react like the proverbial frog: when placed in boiling water, the frog leaped out of danger; but when placed in cold water that is gradually heated to boiling point, the complacent frog gets used to the changing conditions – and dies.

By contrast, in the GEOPolity world a series of real and perceived problems help wake people up to the dangers of an overly narrow economic model. In this future, the fact that governments have lost credibility as problem-solvers means that people initially expect multinationals to step into the breach. But the business sector is unable or unwilling to respond adequately. At the same time, there is growing interest in such concepts as 'sustainable cities' and 'sustainable national accounting', but few business leaders are prepared to invest in making these things happen.

In the absence of leadership from business or traditional forms of government, new institutional systems start to emerge. Corporate Butterflies and Honeybees are among those lobbying for new forms of global and corporate governance. One is the Global Ecosystem Organization (GEO). This is given – or assumes – broad powers to design and enforce global standards and measures to preserve the environment and society, even if doing so requires economic sacrifice.

Over time, governments are rejuvenated as focal points of civil society. They begin to come down hard on Corporate Caterpillars and Locusts that have run amok in the intervening period. And they increasingly create market conditions favorable to the development of business of all sizes that adopt and adapt Corporate Butterfly and Honeybee value creation models.

And then there's the third scenario, Jazz. As WBCSD puts it, "this is a world of social and technological innovations, experimentation, rapid adaptation, much voluntary interconnectedness, and a powerful and ever-changing global market. What enables the quick learning and subsequent innovation in Jazz is high transparency – the widespread availability of information about ingredients in products, sources of inputs, company financial, environmental, and social data, government decision-making processes, and almost anything else concerned consumers want to know."

In this highly competitive and interconnected world, businesses increasingly see strategic advantage in being perceived as – and being – environmentally and socially responsible. As a result, many become pro-active leaders in responding to a wide range of social and environmental challenges. This is a world in which NGOs, governments, concerned consumers and businesses learn to act as partners and to operate mainly through market mechanisms – or everybody fails.

This is a high-risk world for Corporate Locusts – and for any Corporate Caterpillars that are slow to adapt. It is also a turbulent, risky world for many Corporate Butterflies, simply because of the speed and unpredictability of change. "Achievement of the new environmental and social standards occurs largely out of self-interest," the WBCSD team explained. "The public is made aware of transgressions and quickly acts against companies or countries that violate standards." Interestingly, Corporate Butterflies and Honeybees become increasingly sensitive to problems elsewhere in their value webs, monitoring their relationships with both suppliers and customers. Where problems begin to emerge, risky partners are dropped with little room for appeal.

Clearly, none of these three visions of the future is likely to play out in full. The future is likely to be a mix of all three scenarios – and of others we can hardly even guess at today. But the use of such scenarios certainly helps companies and other business organizations to fine-tune their radar screens, so they detect early warning signals among the background noise. And that's a process which can also be boosted by people, including so-called 'tempered radicals', who understand the new agendas – partly, as we see in Chapter 13, because they have helped to create them.

Box 17: Blips on the screen

Intergenerational politics

Passing through airports, I scoop up armfuls of magazines. On a recent trip to Brussels, I grabbed the latest *Foreign Affairs* – partly because of its feature on the global aging crisis. Aging had been on my mind, perhaps not unconnected with the fact that this was my fiftieth year. But I am also interested in the impact that the graying of western populations will have on our capacity to address the social and environmental challenges we now face.

In *The Green Wave*, a report I wrote for Earth Day 1990, I warned of the environmental implications of this 'graying' trend. "One could ask whether the baby boom generation will remain as environmentally committed as it grows longer in the tooth," I mused, "but there are a number of more serious implications posed by the growing number of elderly people in our societies." Among looming intergenerational friction points, I warned, would be health care, welfare and pension rights.

The article that caught my eye in Heathrow was "Gray Dawn: The Global Aging Crisis," by Peter Peterson, deputy chairman of The Federal Reserve Bank of New York. "Unlike with global warming," he argues, "there can be little debate over whether or when global aging will manifest itself." The impact, he predicts, will "spark economic crises that will dwarf the recent meltdowns in Asia and Russia." The cost will run into quadrillions of dollars over the next century, massively affecting – my words, not his – our ability to tackle the SD agenda.

Peterson talks of the "Floridization" of the world, with country after country mimicking that state's huge concentration of senior citizens. In Florida's case, they now account for 19 percent of the population. Italy will hit this mark in 2003, Japan in 2005, Germany in 2006. France and Britain will pass present-day Florida around 2016, while the USA and Canada are forecast to do so in 2021 and 2023. This trend is revolutionary: until the Industrial Revolution, people aged 65 and over never amounted to more than 2–3 percent of the population.

We all know the results will include an unprecedented burden on working-age people, but do we really understand to what extent? The number of the 'old old' (over 85), demanding much greater health care resources, will explode. The 'old old' consume dramatically more health resources than the 'young old', aged 65–84. Worker shortages will likely spur huge immigration, taxing the ability of societies to maintain their cultural identity and social priorities.

Will our societies retain the will – let alone the resources – to tackle international security threats, military or environmental? Will we see the Old/Young divide rivaling the North/South divide? If we fail to prepare for the 'Gray Dawn', the prospects are gloomy. Some warn, for example, that the unfunded pension rights in many EU countries represent a clear and future danger as deadly as the iceberg was to the *Titanic*. Peterson believes the European Central Bank, the euro and half a century of progress towards European unity could founder as a result. SD is about intergenerational equity, a concept some see as diffuse, distant. Not so. Intergenerational tensions will be the very stuff of the 21st century politics.

PANEL 12

Transformed worlds

Consider: Was it accidental that 1997's Nobel Prize winners for economic science were soon at the epicenter of the market-wrenching Long Term Capital Management débâcle? And was it accidental that 1998's prize went to someone with radically different ideas? Hardly. The 1997 prize went to Myron S. Scholes and Robert C. Merton for their work on options-pricing theory, the 'rocket science' underpinning hedge funds like LTCM. They literally wrote the book on financial derivatives. Yet their spectacular failure brought world financial markets to the brink of a chasm. LTCM's mathematical models did for global financial markets what that proverbial butterfly's wings in the rainforest did for the world's weather.

Which brings us to the 1998 winner, Amartya Sen. Professor Sen, whose ambition is to restore an ethical dimension to the discussion of vital economic problems, started as a rank outsider. His work was seen as wildly unfashionable. As *The New York Times* put it, he was "out of step with the value-free, specialized approach that the economics profession values so highly." However, helpfully, the Royal Swedish Academy of Sciences made sweeping changes in its prize rules, accepting non-economists on the prize committee.

Great, but why is this important? Well, answers began to crystallize in my brain when I was in Washington DC, attending a landmark conference organized by the World Resources Institute (WRI). Allen Hammond, a key player in a fascinating WRI research program called "Project 2050", kicked off, drawing heavily on his just-published book, *Which World? Scenarios for the 21st Century*.[19] And his conclusions and recommendations would have made a lot more sense to Sen than to Scholes and Merton.

The economic, social and environmental downsides of current forms of development haunt such organizations as WRI. In response, they deploy policy proposals and rafts of peer-reviewed data to underpin their argument that key world regions are going down the tubes. But theirs is a well-shaken cocktail of optimism and pessimism. For example, they believe that SD will be delivered through markets, with business helping to create markets and delivering the necessary finance, technology, products and services.

Their first scenario, *Market World*, assumes economic reform and technological innovation will drive rapid economic growth – and that developing countries will be successfully integrated into the global economy. Anyone who reads the *Wall Street Journal* or *Economist* will know how the arguments might run.

The second scenario, *Fortress World*, is much gloomier. Markets and governments fail to address looming environmental disasters or to redress the ever-widening chasm between haves and have-nots. Result: "islands of prosperity in oceans of poverty". Some people successfully attempt stealth wealth, but the chasm between these different worlds will become painfully – dangerously – obvious.

Happily, there is a third option, *Transformed World*. And, no, this isn't a Disneyworld confection. It envisions a future in which power and wealth are much more evenly shared. Grass-root coalitions, massively boosted by the internet, powerfully shape how governments, business and communities behave. Like the 'Long Boom' scenario developed by GBN, this is a positive meme, designed to infect a wider world.

In this third scenario, the butterfly effect operates with increasing power. New forms of governance emerge, often starting on the political margins. Remember how the anti-landmines campaign threw governments and arms-makers on the defensive? Inevitably, the 21st century will mix all three scenarios – and others. But the ideas of Hammond, WRI and Sen are crucial because they encourage us (and the world's growing number of Citizen CEOs) to believe that we can choose at least some elements of the future we want.[20]

CHAPTER 13

Kaleidoscope
A dipstick survey of SD thought-leaders

It's messy inside a chrysalis, but this is where metamorphosis happens. And it's the same inside Corporate Chrysalids. Prize open these cocoons, and you find corporate change agents playing the same sort of role that hormones and 'imaginal cells' play inside a chrysalis. Ask them what they are trying to do, and some will offer road-maps or balanced scorecards like those consultants use to boil down complex processes (Figure 13.1). Fine, helpful even, but – although it's always comforting to see things in boxes – the real world isn't like that. It's organic.

So, to get a better sense of where we may be headed, I surveyed some of those who work alongside Corporate Chrysalids, helping guide Citizen CEOs. These people often create value by bringing the outside world in to companies. And one thing they can never afford to forget is that no battle is ever totally won. August management journals like the *Harvard Business Review* run articles with titles like:

Figure 13.1   Sustainability balanced scorecard.
Source: KPMG.

"Why Good Companies Go Bad."[21] The immediate sense of crisis wears off, an SD-aware CEO moves on, market conditions change.

Treat what follows like a kaleidoscope. I took a set of interesting perspectives and gave them a good shake. This is how they ended up looking to me. But try picking your own set of perspectives and giving them a shake, too. Know, too, that all of this should come with a health warning. It's not to do with statistical rigor; it's to do with our ability to change the world. One of the world's top business gurus admits that even the best advice isn't necessarily going to work miracles. "The whole secret to our success," Tom Peters told *Fortune*, "is being able to con ourselves into believing that we're going to change the world, because statistically we are unlikely to do it."[22] Well, again fine, self-criticism can be healthy, but most of those I talked to are confident they are making a difference.

Most say they have worked with business leaders for at least five years, with a fair number having started at least 10 years ago. Several claim track records of around 20 years. Wouter van Dieren of IMSA says he began tackling CEOs as early as 1970, aged 28, as the new chairman of Friends of the Earth Netherlands. There's a difference, though, between challenging and *advising* CEOs. Only Thilo Bode, who led Greenpeace International for a long stint, explicitly mentioned making it to the CEO's Mecca, at the World Economic Forum in Davos (page 203), challenging business leaders just when they thought they were safe. But Australian Molly Harriss Olson, who we will hear from in a moment, is also something of an old Davos hand.

So what sort of companies do these people actually advise? They came up with an A-to-V: ABB, Ahold, Akzo-Nobel, Algol, Allianz, Banque Cortal, BASF, Ben & Jerry's, Bosch, BP, Carrefour, Chiquita, Coca-Cola, Daimler-Benz (now Daimler-Chrysler), Danone, De Beers, Dow Chemical, Dutch Railways, Electrolux, Eroski, The Gap, Heineken, Hoechst (now part of Aventis), Iceland, ICI, Interface, KBB, Lafarge, Levi Strauss & Co., Monsanto, Nike, Norsk Hydro, Procter & Gamble, Renault, the Schmidheiny Group, Seagrams, Shell International, Shell USA, SITA, Svenska Cellulosa, Swatch, Tetra Pak, and Volkswagen. And the list would have been much longer if I had probed.

Wouldn't you just love to be able to click on each company name and hear the inside story of what really happened, or didn't? To find out how change agents decide whether or not to work with a particular CEO or company? "I have learned to trust my feelings," explains Elisabeth Laville of Paris-based Utopies. "If the CEO or board member in front of me is not sincerely committed to SD, then he/she won't have what it takes. Incidentally, I don't think that companies are evil, and since I really am optimistic, I believe that almost any company run by sincere, committed people (except probably one producing land-mines) can take significant steps towards sustainability."

These people's life-stories would make fascinating reading. Some who came from the business side say their colleagues accused them of joining the "beads and sandals brigade". Claude Fussler, once of Dow Chemical and then seconded to the World Business Council for Sustainable Development (WBCSD), recalls: "Sometimes my business colleagues looked at me like I had been 'buying in' to SD initiatives too lightly." But those from the NGO side got a rather rougher ride. "Radical NGOs have accused me of 'sleeping with the enemy,'" says Sir Geoffrey Chandler, who has chaired the UK business group of Amnesty International (and is a rare bird indeed, in that he has worked at high levels for industry, government and NGOs). But he stresses that "if companies need NGOs for their knowledge, NGOs also need companies for their influence if we wish to change the world."

In some cases, things got nastier. "While I haven't been accused of selling out," says Bob Dunn of Business for Social Responsibility (BSR), "I have been attacked publicly at various times as I sought to work through difficult situations. While I was working for Levi Strauss & Co., for example, social activists threw rocks and tried to overturn a car I was driving." Since he joined BSR, the criticisms have been because BSR "won't comment publicly on the work we do with companies without their permission."

The assaults on Wouter van Dieren of eco-consultants IMSA were even more energetic. "Indeed," he muses, "I have frequently been accused of selling out, by my former NGO friends, by the Dutch Parliament, by all sorts of people. One group said industry was the enemy, comparable to the Nazis, while the NGOs are the Resistance. So an NGO person who comes 'out of the bush' to advise industry is automatically a traitor. In 1988, a full-page article in *De Volksrant* laid this claim against me. I lost numerous friends, and 70 percent of IMSA's staff left."

Other change agents, from different backgrounds, haven't had quite these problems. "My credentials as a narrow minded economist are unchallenged!", quips Ulrich Steger, who has served as a German state economics minister, an environment director at Volkswagen and, now, as a business school professor. But what goes around, comes around. "Today," van Dieren notes, tongue firmly in cheek, "my prestige is untouchable, the press now naming me the national Green Guru, or even the Green Pope. This last nickname I like best," he says, "as it fits my image of an old patriarch, ignorant of reality and worldly affairs!"

Some activists who have "come in from the cold" have turned on old colleagues. Others have simply been dismissive. Des Wilson, who founded Shelter and chaired Friends of the Earth UK, put it this way when he later worked at British Airports Authority (BAA): "If you want to stand outside BAA with leaflets and a banner, you'll get wet, you'll get cold and no one will take any notice. The momen you walk in the door, people will listen."[23]

Well, maybe, but if we have learned anything, it is that driving radical chang in companies, value-webs and economies takes every sort of pressure, internal an external. Often we don't know what will work until something quite unexpecte creates a breakthrough. And it is in the very nature of politics and business that som of yesterday's radicals become today's insiders, as Van Dieren and Wilson both did.

Professor Debra Meyerson calls such people "tempered radicals" [24]. Lik 'Chrys' (panel 1, page 9), they challenge the status quo. So, is there a rule book fo such change agents? Well, Meyerson does offer the following tips: *Seek small wins* break the problems up into smaller, more manageable pieces. *Act locally an authentically*: change comes because change agents stay true to their ideals. *Speak th language*: people respond better if they can understand and empathize with what yo are saying. And *build affiliations*: recognize that radicalism can be isolating, so buil networks. And Geoffrey Chandler insists I add here: "Seek multipliers, or th 'infection' factor."

Now, for those who aspire to become Citizen CEOs, for those who work wit such leaders, and for those who recruit people to drive corporate culture chang processes, here are some results of our dipstick survey of change agents:

WHAT'S THE #1 GLOBAL ISSUE FOR BUSINESS?

On this, at least, there was consensus. The S-word was on every tongue, the SL agenda being seen as central for companies operating in a wide range of sectors. Som may see corporate sector development (CSR) and sustainable development (SD) a interchangeable, but one CEO noted recently that "CSR can be read as 'business a usual plus 5 percent', whereas you know that SD has to be about fundamenta change." And the triple bottom line definition of SD was universally accepted.

IS THIS GETTING THROUGH TO BOARDS?

Yes, CSR and SD priorities are percolating up inside companies, driven by bot internal and external pressures. "We are living in a period of great expectations," says Doug Miller, managing director of Toronto-based Environics International, "with people expecting to improve the quality of their lives and believing they can get it all." He notes: "I visit [many] boardrooms [each] year and I can tell you, the members o the board are living in fear of getting their corporate reputations blown away in two months on the internet."[25]

But many CEOs and board members still don't get it, even when presented with the facts by leading experts. "CEOs have short attention spans," comments Paul Hawken of the California-based Natural Capital Institute, "and the work I am involved with doesn't lend itself to sound-bites. Many a time, I have presented to senior management and felt slightly soiled afterwards. The stony faces, the blank looks, the boredom. And then, every so often, you get a group that is interested, aware, and open. We have to face the fact that boards of directors are not necessarily the sharpest knives in the drawer."

SO, WHAT SWITCHES THEM ON?

The bad news is that crises and fear are still seen as the most effective ways of waking up CEOs and boards. Hawken lists the real drivers as follows: "Activism, boycotts, protests, litigation and legislation." Oddly, international stock market listings can also help. South African Breweries recently decided to list on the London Stock Exchange. Its CEO, Graham Mackay, notes that he now spends 40 percent of his time on stakeholder relations, compared to no more than 15 percent when SAB was listed in South Africa.[26]

Some see consumer power and wider citizen pressures as crucial. One change agent quoted Philippe Starck to the effect that: "The average consumer does not exist. She is my mother or my daughter. And I would not dare to sell her bad products." Others remain skeptical. "Campaigners fool themselves if they think the odd triumph against a Monsanto, Shell or Nike is evidence of some radical consumerate (i.e. an electorate that prefers to shop than vote)," warns Forum for the Future's Jonathon Porritt.[27]

That said, first mover advantage has proven to be very profitable for Australian CEOs according to Molly Harriss Olson of Eco Futures. Richard Pratt of Visy Industries set up Australia's first office and curbside recycling programs, and this is now a billion dollar business turning waste to profits. Similarly, she says, Doug Shears, CEO of ICM, Australia's largest privately held integrated agri-business, has positioned his company at the forefront of the food safety issue, knowing that this is increasingly important to young people – and that ICM's profitability in the future will likely be driven by the consumer choices these people make.

Peter Senge of MIT is also positive, observing that several factors helped the Society for Organizational Learning (SoL), which he chairs, to successfully launch its new Sustainability Consortium. "Looking back," he says, "I believe three currents converged to create the Consortium: new guiding ideas about business and the 'Next

Industrial Revolution', knowledge and experience in sustaining transformational change, and a group of firms committed to leading through action."[28]

As an example of guiding ideas, he instances the 'natural capitalism' work of Paul Hawken, in collaboration with Amory and Hunter Lovins, and the work of eco-architect Bill McDonough and his colleague Michael Braungart, co-founders of McDonough Braungart Design Chemistry. McDonough is working with Bill Ford on an ambitious environmental regeneration scheme for Ford's massive old Rouge production site. In relation to transformational change, Senge notes the growing interest in mental and business models. And he points to the growing membership of the SoL Sustainability Consortium, with members required to make sustainability a strategic cornerstone, as evidence of the commitment of at least some companies to action.

WHICH CEOs GET IT?

Top business people – really top people – struggle to get their minds around the SD agenda, says Wouter van Dieren. "They see green as left-wing, and tend to suspect every part of it." But some are overcoming this "paranoia" – and growing numbers come from a new generation, less affected by it. One result: the business leaders nominated as "getting it" (but see page 180) are a slightly weird, kaleidoscopic mix of Corporate Locusts, Caterpillars, Butterflies and Honeybees.

Among those named at least once: **Ray Anderson** (Interface), **Jaime Augusto Ayala** (Ayala Corporation, Philippines), **Percy Barnevik** (ex-ABB), **Tom Chappel** (Tom's of Maine), **Ben Cohen** (Ben & Jerry's), **Douglas T. Dean** (Collex), **Bill Ford** (Ford Motor Company), **Sir John Browne** (BP), **David George** (United Technologies), **Lou Gerstner** (IBM), **Seth Goldman** (Honest Tea), **Danny Grossman** (Wild Planet Toys), **Chad Holliday** (DuPont), **Chantal Jaquet** (Carrefour), **Guilerme Leal** (Natura), **Francois Lemarchand** (Nature & Découvertes), **Göran Lindahl** (when with ABB), **Erling Lorentzen** (Aracruz Celulose, Brazil), **Aarnout Loudon** (when with Akzo), **Graham Mackay** (South African Breweries), **John McGrath** (ex-Diageo), **Jerome Monod** (Suez Lyonnaise des Eaux), **Sir Mark Moody-Stuart** (Shell International), **John Morgridge** (Cisco Systems), **Mads Øvlisen** (Novo Nordisk), **Jacques Pétry** (SITA), **Pasquale Pistorio** (STMicroelectronics), **Bill Platt** (formerly at Hewlett-Packard, now at Kendall-Jackson Winery), **Richard Pratt** (Visy Industries), **Anita Roddick** (Body Shop International), **Stephan Schmidheiny** (founder of Business Council for Sustainable Development), **Doug Shears** (ICM International), **(Lord) David Simon** (ex-BP), **Ratan Tata** (Tata Industries), **Phil Watts** (Royal Dutch/Shell),

John White (Global Renewables), **Judy Wicks** (White Dog Enterprises), **Dr Herman Wijffels** (when with Rabobank) and **Robert Wilson** (Rio Tinto).

When I showed this list to colleagues, there were a fair number of "Yes, but" comments. But if you are a CEO or board member wanting to move up the Citizen CEO learning curve, those are some people you might want to track down PDQ as potential models or even mentors. And it's interesting to see how the cross-connects between the CEO and sustainability worlds are developing: for example, shortly after stepping down from ABB, Göran Lindahl said he would chair the international advisory board of the Alliance for Global Sustainability, backed by MIT, the Swiss Federal Institute of Technology and the University of Tokyo.

WHAT CEO CHARACTERISTICS HELP?

Leadership characteristics most often mentioned were: *Vision. A values orientation. An ability to see the company as others see it. Passion. Courage. Freedom from group-think. Personal commitment. Honesty. Candor. Openness. An inquiring mind. An ability to learn. A willingness to lead, and to walk the talk. A focus on legacy. A recognition that business as usual is putting the planet out of business. An understanding that you cannot have a sustainable company in an unsustainable world. And a sense of humor.* Anyone head-hunting CEOs or board members might want to run candidates off against this checklist.

WHAT ABOUT CEO OR BOARD MEMBERS WHO DON'T GET IT?

Not an unknown problem. One imaginative suggestion comes from WBCSD's Claude Fussler, who suggests a recalcitrant CEO should spend "a month as an NGO front-line volunteer." Paul Hawken offers an even more striking idea. "The most interesting process I heard of recently for waking up a board," he says, "was proposed to the senior management of a huge office supply chain by Michael Marx of the Coastal Rainforest Coalition. As a condition for them to stop being picketed for their use of non-recycled paper and their use of paper made from fiber from old growth forests, they had to fly over clear-cut primary forests, as well as walk the land, see the silted streams, watch the dying salmon unable to spawn. In other words, they had to do a hands-on visit to the results of their purchasing decisions."

WHAT OF MARKETS?

Broadly, there is now strong interest in the role of markets, although the often difficult interplay between values and value creation surfaced time and again in the

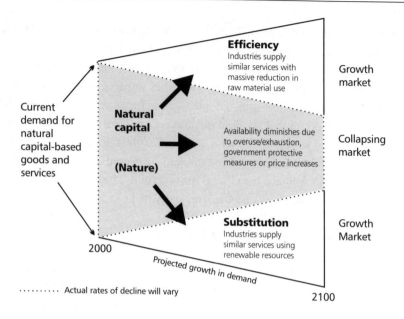

Figure 13.2   Natural capitalism, 2000–2100.
Source: Paul Hohnen, Greenpeace International.

replies. "The real problem," Jane Nelson concludes, "is that too many business people still think in 'boxes' and there is a box for values and one for value creation, rather than looking at one (values) underpinning the other (value creation)."

But change is in the air. Much media attention has been focused on anti-capitalism, but a considerable rump of the SD movement is interested in the potential positive power of markets. Many change agents are watching the internal carbon trading schemes evolving in companies like BP and Shell. There is real interest in seeing whether schemes like STEPS, the Shell Tradable Emission Permit System, can cut the giant oil company's greenhouse gas emissions by 10 percent by 2002 from 1990 levels. And, whatever the short-term outcomes, there is a sense that at last the costs of carbon are beginning to be taken into account.

The Big Squeeze that will be a crucial factor in creating and driving the Chrysalis Economy will operate on a longer time-scale than the 2000–2030 period we take here. Indeed, Paul Hohnen of Greenpeace offers the diagram shown in Figure 13.2, with a 100-year time-scale. He argues that efficiency and substitution measures will progressively squeeze unsustainable technologies, business models and industries through the next century.

WHO BACKS NEW TECHNOLOGY?

Most of these people back at least some forms of new technology, but don't expect them to give you tips on which sustainable technologies to invest in. That said, Paul Hawken, Amory Lovins and Bill McDonough are all happy to lay out likely characteristics of tomorrow's sustainable technologies. In simple terms, what they dub the 'Next Industrial Revolution' will be based on materials and products that increasingly behave as natural materials and products do.

The new business model, they say, will not only be about *eco-efficiency* (making things less bad for the environment) but also about *eco-effectiveness* (making them increasingly beneficial to the environment, like the leaves of a forest).[29] What these people are wary of doing, however, is betting on one market mechanism, one technology, over all others. Rather, most sense the wisdom of backing several horses.

As a general principle, Lovins notes that: "Natural capitalism businesses take their values from their customers, their designs from nature and their discipline from the marketplace. For them, there is no contradiction between what people do on the job and what they want for their kids when they go home."[30]

WHAT'S THE SINGLE GREATEST BARRIER TO SD?

Not technology, it seems. "Boardroom myopia," suggests Geoffrey Chandler (ignoring the question and listing *three* barriers), coupled with "the myth that there is a 'free' market which we constrain at our peril, and the fallacy that the purpose of a company is to provide value to shareholders, so confusing ends and means, and making money the sole measure of performance." In fact, most answers clustered around problems created by short-term pressures exerted by the financial markets.

"This calls for more leadership on the part of CEOs and boards," argues Jane Nelson, "and more efforts to boost understanding of the 'business case'." "Courage," adds Molly Harriss Olson. "It is a rare quality at the best of times and highly endangered in turbulent times for business."

A second order problem, but one likely to grow in importance, is behind-the-scenes corporate lobbying. Increasingly, the focus will be on "business lobbying," say Thilo Bode (ex-executive director) and Paul Hohnen (special adviser) of Greenpeace International, "or support for government regulations which permit, or even encourage, large-scale environmental degradation and pollution."

Another issue is that, as the agenda moves on, previous public interest groupings often become entrenched, becalmed. You see this most clearly where you have different generations of the same family working in the same company. One person I have worked with at Ford is Dave Berdish. His grandfather, Rufus, started work at Ford's Rouge Complex in the 1930s. He was a trade union activist, and was beaten up at the 'Battle of the Overpass' by Ford security people in 1937. Later, Dave recalls, Rufus used to write "under pseudonyms like Karl, Lenin, Marx." As a result, "the Government knew him. When I was hired by Ford Aerospace in 1983, I had to be cleared for classified jobs for the CIA and NSA. I had to go through extensive lie detector tests to prove that I was not influenced by a man I barely knew."

In retrospect, the union movement failed to respond in time to the wider agendas that began to evolve in the 1960s. So what would Red Rufus think of Green Dave? "I'm pretty sure he'd be proud of the work I am doing on sustainability," Dave replies, "and pleased that I'm supporting the Rouge greening initiative proposed by Bill McDonough. But if he knew I was part of management, he'd be rolling in his grave!"

As I developed this chapter, I even began to wonder whether there might be a gene for change agents? Talking to Sarah Severn, Director for Corporate Responsibility at Nike, I found that she was related to William Cobbett, the extraordinary English journalist and MP who hounded the British Establishment during the period when the country was being rapidly transformed by the Industrial Revolution. But the evidence suggests that, whether it's a question of nature or nurture, there is a huge wave of new change agents coming through who can't easily track their family lines back to a 'Red Rufus' or, as Cobbett's opponents dubbed him, a 'Peter Porcupine'.[31]

CAN CORPORATE CULTURES CHANGE – AND HOW?

Given enough time, any corporate culture can change – although it is amazing how resistant to change some companies can be. Interestingly, some CEOs seem to think you can change corporate cultures at the flick of a switch. The evidence suggests that most can't.

One interesting change agent in this area is Alan AtKisson, co-founder of Sustainable Seattle. He sees organizational cultures like amoebas. When a new piece of food comes along, an amoeba buds off a 'pseudopod', which tests and then engulfs the morsel. In the same way, different people in an organization play different roles in cultural adaptation. The *Innovator* is first on the scene, but often has difficulty selling a new idea internally. *Change Agents* are deeper into the culture, helping achieve buy-in. *Transformers* are the real doorkeepers, however, adapting new thinking so it can be adopted by *Mainstreamers*.[32]

One example of a transformer might be an effective Chief Sustainability Officer. Slowing things down, meanwhile, are *Laggards*, *Spiritual Recluses* and *Curmudgeons*. Indeed, it's no accident that corporate culture change experts have started to talk about 'stability structures' and 'shock absorbers'. Too many companies are already suffering from change fatigue.[33]

To help cope with such problems, AtKisson has evolved 'The Innovation Diffusion Game', to help teams understand how innovation can spread through cultures and organizations. This includes 'The Amoeba Game', giving players first-hand experience of what it is like when parts of an organism – or organization – try to race ahead of the main body. So has he ever tried it with a corporate board? "Not yet," he says, "but it would be well suited to one, if the group were large enough: 25 is a good number."

AND THE NEW ECONOMY?

Mixed views here. Some say it is a sideshow, while others see the internet as a powerful lever for CSR and SD. That said, few change agents surveyed had yet worked with new economy companies, with most efforts concentrated on old economy players. And it's interesting that most of the CEOs nominated as "getting it" were also old economy folk, an interesting exception being Pasquale Pistorio of STMicroelectronics. An opportunity space to be invaded? Among those now diving in are the World Resources Institute and Forum for the Future, with its *digital futures* initiative.

WHAT VALUES DRIVE YOUR WORK?

A wide range of values surfaced. So, based on the replies, if you were writing a job description for a top-notch corporate change agent, what values would you specify? Change agent responses included: commitment; an appreciation for diversity; a spirit of cooperation; courage; enthusiasm; fairness; honesty; humility; inclusiveness; initiative; inspiration; integrity; justice; open mindedness; respect; responsibility; and "unrealistic ambition".

In relation to that last item, many of these business leaders are in the "unrealistic" process of creating new market realities. But, I would venture that most change agents are also driven by a conviction that even such business leaders still have much to learn about the CSR and SD agendas, representing a huge opportunity to engage, learn and make a difference.

In the process, they act as ambassadors for the future and for respect. "If the sustainability movement is to succeed," says Paul Hawken, "which I think it will, it needs to model, as Gandhi said, what it wants the world to become. At the very heart of sustainability is respect, the unconditional respect for other human beings even if we do not agree with them. I should probably say, especially if we don't agree with them. That respect must be at the very heart and foundation of sustainability, or we will simply end up as another marginal movement that thinks it is right."

WHERE DO NUMBERS FIT IN?

Visions and values will only get us so far. One of the most interesting responses came from Rupert Howes of Forum for the Future. Working with companies like Anglian Water, cider producer Bulmers, construction company Carillion, and Ray Anderson's Interface, he and his colleagues have found that if you want to catch board-level attention, putting numbers on key aspects of the SD agenda helps enormously. Howes, who I watched in action at a meeting of the sustainability committee of Anglian Water's board, originally trained as an accountant. And, helpfully, it shows.

These companies have already signed up to sustainability, he notes, as illustrated by the fact that Anglian has a sustainability committee, or that Bulmers has a sustainability director. But the real challenge is getting all this into the mainstream. And that means engaging the finance department. Although the work started with the preparation of environmental external cost accounts, Howes has been asked in each case to extend the accounts to aspects of the company's social performance.

So how much would such companies have to pay or invest if they were to turn the environmental dimension of their triple bottom line performance neutral? Based on his work to date, Howes reckons that the answer would be around 3 percent of turnover and between 8 and 15 percent of profits. That's a lot of money, but nothing like as much as some of these board members had been fearing. That said, the latest Interface accounts are more thorough, he notes, and the proportion of profits has slid up to 20 percent.

WHERE WILL THE REAL ACTION BE?

Most readers of *The Chrysalis Economy* live and work in the OECD world, the rich world. So the temptation is to focus on the OECD world when thinking of what to do next. But wait a moment! Remember the Sustainability Triangle, shown as Figure 7.1

on page 132? Look at the bottom line, the 'Raise the Bottom' fractal. The real opportunities for strategic growth are often going to lie there, say professors C.K. Prahalad and Stuart L. Hart.[34] Some folk are even beginning to talk of a B24B model, focusing on the needs of the world's poorest four billion people.

We have been blind to these opportunities for creating market opportunities out of the very real SD needs of the poor countries, they say, because major companies assume their current cost structures as a given, focus on products not functionality (e.g. on detergents, not cleanliness), think of product rather than business innovations, and tend to switch off when a new market opportunity has a humanitarian element.

Yet the emergence of what Prahalad and Hart call the 'Tier 4' market, made up of four billion people, represents one of the most important new realities of the 21st century. And this isn't simply a question of opportunities. There are threats, too. Either we work out ways of making this market work, or some of these billions of people are going to make life a lot less comfortable in the rich world.

ANY ADVICE FOR NEW KIDS ON THE BLOCK?

The 'Chrysalis Effect' will only make companies and their value-webs more sustainable over time if the relevant political (and regulatory) pressures are sustained over time. For this to happen, new generations of change agents must be recruited, trained and deployed. Much of the running to date has been made by the Sixties generation, my generation (panel 13, page 256), whereas the sheer scale of the opportunity space now emerging will demand huge numbers of new entrants.

Happily, new voices are coming into the conversation. The surprise best-seller *No Logo*, by Naomi Klein, is a great example of the way in which the anti-corporate movement continues to evolve and recruit.[35] Another powerful critic of what he calls "extreme capitalism" is Thomas Frank, who in his book *One Market Under God* also attacks the notion that markets can solve all our problems.[36] But anyone who sees a central role for business in SD must acknowledge a future for brands. A 'No Logo' world would not necessarily be a more responsible world. "Brands have a reputation to protect that can be worth billions," says Marcel Knobil, global chairman of Superbrands. "The owners of unbranded goods would be anonymous and would have little or no reputation to protect." No brand, no leverage for campaigners and other change agents?

So, what advice would today's leading change agents offer those following in their tracks? Here are some of their suggestions:

The challenge of steering Supertanker Earth towards an environmentally sustainable course is the greatest, most exhilarating, most important challenge of the 21st century. Get involved. Be prepared to be frustrated, curious, creative and open. And, to MBA students: It's not just about money. Use your entrepreneurial skills to advance something bigger than your company's market share. Remember the caution: unlimited growth is also the philosophy of the cancer cell.

Thilo Bode and **Paul Hohnen** (Greenpeace International, The Netherlands)

Get practical experience of business. Bring your own personal values to the work and don't surrender them to an unacceptable corporate ethos. Avoid arrogance, and understand what has created it. Remember, for yourself and for the company, that there are values more important than money.

Sir Geoffrey Chandler (Amnesty International, UK)

It can only be done if you believe in some end target. If you are willing to learn a thousand skills. If you are broadly equipped with both technical and educational or communication talents. And if you do not want to make quick, big money. But it is very rewarding work indeed.

Wouter Van Dieren (IMSA, The Netherlands)

I'd encourage them to learn the fundamentals and culture of the world of business. Without this, it's very difficult to be a successful agent for change. I'd also urge them to bring to business responsibilities a broad knowledge of our society and its aspirations, because that's the only way to ensure the ongoing viability of business as an institution. Ultimately, though, this work is about acquiring wisdom, not knowledge. There's an old quote I like, but I don't know the source: 'For every complex problem, there is a simple solution that is wrong.'

Bob Dunn (Business for Social Responsibility, USA)

"Stick to whatever seems most exciting to you – and beware of whatever bothers you."

Elisabeth Laville (Utopies, France)

Remember that SD makes for strange bedfellows. Expect the unexpected. John Browne did more in one speech to transform the global debate on Climate Change than the IPCC and Greenpeace had been able to do with years of effort.

Molly Harriss Olson (Eco-Futures, Australia)

Engage your head and your heart. Don't be shy to talk about values to business leaders and about profits to anti-capitalism campaigners. Celebrate diversity. Embrace complexity. Build learning networks and alliances. And work with a sense of urgency. It helps if you enjoy roller coaster rides. But you'll never be bored.

Jane Nelson (International Business Leaders Forum, UK)

Which is a great platform from which to jump to **Paul Hawken** (Natural Capitalism Institute, USA): *"Find a mentor,"* he suggests, *"carry her bag, listen up, read voraciously, get tapes, go to meetings, know how a business works, and if you don't, work in one. Get every experience possible before thinking you can walk into a boardroom."*

And so, after a final vigorous shake of the kaleidoscope, what are my own concluding suggestions?

- First, learn from some of the real achievements of the new economy and work on *scalability*. In this case, whatever we do, at whatever level, must be able to scale up to an equitable, sustainable world of 10 billion people.
- Second, remember to *think small*. Working with a BP or GM may thrill, but vital SD contributions will also come from business that are much less visible, particularly so-called 'sliver' companies. Though small, these leverage the internet, developing and selling products and services on a global scale.[37] Think of Denmark's wind-power company Vestas, or Norway's reverse-vending and recycling company Tomra.
- Third, *focus continuously on developing the 'generative cocoon'* needed to drive the incubation process. This will involve working with politicians and government agencies to reshape markets, not least by changing price signals and tax systems to favor SD investment and initiatives.

Here, again, we may have something to learn from the social insects. Instead of forcing hive or colony members to do things, ants, bees and termites lay chemical guide-rails.[38] So, for example, web-site designers now use 'digital pheromones' to guide e-surfers. Engineers are learning from wasps how to make swarms of tiny mobile satellites that can self-assemble into larger structures in space. So perhaps instead of swatting at individual Corporate Locusts or Wasps, we can work out how to program entire economic hives or swarms? It's time to use legitimate sweeteners, such as fiscal and financial incentives, to get business moving into, through and out of the Chrysalis Economy.

PANEL 13

Pawns in their game?

"I am going to a Bob Dylan concert tomorrow night," ICI CEO Brendan O'Neill told the *Financial Times* recently.[39] "I do not expect to see many FTSE chief executives there." No, but as it happens, I was also headed in the same direction. Here's why. Few people had such a profound impact on my generation as Robert Allen Zimmerman, a.k.a. Bob Dylan. Kicking off his career with protest songs like "Blowing In the Wind", "A Pawn in Their Game" and "The Times They Are A-Changin'", he soon dismayed early fans by going electronic. In the same way, you could say, many early activists also later dismayed purists by crossing the divide and deciding to work with business.

The man, the myth and the cross-over issue were on my mind as I watched this living legend in concert at Wembley, alongside long-time friend and colleague Steve Warshal. Many years before, Steve had broken new ground for the environmental lobby by launching the newsletter *Greenpeace Business,* together with a highly successful series of annual Greenpeace conferences featuring leading Citizen CEOs.

Greenpeace first started providing 'environmental intelligence' to business in 1987, with *PowerLine*. Produced in collaboration with Friends of the Earth, this briefed financial analysts on liability issues surrounding nuclear power stations, which the UK government wanted to privatize. Then, in the late 1980s, Greenpeace activists sat down with ICI executives to discuss the CFC issue. "After the meeting," Warshal recalls, "the campaigners realized they knew more about the dangers of CFCs and about possible alternatives than the ICI executives did." Soon, Greenpeace was complementing its "don't do that", problem-focused campaigns with "try this" solutions-focused campaigns, including the 'Greenfreeze' technology offered as an ozone-friendly alternative to CFC and HFC refrigerants.

Later, *Greenpeace Business* evolved as a new way of getting through to business and the consultancy world. "The annual Greenpeace Business conference is simply an extension of this concept," explains Warshal, "providing Greenpeace information to the business community in language and settings they understand and are comfortable with." The first conference, entitled "Brent Spar ... and After," was held in 1996.

When I chaired a session at the 1997 event, the featured CEO was BP's John Browne. As he took the podium, he joked that it made a change for BP to occupy a Greenpeace platform, rather than the other way around! Other CEOs spotlighted in this way have included Ray Anderson of Interface, Bob Shapiro of Monsanto, Malcolm Walker of Iceland and Bill Ford, Jr. of Ford.

"As a Greenpeace member, I'm the opposite of what people expect," Walker told the 2000 event. "I run a company. I believe in profit. I'm not left wing, I wear a suit, I eat meat, I shoot pheasants. I even smoke an occasional cigar!" Building bridges to companies such as Iceland (which spearheaded the campaign to get ozone-friendly refrigerators onto the UK market) represents useful progress, no question. But the fact that Walker was soon ejected from the company he founded (part of the problem was that he tried to push the organic food strategy too far, too fast) does raise at least a small question mark over the 'engage-the-CEO' strategy.

Meanwhile, some in the campaigning world must wonder whether Greenpeace – and the other sustainability guides surveyed for this chapter – have sold out? For them, seeing campaigners turn up at Greenpeace conferences wearing suits is about as strange as it was for those hearing Dylan going electric for the first time. Indeed, they could be forgiven for wondering whether "A Pawn in Their Game" might not be the appropriate Dylan track here?

Cynics might even link what is happening in the worlds of rock'n'roll and public interest campaigning. In the rock'n'roll world, long-standing counter-cultural figureheads like the Rolling Stones, Carlos Santana and even Dylan himself are succumbing to corporate largesse from the likes of IBM, General Motors, Pepsi and Microsoft.[40] Dylan, and his son Jakob, were reputedly paid $1 million in 1998 to play for 15,000 employees of the Silicon Valley semiconductor company Applied Materials.

So does Steve Warshal think Greenpeace has sold out with its willingness to showcase leading corporations? "No," he says.

"Dialogue doesn't preclude the use of direct action. We have an ongoing schizophrenic relationship with a fair number of companies. For example, we support BP's solar and renewable energy activities, and yet totally oppose their plans for oil exploration, especially in the Arctic region, Alaska and the North Sea. Or, to take another example, we have worked with Unilever on Greenfreeze – and against them on GM foods."

So how does Greenpeace choose CEOs to feature at these events? "We look for 'best of breed'," Warshal explains, "company executives who are showing leadership by publicly adopting positive environmental stances. IKEA was one of the first companies to go PVC-free, Iceland has adopted a strong GM-free stance, Cargill Dow are creating renewable polymers, Vestas is Denmark's largest offshore wind producer, and so on."

And there's another side to it all, too. "The very public nature of a business conference gives campaigners the confidence to make their case in front of a business audience," Warshal confides. "Where else could we stand toe to toe with our opponents, such as Robert Shapiro of Monsanto?" Shapiro arrived at the 1999 event via satellite. The consensus? If you're going to take this particular Greenpeace platform, turn up in the flesh. Judiciously adjusted, satellite imagery and sound still has the capacity to make you look like a visiting alien.

CHAPTER 14

Afterword
Can civilizations be 'built to last'?

Since childhood, I have often walked through the dust and rubble of ancient civilizations – just as future feet will undoubtedly walk through the dust and rubble of ours. So what if the future is still FROG!? Even before I began writing *The Chrysalis Economy*, my editor, Capstone's Mark Allin, was insisting that I write an afterword. His reasoning ran somewhat along the lines suggested by Arthur Miller in panel 14 (page 261): it's time to re-examine the impossible. What if?, Mark asked. What if none of this comes to pass? What if the business case for sustainable development fails to materialize? What, to put it bluntly, if you are wrong?

Well, I decided later, I could be wrong in at least three interesting ways. First, I could be wrong because we were hit by a problem from 'outside the box'. Second, I could be wrong because I have been over-pessimistic, in the sense that the Catch-23 challenge turns out to be less problematic than imagined. Or, third, I could have been over-optimistic: despite every warning, the human species might still fail to act in time.

First, problems from outside the box. These are almost guaranteed, although most are likely to make our problems worse, not better. Films like *Deep Impact* have dramatized the risk of an asteroid hitting the Earth from space, triggering another mass extinction. Given the pattern of impacts in the geological record, this seems a virtual certainty, some day. I'm less convinced, though, by the dates that people have been trying to put on such events. 21 September 2030 is one date we are being asked to hold, when there is apparently a one-in-500 chance that an asteroid will hit Earth with the force of many nuclear bombs.[41]

But who needs to wait for an asteroid? Although scientists squabble over what constitutes a 'mass extinction event', the current level of species extinctions is already going off the scale. And our species is largely to blame. Indeed, if human population numbers continue to grow, extinctions will soon be running at anywhere between 100 and 1000 times the 'normal' levels.[42]

So on to our second option, in which things turn out for the best. No one who has lived through recent decades would deny that the world has a way of catching us totally off guard. Few of us predicted the sudden collapse of communism. And Michael Porter introduced his recent book *Can Japan Compete?* by noting that it would have been unthinkable even a few years earlier to have posed the question his book raises about this once-invincible economic predator.[43] So maybe it's pixie-dust time? I am happy to consider this second option, but the likely doubling of world population throws a dark shadow over this fairy-tale scenario.

Third, despite all the warnings and all the efforts of Citizen CEOs, there is a real risk that we will fail to get our act together. So what if the future turns out to be something like the FROG! scenario covered in Chapter 12? Then, sadly, our civilization would go down in flames. Indeed, I have often thought that we need to fit our civilizations with 'black boxes', like aircraft. We might begin to pay more attention to how they operate.

"If history is anything to go by," as Felipe Fernández-Armesto concludes in *Civilizations*,[44] "it must, like all earlier civilizations, end by being ruined – or transformed. For the history of civilizations is a path picked among ruins. No civilization has lasted indefinitely." The "civilizing ingredient," he argues, is the "systematic refashioning of nature." Some civilizations have done this more sustainably than others. But Fernández-Armesto doesn't believe that this means we should shut up shop. "Just as I would rather live strenuously and die soon than fester indefinitely in inert contentment," he says, "so I would rather belong to a civilization which changes the world, at the risk of self-immolation, than to a modestly 'sustainable' society."

Me too, up to a point, but I would rather not know that I had failed to spot an opportunity to help prevent our civilization collapsing. And here lies a fairly fundamental problem with human evolution to date. Paul Ehrlich, one of the main architects of the 'Environmental Revolution', now talks of the growing need for *conscious evolution*.[45] To date, he says, biological evolution tended to favor the development of quick reflexes and perceptual processes that hold the background steady while we identify an immediate, short-term threat – like a charging lion, a speeding car or a looming competitor. The problem: many of the most serious threats now facing us are different. Instead of leaping out at us, they tend to creep up on us over decades – or even centuries. Indeed, that's the key characteristic of FROG!

Unfortunately, human nature is poorly engineered to pick up these weak, background signals. Time and again, we miss – or choose to ignore – the early signals. Think of the 57 tire-bursts, six leading to punctured fuel-tanks, before a Concorde finally crashed, killing 109 people.[46] And the busier our world, the more likely it is that such signals will be buried in the background noise. Dramatically bigger impending problems to which we seem equally blind include such things as population growth, climate change, species loss and the spread of knowledge on how to make nuclear bombs and germ warfare weapons.

There are many ways in which we can learn to detect early warnings. Scenarios, as we have seen, can help sensitize our brains to emergent patterns in apparent chaos. Stakeholder dialogue sessions can alert us to risks and opportunities we might otherwise miss. Greater integration across companies and value-webs can also help ensure that we are not blind-sided. And we can work out how to present complexity to decision-makers in ways they can 'see' and manage. Edward Tufte has done fascinating work in this area, showing, for example, how the way engineers presented data on the risks facing the ill-fated *Challenger* space shuttle almost guaranteed that the thing would fly and blow apart.[47]

Those at the controls of Spaceship Earth – and in these days of consumer markets that increasingly means most of us – need better 'head-up' displays. The only thing that didn't come with our spaceship, as Buckminster Fuller used to say, is a control manual. Meanwhile, too much information is being thrown at us all, making it difficult to pick out the real priorities, risks and opportunities. The problem is generic. The Boeing 747 cockpit, for example, can contain nearly 1000 indicators and buttons.[48] The latest version, the B747-400, contains just 500, so the pilot can concentrate on navigation. A lesson to be learned?

But, for me, the best way to make sense of the future is not just to have good data displays, but to actively choose to ride the right waves of change. Although it is true that we risk being blasted away by asteroids, or terrorist nukes, the sustainability wave is now building. To switch metaphors, we appear to have a once-off "window of opportunity." For example, the decarbonization of the global economy is now a priority challenge.[49] Like Arthur Miller listening to the faint signals on his telephone line through the Iron Curtain (panel 14), it's time to hear the future calling and act. The Chrysalis Economy is our destiny. But what emerges from it will very much depend on us.

PANEL 14

Re-examine the impossible
Probably best remembered as Marilyn Monroe's brainiest husband, Pulitzer Prize-winning playwright Arthur Miller heard a distant butterfly's wing-beat in 1986. "My phone rings," he recalls. "The caller's voice seems so distant that I imagine the wind is carrying it. And, indeed, he says he is calling from Kirghizia. I am not sure

where that is, but I recall hearing that it is a vast and nearly empty space somewhere along the Chinese border."[50]

The caller turns out to be a novelist Miller met recently in Moscow, with an invitation to visit. And Chingiz Aimatov promises something unheard of: "There will be no party supervision." But what neither man yet knows is that they are about to get an early, privileged warning of one of the biggest transformations of the 20th century.

Arriving at the event, Miller found "a certain hyper-expectancy among the Soviet writers, a waiting-for-the-other-shoe-to-drop, due no doubt to this newly liberated system under which we were all operating." Those assembled enjoyed a fine couple of days at a health resort, savoring their first taste of mare's milk and watching some extraordinary horsemanship by both men and women. Then came the shock: "On the morning of our departure, a message was relayed by one of the Soviets that we were invited to meet with Chairman Gorbachev in Moscow that afternoon."

Arriving in the Soviet capital, the visitors – "American, British, French, Italian, Ethiopian, and several other nationalities" – gathered round a "mile-long conference table high up in the central Communist Party headquarters skyscraper." To begin with, Miller sat back and listened. Then it struck him: Gorbachev was trying to deliver a message to the world. Miller could hardly believe his ears. He began to scribble furiously, trying to keep track of the momentous announcements.

Gorbachev began by saying that "this was a new age, unforeseen by Marx, who knew nothing of atomic power, electronics, or any of the other inventions that have transformed post-World War II societies." The Soviet leader argued that the time had come to abandon the old thinking. "We must work from realities," as Miller summed it up later, "not textbooks or dogma, and those realities were unknown to 19th-century thinkers, including Marx, who was a genius, to be sure, but not a mystical prophet."

What was really interesting, however, was not just what Gorbachev said, but the US media's response when Miller got back home. Told by a retired *New York Times* reporter who had spent a decade or so in Moscow that he had a "fantastic scoop", Miller wrote an article and sent it first to the *Times* and then, when they turned it down, to the *Washington Post*. The *Post*, too, refused to print the story. They appeared to have no sense that this was a distant wing-beat that heralded the end of the world as they had come to know it.

"Clearly," Miller notes, "the American mind-set had been so calcified by nearly two decades of Cold War that it was simply not conceivable for the head of the Soviet Union to be speaking as I reported." Miller began to understand why Gorbachev had convened that group of artists in the first place. "He no doubt had been finding it impossible to penetrate the Western mind – at least its press and diplomatic representatives – with his new concept of what was real."

No one, and this was also true of Gorbachev, could imagine a future in which the Soviet Union would break into pieces. But as the Communist Party's monopoly on power imploded, so did the Soviet Empire. The lesson? Perhaps the message should have been relayed by a seductive, blonde Hollywood sex symbol? Miller, however, has other ideas: "I think it is that one has to endlessly reexamine what one is absolutely sure is beyond possibility. And so I open the papers now, ever since this experience, wondering what else is real but not reportable. What else does our fixed mind-set find too incredible to print?"

PART V

SOURCE$

Where did the information in *The Chrysalis Economy* come from?

Key books, reports and web-sites are referenced on pages 266–276

A number of SustainAbility research and consultancy programs are briefly described on pages 264–265

The Chrysalis Economy has covered a lot of ground. Before listing the sources and references used, section by section, it may be helpful to say something about the SustainAbility programs on which key parts of the book are based. A 28-page booklet published in 2001 (Sketchbook 01) is available on request from: SustainAbility, 11–13 Knightsbridge, London SW1X 7LY, United Kingdom or on +44 207 245 1116. Alternatively, send an e-mail request to: info@sustainability.co.uk

To help build the networks, our website (www.sustainability.com) provides links to a growing number of other companies and organizations active in this area. It also covers, among other things, the following research and outreach programs:

Radar is SustainAbility's subscription-only intelligence service, which has been evolving for nearly ten years. It is based on ten triple bottom line briefings a year, aimed at business and the wider stakeholder community.
Further details from: www.sustainability.com/radar

The Chrysalis Program is new, focusing on the corporate, market and cultural transformations required for the sustainability transition. *The Chrysalis Economy* is its first product.
Further details from: www.sustainability.com/chrysalis

Trimaran is an action research program, developed in partnership with the International Business Leaders Forum (IBLF), and focusing on corporate and global governance. The program's first output was *The Power to Change: Mobilising Board Leadership to Deliver Sustainable Value to Markets and Society*.
Further details from: www.sustainability.com/trimaran

The Business Case Program is a foundation stone for Sustain-Ability's ongoing consultancy work with both private and public sector clients.
Further details from: www.sustainability.com/business-case

Engaging Stakeholders is our longest-running research program, dating from 1994, and developed in partnership with the United Nations Environment Programme and over 20 companies. The focus is on corporate accountability and reporting across the triple bottom line agenda.
Further details from: www.sustainability.com/engaging

The Global Reporters Program is our international benchmark survey series on corporate sustainability reporting. Its first output, *The Global Reporters: The first international survey of corporate sustainability reporting* (2000).
Further details from: www.sustainability.com/engaging

The Janus Program, developed in partnership with Government Policy Consultants (GPC), focuses on the ways in which corporations and industry federations influence public policy. The program's concept paper: *Politics and Persuasion* (2000).
Further details from: www.sustainability.com/janus

The Emerging Economies Program is SustainAbility's newest research venture. Launched in 2001, it focuses on the great divides between the world's haves and have-nots. Further details from: www.sustainability.com/emerging-economies

Notes

Notes to Part I

1   Global Capitalism, *Business Week* special report, 6 November 2000.
2   Too much corporate power?, *Business Week*, 14 September 2000.
3   Andrew Campbell, The value of corporate mortality, *Strategy + Business*, Fourth Quarter 2000.
4   John Elkington, *Cannibals With Forks: The Triple Bottom Line of 21st Century Business* (Capstone: Oxford, 1997; New Society: Gabriola Island, Canada, 1998).
5   When was the word 'sustainability' first used in its current sense? I am grateful to Laurent Marriott Leduc for tracking it back at least to 1975, when the World Council of Churches, meeting in Nairobi, called for "Justice, Participation and Sustainability." But when my colleagues and I founded SustainAbility in 1987, the term was still virtually unknown. Much of our time was spent spelling the word for people who had never come across it.
6   Wall Street's old order changes, *The Economist*, 16 September 2000.
7   Michael Arndt, Let's talk turkeys, *Business Week*, 11 December 2000.
8   Art Kleiner, *The Age of Heretics: Heroes, Outlaws, and the Forerunners of Corporate Change* (Nicholas Brealey: London, 1996).
9   Demerger Document, Board of Directors, Novo Nordisk A/S, Bagsvaerd, Denmark, 16 October 2000.
10 William Hall, Novartis pins hopes on new leukaemia drug, *Financial Times*, 4 December 2000.
11 Roger Boyes, Stasi blamed for "River of Death" pollution, *The Times*, 21 November 2000.
12 A correspondent, Mankind extinct in 1,000 years, *The Times*, 30 September 2000.
13 World Commission on Environment and Development, *Our Common Future* (Oxford University Press: Oxford, 1987).
14 *People, Planet & Profits: An Act of Commitment*, The Shell Report 1999, Royal Dutch/Shell Group.
15 Donnella H. Meadows, Dennis L. Meadows and Jørgen Randers, *Beyond the Limits: Global Collapse or a Sustainable Future* (Earthscan: London, 1992).
16 James Lovelock, *Gaia: The Practical Science of Planetary Medicine* (Gaia Books, 1991).
17 *State of the World 2000*, WorldWatch Institute, Washington, DC, 2000.
18 *World Resources*, World Resources Institute, Washington, DC, 2001.
19 *Human Development Report 2000*, United Nations Development Programme (Oxford University Press: Oxford, 2000).
20 Tim Radford, Hole in Antarctic ozone now three times size of US, *The Guardian*, 9 September 2000.
21 Mark Henderson, Ozone hole will heal in 50 years, *The Times*, 4 December 2000; Vanessa Houlder, Hole in ozone layer may close up within 50 years, *Financial Times*, 4 December 2000.
22 Lester Brown, Christopher Flavin and Hilary French, *State of the World 2000* (W.W. Norton: New York and London, 2000).
23 Unless otherwise identified, all statistics come from *State of the World 2000*.
24 Anthony Browne, The last days of a white world, *The Observer*, 3 September 2000.
25 Vanessa Houlder, Urgent warning on climate change, *Financial Times*, 22 January 2001.
26 Theodore C. Bestor, How sushi went global, *Foreign Policy*, November/December 2000.
27 Stephen Castle, EU may impose 75% cuts in fishing quotas, *The Independent*, 2 December 2000.
28 American Association for the Advancement of Science, *Atlas of Population and the Environment* (AAAS, 2001).
29 Amelia Gentleman, Tragedy of Chernobyl does not end with simple switch-off, *The Guardian*, 16 December 2000.

30   Nigel Hawkes, El Niño fiercer last century than for 130,000 years, *Financial Times*, 26 January 2001.

31   See www.elnino.noaa.gov, or www.elnino.com. See also Brian Fagan, *Floods, Famines and Emperors: El Niño and the Fate of Civilizations* (Pimlico/Random House: London, 2000).

32   Vanessa Houlder, Europe's poorest face worst climate effects, *Financial Times*, 2 November 2000. See also *Assessment of the Potential Effects and Adaptations for Climate Change in Europe*, Jackson Environment Institute, University of East Anglia, Norwich, November 2000.

33   Paul H. Ray and Sherry Ruth Anderson, *The Cultural Creatives* (Harmony Book: New York, 2000).

34   Most of the information in this section is drawn from UNDP's *Human Development Report 2000*.

35   Francesco Guerrera, De Beers: all that glitters is not sold, *Financial Times*, 11 July 2000.

36   Jamie Doward, Oryx float killed by FO, *The Observer*, 11 June 2000.

37   Sarah Boseley, Glaxo stops Africans buying cheap AIDS drugs, *The Guardian*, 2 December 2000.

38   Paul Wilkinson, Internet cameras cut crime on estate by half, *The Times*, 27 December 2000.

39   Michael Katz, All-knowing eye, *Forbes Global*, 11 December 2000.

40   David Kirkpatrick interviewing Ross Adey, *Fortune*, 9 October 2000.

41   Fareed Zakaria, No, economics isn't king, *Time*, Issues 2001: Special Edition, December 2000–February 2001.

42   Christopher Brown-Humes, Nokia's dominance of economy prompts worries in Finland, *Financial Times*, 3 January 2001.

43   Paul Rauber, The green menace, *Sierra*, November/December 2000.

44   Peter Thal Larsen, Russian aluminium group faces US lawsuit, *Financial Times*, 20 December 2000.

45   Patrick Cockburn, A city still blighted by anthrax disaster, *The Independent*, 29 July 2000.

46   Jeanne Guillemin, *Anthrax: The Investigation of a Deadly Outbreak* (University of California Press, 1999).

47   Robert Lenzer and Tomas Kellner, Corporate saboteurs, *Forbes*, 27 November 2000.

48   Anti-capitalist protests, *The Economist*, 23 September 2000.

49   Robert Wright, *Nonzero: The Logic of Human Destiny* (Pantheon Books: New York, 2000).

50   Benjamin Barber, *Jihad vs. McWorld* (Times Books, 1995).

51   Robert Wright, Planet Earth goes for the big one, *Sunday Times*, 27 February 2000.

52   John Plender, Russia hears the gospel of governance, *Financial Times*, 24 November 2000.

53   *Governance for a Sustainable Future*, a report of the Commissions of the World Humanity Action Trust, London, 2000 (www.what.org.uk).

54   Manuel Castells, *The Information Age: Economy, Society, and Culture* (Blackwell: Oxford, 1996–1998).

55   Eric Nee interviews Manuel Castells, *Fortune*, 9 October 2000.

56   Amelia Gentleman, Millions fear killer dust clouds from dried-up sea, *The Observer*, 10 September 2000.

57   Alexander Nicoll, Change in climate 'may spark future wars', *Financial Times*, 8 February 2001.

58   Elaine Sciolino, 2015 outlook: enough food, scarce water, porous borders, *New York Times*, 18 December 2000.

59   Hernando de Soto, *The Mystery of Capital: Why Capitalism Triumphs in the West and Fails Everywhere Else* (Bantam Press: London, 2000).

60   *Governance for a Sustainable Future*, a report of the Commissions of the World Humanity Action Trust, London, 2000 (www.what.org.uk).

61   Norman Myers, *Perverse Subsidies*, International Institute for Sustainable Development, Winnipeg, 1998.

62   Thomas Kuhn, *The Structure of Scientific Revolutions* (University of Chicago Press: Chicago, 1962).

63   Paul Harris, 'Insane' daredevil skis down Everest, *The Observer*, 8 October 2000; Jack Grimston, Skier masters Everest from top to bottom, *Sunday Times*, 8 October 2000.

64   Richard Waters, The pleasures and the pain in a year of market mania, *Financial Times*, 23 December 2000.

65   Ian McDonald Wood, *The Bucks Start Here: How Great Digital Companies Create Lasting Business Value* (Capstone: Oxford, 2000).

66   Kenichi Ohmae, *The Invisible Continent: Four Strategic Imperatives of the New Economy* (Nicholas Brealey: London, 2000).

67   Untangling e-conomics: A survey of the New Economy, *The Economist*, 23 September 2000.

68   Michael J. Mandel, The next downturn, *Business Week*, 9 October 2000.

69 Don't say 'new economy', *The Economist*, 6 January 2001.
70 Peter Martin, After the bubble, *Financial Times*, 28 December 2000.
71 Michael J. Mandel, *The Coming Internet Depression: Why the High-Tech Boom Will Go Bust, Why the Crash Will be Worse Than You Think, and How to Prosper Afterwards* (Basic Books: New York, 2000).
72 Joseph Schumpeter, *Business Cycles* (McGraw-Hill: New York, 1939).
73 *The New Economy*, The Future 500, www.globalfutures.org.
74 William A. Sahlman, The New Economy is stronger than you think, *Harvard Business Review*, November–December 1999.
75 Sahlman, *ibid.*
76 Richard Tomkins, A virtual investment, *Financial Times*, 5 December 2000.
77 Jim Kerstetter *et al.*, Finding the right formula, *Business Week*, 23 October 2000.
78 Irwin Stelzer, Tulip mania holds lessons for dotcoms, *Sunday Times*, 10 December 2000.
79 Gary Hamel, Revamping the corporation from inside out, *Business2.com*, 26 September 2000.
80 Amar Bhidé, David and Goliath, reconsidered, *Harvard Business Review*, September–October 2000.
81 Gary Hamel, *Leading the Revolution* (Harvard Business School Press: Boston, 2000).
82 Grady Means and David Schneider, *MetaCapitalism: The e-Business Revolution and the Design of 21st-century Companies and Markets* (John Wiley:, New York, 2000).
83 Joan Magretta, The power of virtual integration: an interview with Dell Computer's Michael Dell, *Harvard Business Review*, March–April 1998.
84 Michael S. Dell, Creating and managing hypergrowth, in *Wisdom of the CEO* (Pricewaterhouse-Coopers, John Wiley: New York, 2000).
85 Simon Caulkin, More dash than full stop for dotcoms, *The Observer*, 26 November 2000.
86 Don Tapscott *et al.*, *Digital Capital* (Harvard Business School Press: Boston, 2000).
87 Paul Saffo, Commerce isn't about buying stuff, *Fast Company*, September 2000.
88 Simon Zadek, Niels Hojensgard and Peter Raynard, *The New Economy of Corporate Citizenship*, The Copenhagen Centre, 2000 (www.copenhagencentre.org).
89 Jeremy Rifkin, *The Age of Access: How the Shift from Ownership to Access is Transforming Capitalism* (Penguin Books: London, 2000).
90 Bill Joy, Design for the digital revolution, *Fortune*, 6 March 2000.
91 Ed Vulliamy, IBM accused of helping Nazis automate the Holocaust, *The Observer*, 11 February 2001; Edwin Black, IBM's guilty past, *Sunday Times*, 11 February 2001. Both articles based on Edwin Black, *IBM and the Holocaust* (Little, Brown: New York, 2001).
92 Po Bronson, *The Nudist on the Late Shift* (Vintage: London, 2000).
93 James Salzman, Beyond the smokestack: environmental protection in the service economy, *UCLA Law Review*, vol. 47(2), December 1999.
94 I am grateful to Titus Moser of Shell for permission to use this diagram from his thesis – and impending book, to be published by Earthscan.
95 Simon Caulkin, Accounting for very little, *The Observer*, 29 October 2000.
96 Stan Davis and Christopher Meyer, *Future Wealth* (Harvard Business School Press: Boston, 2000).
97 Michael Peel, A renaissance in accounting, *Financial Times*, 21 December 2000.
98 Robert Repetto and Duncan Austin, *Coming Clean: Corporate Disclosure of Financially Significant Environmental Risks*, World Resources Institute, Washington, DC, 2000.
99 This panel is partly based on Daniel Pinchbeck, The fire this time, *Rolling Stone*, 9 November 2000.
100 Scott McNealy, Business built on metaphors still need value, *Forbes ASAP*, 2 October 2000.

Notes to Part II

1 *Putting Values into Action*, Novo Nordisk Environmental and Social Report 1999, Bagsvaerd, Denmark (www.novo.dk).
2 Ian Burrell, Slavery 'worse now than under Roman Empire', *The Independent*, 2 December 2000. Link to anti-slavery sites through www.independent.co.uk/links/.
3 Francesco Guerrera and James Mackintosh, Huntingdon secures new lifeline from US backer, *Financial Times*, 20 January 2001.
4 Steve Connor, If tests go elsewhere, the suffering may be greater, *The Independent*, 20 January 2001.

5   Who will be next target of Huntingdon terror tactics?, *Sunday Times*, 21 January 2001.

6   Jean Eaglesham, A lost connection, *Financial Times*, 21 November 2000.

7   Jean Eaglesham, Yahoo! yields to ruling by French court, *Financial Times*, 4 January 2001.

8   Richard Barrett, *Liberating the Corporate Soul: Building a Visionary Organization* (Butterworth-Heinemann: Woburn, MA, 1998).

9   Further details can be found at www.corptools.com.

10   Stephen R. Covey, *Seven Habits of Highly Effective People: Powerful Lessons in Personal Change* (Fireside: New York, 1990).

11   Robert S. Kaplan and David P. Norton, *The Balanced Scorecard: Translating Strategy into Action* (Harvard Business School Press: Boston, 1996).

12   *Values in Action: Formalizing Your Company's Values* (Business for Social Responsibility: San Francisco, 2000).

13   Charles Hampden-Turner and Fons Trompenaars, *The Seven Cultures of Capitalism* (Doubleday, 1993).

14   The ethics gap, *The Economist*, 2 December 2000.

15   H.C. Skip Smith, *The Illustrated Guide to Aerodynamics*, 2nd edn (TAB Books: Blue Ridge Summit, PA,1992).

16   Stan Davis and Christopher Meyer, *Future Wealth* (Harvard Business School Press: Boston, 2000).

17   Conversation: Chief Privacy Officer, *Harvard Business Review*, November–December 2000.

18   Jonathan Wright, Tim Berners-Lee: the quiet revolutionary, *Business 2.0*, December 2000.

19   The definitions are partly based on *The Capitals Model: A Framework for Sustainability*, paper produced for the SIGMA Project, London, 2000.

20   See Robert D. Puttnam, *Making Democracy Work: Civic traditions in Modern Italy* (Princeton University Press: Princeton, 1993); and Francis Fukuyama, *Trust: The Social Virtues and the Creation of Prosperity* (Hamish Hamilton: London, 1995). See also Puttnam's latest book, *Bowling Alone* (2000).

21   Quoted in Paul Hawken and Amory and L. Hunter Lovins, *Natural Capitalism* (Little, Brown: Boston, 1999).

22   John T. Landry, Supply chain management: the value of trust, *Harvard Business Review*, January–February 1998.

23   Anthony Browne, The last days of a white world, *The Observer*, 3 September 2000.

24   Chris Hewett, Small is beautiful, *The Guardian*, 22 November 2000.

25   Peter Senge, *The Fifth Discipline: The Art and Practice of the Learning Organization* (Doubleday: New York, 1990). See also Bert Frydman, Iva Wilson and JoAnne Wyer, *The Power of Collaborative Leadership: Lessons for the Learning Organization* (Butterworth-Heinemann: Boston, 2000).

26   World Commission on Environment and Development, *Our Common Future* (Oxford Paperback: Oxford, 1987).

27   Richard Barrett, *Liberating the Corporate Soul* (Butterworth-Heinemann: Boston, 1998). See also James C. Collins and Jerry I. Porras, *Built to Last: Successful Habits of Visionary Companies* (Century Business, 1994).

28   Gregory Zuckerman, Asbestos litigation hits US stocks, *Wall Street Journal Europe*, 2 January 2001.

29   Laura Landro, Ethics for the Internet age, *Wall Street Journal*, 6 November 2000.

30   John Elkington, *Cannibals with Forks: The Triple Bottom Line of 21st Century Business* (Capstone: Oxford, 1997/99; New Society: Gabriola Island, Canada, 1998).

31   In the three months to September 2000, on an annualized basis. See Gerard Baker and Peronet Despeignes, US economy eases past landmark, *Financial Times*, 28 October 2000.

32   Amelia Hill, SBOXs buy value, not values, *The Observer*, 1 October 2000.

33   One in seven consumers say ethical concerns influence decisions, *ENDS Report 309*, October 2000. See Co-operative Bank, Who are the ethical consumers?, www.co-operativebank.co.uk.

34   Based on a survey by Wharton Business School, Ernst & Young and *Forbes ASAP*.

35   *A Responsible Investment? Overview of the Socially Responsible Investment Community*, SustainAbility and the Centre for Business Performance, London, 2000.

36   Nicholas George, Ethical practice may have kept Sweden clear, *Financial Times*, 30 November 2000.

37   Stan Davis and Christopher Meter, *Blur: The Speed of Change in the Connected Economy* (Capstone: Oxford, 1998).

38   Robin Wood, *Managing Complexity: How Business Can Adapt and Prosper in the Connected Economy* (The Economist/Profile Books: London, 2000).

39   *Realising the Business Value of Sustainable Development* (Arthur D. Little: London, 1999). See also Measuring progress towards sustainability, *ENDS Report 296*, September 1999.

40   Keith H. Hammonds, Practical radicals, *Fast Company*, September 2000.

41   For further details, see or .

42   Julia Butterfly Hill, *The Legacy of Luna: The Story of a Tree, a Woman, and the Struggle to Save the Redwoods* (HarperSanFrancisco: San Francisco, 2000).

43   See, for example, Heather Millar, Generation Green, *Sierra*, November/December 2000.

44   See also their book, *Microcosmos: The Invisible World of Insects* (Stewart, Tabori & Chang: New York, 1996). The description of the chrysalis process is largely based on theirs.

45   John Wyndham, *The Chrysalids* (Michael Joseph: London, 1955; Penguin: London, 1975).

46   Erich Hoyt and Ted Schultz, *Insect Lives* (Mainstream: Edinburgh, 1999).

47   Gilbert Waldbauer, *Millions of Monarchs, Bunches of Beetles* (Harvard University Press: Cambridge, MA, 2000).

48   Waldbauer, *ibid.*

49   Peter Thal Larsen and Peter Spiegel, ABB sets aside $430m for asbestos claims, Financial Times, 5 April 2001.

50   See John Elkington, *A Year in the Greenhouse* (Gollancz: London, 1989).

51   Peter Thal Larsen, Russian aluminium group faces US lawsuit, *Financial Times*, 20 December 2000.

52   René Haller and Sabine Baer, *From Wasteland to Paradise* (Koschany Verlag: München, 1995).

53   A new focus on drugs in the environment, *ENDS Report 304*, May 2000.

54   Kevin Brown and Matthew Jones, BNFL plans executive cull to save partial sale, *Financial Times*, 29 February 2000.

55   Nick Paton Welsh and Oliver Morgan, New review adds extra £5bn to Sellafield's clean-up bill, *The Observer*, 10 December 2000.

56   Matthew Jones, Tough love for the nuclear family, *Financial Times*, 9 February 2001.

57   Tom Rhodes, The smoking gun, *Sunday Times*, 12 March 2000.

58   Patti Waldmeir, Healthy smokers sue tobacco industry, *Financial Times*, 8 January 2001.

59   Cyanide spill sends Aussie mine co into administration, *ninemsn*, 16 March 2000.

60   Michael Shari and Sheri Prasso, A pit of trouble, *Business Week*, 31 July 2000.

61   Rosie Waterhouse, British firm linked to global BSE, *Sunday Times*, 4 February 2001.

62   Simon Caulkin, How to steer Britain on the wrong track, *The Observer*, 10 December 2000.

63   Steve Boggan, Nightmare network, *The Independent*, 2 December 2000.

64   David Parsley and Jon Ungoed-Thomas, Cracked rail risks were known 'months ago', *The Guardian*, 5 November 2000.

65   Joanna Walters, How a broken rail exposed the cracks in a fragmented industry, *The Observer*, 29 October 2000.

66   Peter Briggs, United for a sustainable future, *Review*, Rio Tinto, December 2000.

67   Kurt Johnson and Steve Coates, *Nabokov's Blues: The Scientific Odyssey of a Literary Genius* (Zoland Books: Cambridge, MA, 1999).

68   George John Romanes, Caterpillars on the line, in Erich Hoyt and Ted Schultz, *Insect Lives: Stories of Mystery and Romance from a Hidden World* (Mainstream: Edinburgh, 1999).

69   Christopher Bowe, Challenge to an integrated approach, *Financial Times*, 15 December 2000.

70   Scotchguard chemical confusion, *BBC Online*, 19 December 2000.

71   Interface Europe: leading the way with environmental accounts, *ENDS Europe 304*, May 2000.

72   Jack Tresidder, *The Hutchinson Dictionary of Symbols* (Helicon: Oxford, 1997).

73   Gilbert Waldbauer, *Millions of Monarchs, Bunches of Beetles* (Harvard University Press: Cambridge, MA, 2000).

74   Stephen L. Buchmann and Gary Paul Nabhan, *The Forgotten Pollinators* (Island Press/Shearwater Books: Washington, DC, 1996).

75   Johnson and Coates, *Nabokov's Blues, op cit.*

76   My thanks to Janet Ranganathan of WRI for this nomination and for that of ODE, which follows.

77   Patagonia, in Lorinda R. Rowledge, Russell S. Barton and Kevin S. Brady, *Mapping the Journey: Case Studies in Strategy and Action Towards Sustainable Development* (Greenleaf: Sheffield, 1999).

78   Jane Hughes, Green textiles, *The Guardian*, 22 November 2000.

79   See www.climatex.com.

80   Johnson and Coates, *Nabokov's Blues, op cit.*

81   Johnson and Coates, *Nabokov's Blues, op cit.*

82   Jim Steiker and Michael Golden, Hot fudge partners, *Business Ethics*, May/June 2000.

83   Tresidder, *op. cit.*

84   Tim Radford, Bees can think say scientists, *The Guardian*, 19 April 2001

85   Karl von Frisch (with Otto von Frisch), *Animal Architecture* (Harcourt Brace Jovanovich: New York, 1974).

86   Eva Crane, *A Comprehensive Survey of Honey* (Heinemann: London, 1975).

87   *Next Generation Goals: Implementation Guide*, Johnson & Johnson, 2000.

88   Due out later in 2001 is *The Next Industrial Revolution*, by William McDonough and Michael Braungart.

89   Cargill Dow Polymers: Turning plastics from plants into a sustainable business, *ENDS Report 300*, January 2000.

90   Michael Light and Andrew Chaikin, *Full Moon* (Jonathan Cape: London, 1999).

91   Jann S. Wenner with Will Dana, Al Gore: the Rolling Stone interview, *Rolling Stone*, 9 November 2000.

92   See, too, the L.E.A.D.E.R. agenda outlined by Jane Nelson and Peter Zollinger in *The Power to Change: Mobilising Board Leadership to Deliver Sustainable Value to Markets and Society*, The International Business Leaders Forum and SustainAbility, London, 2001.

93   Schlender, op. cit.

94   Boards to CEOs: one strike and you're out, *Fortune*, 26 June 2000.

95   Anthony Bianco and Louis Lavelle, The CEO trap, *Business Week*, 11 December 2000.

96   Jane Nelson, *The Business of Peace: The Private Sector as a Partner in Conflict Prevention and Resolution*, The Prince of Wales Business Leaders Forum with International Alert and the Council for Economic Priorities, London, 2000.

97   Amy Barrett and Louis Lavelle, It's getting lonely at the top. Too lonely, *Business Week*, 13 November 2000.

98   Dee Hock, *Birth of the Chaordic Age* (Berrett-Koehler: San Francisco, 1999).

99   www.chaordic.org.

100   John Heilemann, The truth, the whole truth and nothing but the truth: the untold story of the Microsoft antitrust case, *Wired*, November 2000.

101   Ron Chernow, *Titan: The Life of John D. Rockefeller, Sr.* (Random House: New York, 1998).

102   Anita Roddick, *Business as Unusual* (Thorsons: London, 2000).

103   Andrew Clark and Julia Snoddy, Body Shop makeover flops, *The Guardian*, 13 January 2001.

104   *BC Hydro Triple Bottom Line Report 2000*, BC Hydro, Vancouver, 2000.

105   *1997 Report on Sustainable Development*, Monsanto Company, St Louis, 1997.

106   Joan Magretta, An interview with Monsanto's CEO, Robert B. Shapiro, *Harvard Business Review*, January–February 1997.

107   Dick Dusseldorp, obituary in *The Times*, London, 9 June 2000.

108   Jill Ker Conway, *The Road from Coorain* (William Heinemann: London, 1989) and *True North* (Hutchinson: London, 1994).

109   Virginia Marsh, Jill Ker Conway: Australian pioneer with her own iconic property, *Financial Times*, 30 October 2000.

110   In the interests of transparency, SustainAbility was working for both Ford and Shell at the time of writing, while BP was a sponsor of our Engaging Stakeholders research program.

111   Janet Guyon, A big-oil man gets religion, *Fortune*, 6 March 2000.

112   Sir John Browne, Health and population, the Third Reith Lecture, BBC Radio 4, April 2000.

113   Greenwash Award, *BP: Beyond Petroleum or Beyond Preposterous?*, http://www.corpwatch.org/greenwash/bp2.html.

114   *People, Planet & Profits: An Act of Commitment*, Royal Dutch/Shell Group, London, 1999.

115   Robert Corzine, Clock ticks down as Shell mulls break with tradition, *Financial Times*, 2 November 2000.

116   Amy Barrett, DuPont's big remake may need a remix, *Business Week*, 30 October 2000.

117 Chad Holliday, DuPont is a Science Company, in G. William Dauphinais, Grady Means and Colin Price, *Wisdom of the CEO: 29 Global Leaders Tackle Today's Most Pressing Business Challenges* (John Wiley: New York, 2000).
118 See www.dupont.com.
119 Barrett, *op. cit.*
120 *Report 1999: Studies in Sustainability*, DuPont Canada, 1999.
121 Andrea Spencer-Cooke, Paul Tebo: hero of zero, *Tomorrow*, November–December 2000.
122 *Connecting with Society*, Ford Motor Company, Dearborn, 2000.
123 Ed Helmore, Small-town lawyer who humbled the car giants, *The Observer*, 10 September 2000.
124 Alex Taylor III, Jac Nasser's biggest test, *Fortune*, 18 September 2000.
125 Mike France, The hidden culprit: the US legal system, *Business Week*, 18 September 2000.
126 Ford: a crisis of confidence, *Business Week*, 18 September 2000.
127 Gilbert Waldbauer, *Millions of Monarchs, Bunches of Beetles* (Harvard University Press: Cambridge, MA, 2000).
128 Jean Chevalier and Alain Gheerbrant, *The Penguin Dictionary of Symbols*, trans. John Buchanan-Brown (Penguin Books: London, 1969/1996).

Notes to Part III

1 The five definitions heading Chapters 7–11 are partly drawn from *The Oxford English Reference Dictionary* (Oxford University Press: Oxford, 1995/96). The final definition in each case is the author's.
2 Fish and chips for safer turbines, *Business Week*, 30 October 2000.
3 Peter Popham, Rain gods give Arundhati Roy final chance to save villagers, *The Independent*, 16 September 2000.
4 http://www.essential.org/monitor/mm2000/00december/enemies.html.
5 David Pimental, Lori Lach, Rodolfo Zuniga and Doug Morrison, Environmental and economic costs of nonindigenous species in the United States, *BioScience*, 1 January 2000.
6 Dominic Rushe, The monster stumbles, *Sunday Times*, 17 December 2000.
7 Nicola Lorusso, What a carve-up, *The Independent*, undated.
8 Tim Judah, The new cold war, *Business Life*, British Airways, 2000.
9 Ian Brodie, Fears for Arctic wildlife as land aide is named, *The Times*, 3 January 2001.
10 Anthony Browne, Buy a chair on the high street and you put the Amazon at risk, *The Observer*, 23 July 2000.
11 Jon Swartz, The boom in dot-com riles neighbors, *USA Today*, 18 October 2000.
12 John A. Frisch, The New Economy is both destructive and creative, *Business Week*, 30 October 2000.
13 Sherry Turkle, *Life on the Screen: Identity in the Age of the Internet* (Simon & Schuster: New York, 1995).
14 Tara Lemmey, Your next identity crisis, *Business2.com*, 26 September 2000.
15 Edward Helmore, Be very afraid of the future, *The Observer*, 19 March 2000.
16 Bill Joy, Why the future doesn't need us, *Wired*, April 2000.
17 Rants & raves, *Wired*, July 2000.
18 *Ibid.*
19 Frans Lanting, *Jungles* (Terra Editions/Benedikt Taschen Verlag: Köln, 2000).
20 John Emsley, *The Shocking History of Phosphorus: A Biography of the Devil's Element* (Macmillan: London, 2000).
21 John Elkington, *The Ecology of Tomorrow's World* (Associated Business Press: London, 1980).
22 *Fast Company*, July 2000.
23 Anne F. Pyatak, Job titles of the future, *Fast Company*, April 2000.
24 Interview.
25 Steven Viederman, On the Limits of Corporate Social Responsibility, Conference on Screening Socially Responsible Investing: Towards Improved Methods of Auditing and Reporting Triple Bottom Line Performance, Rotterdam, November 2000.
26 John Elkington, foreword in Lorinda R. Rowledge, Russell S. Barton and Kevin S. Brady, *Mapping the Journey* (Greenleaf: Sheffield, 1999).

27   See Jane Nelson and Peter Zollinger, *The Power to Change: Mobilising Board Leadership to Deliver Sustainable Value to Markets and Society*, International Business Leaders Forum and SustainAbility, London, 2001.
28   Elkington, *Cannibals with Forks, op. cit.*.
29   Michael Wolff, *Burn Rate: How I Survived the Goldrush Years on the Internet* (Orion: London, 1999).
30   Michael Wolff, Got it?, *Forbes ASAP*, 2 October 2000.
31   Julia Butterfly Hill, *The Legacy of Luna, op cit.*
32   Graham Bannock, R.E. Baxter and Evan Davis, *Dictionary of Economics* (The Economist/Profile Books: London, 1972/1999).
33   Dennis A. Rondinelli, IT comes to the aid of environmental managers, *Financial Times: Mastering Management*, 27 November 2000.
34   John Elkington and Julia Hailes, *The Green Consumer Guide* (Gollancz: London, 1988).
35   Ashlea Ebeling, Sue everywhere, *Forbes Global*, 16 October 2000.
36   John Elkington, *The Environmental Audit* (SustainAbility and WWF: London, 1989).
37   John Seddon, The 'quality' you can't feel, *The Observer*, 19 November 2000. Based on Seddon's book, *The Case Against ISO 9000* (Oak Tree Press, 2000).
38   Pamela L. Moore and Diane Brady, A life of fines and beating, *Business Week*, 2 October 2000.
39   Dara O'Rourke, assistant professor, *Monitoring the Monitors: A Critique of PricewaterhouseCoopers (PwC) Labor Monitoring*, Department of Urban Studies and Planning, Massachusetts Institute of Technology, 2000 (downloadable at: http://web.mit.edu/dorourke/www/PDF/pwc.pdf.
40   *Comparison of Selected Corporate Social Responsibility Related Standards*, Business for Social Responsibility, San Francisco, November 2000.
41   For a detailed account of the standard, see Christopher Seldon (ed.), *ISO 14001 and Beyond: Environmental Management Systems in the Real World* (Greenleaf: Sheffield, 1997).
42   Rondinelli, IT comes to the aid of environmental managers, *op cit.*
43   Thomas A. Stewart, Why values statements don't work, *Fortune*, 10 June 1996.
44   *Values in Action: Formalizing your Company's Values*, Business for Social Responsibility, San Francisco, 2000.
45   Andrew Jennings, *The Great Olympic Swindle: When the World Wanted its Games Back* (Simon & Schuster: New York, 2000).
46   William Echikson, Foul play redux, *Business Week*, 2 October 2000.
47   Peter Fries, Going for green, *Tomorrow*, September 2000.
48   Unilever follows Coca-Cola in Olympics HFC phase-out, *ENDS Report*, London, 2000.
49   Mark Hodson, Bunker beds, *Sunday Times*, 29 October 2000.
50   Ivan Alexander, *The Civilized Market: Corporations, Conviction and the Real Business of Capitalism* (Capstone: Oxford, 1997).
51   Alice Lagnado and Michael Binyon, Letter describes death on the *Kursk*, *The Times*, 27 October 2000.
52   John Elkington and Julia Hailes, *The Green Consumer Guide* (Gollancz, London, 1988).
53   Uta Harnischfeger, Guardian of the family fortune, *Financial Times*, 3 November 2000.
54   Khozem Merchant and David Gardner, Charmer who plans to clean up India, *Financial Times*, 3 November 2000.
55   The full report of the BSE Inquiry, led by Lord Phillips of Worth Matravers, can be found at: www.bseinquiry.gov.uk.
56   Norman C. Finkelstein, *The Holocaust Industry: Reflections on the Exploitation of Jewish Suffering* (Verso: London, 2000).
57   Will Hutton, The state we can't escape, *The Observer*, 29 October 2000.
58   Jeremy Thompson, Now we go live to . . ., *The Observer*, 22 October 2000.
59   Peter Schwartz, Scenarios: consequences too large to imagine, *Red Herring*, 30 October 2000.
60   Jennifer Fonstad, Zero latency is looming, *Red Herring*, 30 October 2000.
61   Edward Harris, The Web helps unite activists world-wide, *Wall Street Journal*, 3 October 2000.
62   Simon Caulkin, Taking over by talking back, *The Observer*, 1 October 2000.
63   Kevin Kelly, *New Rules for the New Economy* (Fourth Estate: London, 1998).
64   *The Global Reporters*, SustainAbility for the United Nations Environment Programme, London/Paris, 2000.
65   John Arlidge, 'Repellent' Olympics TV ad banned, *The Observer*, 1 October 2000.

66   Thomas H. Davenport and John C. Beck, Getting the attention you need, *Harvard Business Review*, September–October 2000.

67   SITA hides from stakeholders while Greenpeace makes hay, *ENDS Report 309*, October 2000.

68   Stakeholder dialogue: is fatigue setting in?, *Ethical Performance*, October 2000.

70   Peter Burrows, The radical: Carly Fiorina's bold management experience at HP, *Business Week*, 19 February 2001.

71   James Dalrymple, The trusting souls who fell into a hellish abyss, *The Independent*, 26 February 2000.

72   Dalrymple, *ibid.*

73   Dalrymple, *ibid.*

74   The Environment Foundation, PO Box 10, Fishguard SA65 9YW, UK. Email: helen.holdaway@which.net.

75   Defined by the WBCSD as "the delivery of competitively priced goods and services that satisfy human needs and bring quality of life while progressively reducing ecological impacts and resource intensity, through the life cycle, to a level at least in line with the earth's estimated carrying capacity." An excellent primer on eco-efficiency and eco-innovation is Claude Fussler's *Driving Eco Innovation* (Pitman: London, 1996).

76   See, for example, Peter S. Pande, Robert P. Neuman and Roland R. Cavanagh, *The Six Sigma Way: How GE, Motorola, and Other Top Companies are Honing their Performance* (McGraw-Hill: New York, 2000).

77   Andrew Fisher, Bewildering change in the boardroom, *Financial Times Survey: FT Director*, 17 November 2000.

78   Scott Leibs, Help wanted (and how), *CFO*, November 2000.

79   Davis and Meyer, *Blur, op cit.*

80   Geoffrey Nairn, Ripples from a quiet revolution bring net gains for manufacturing sector, *Financial Times*, 1 November 2000.

81   Phillip Manchester, The totally digital factory may not be so far away, *Financial Times*, 1 November 2000.

82   Rondinelli, IT comes to the aid of environmental managers, *op cit.*

83   Hugo Dixon, *The Penguin Guide to Finance* (Penguin Books: London, 2000).

84   Dixon, *ibid.*

85   Dixon, *ibid.*

86   *CSR Europe*, The Business Network for Corporate Social Responsibility, Brussels, 2000.

87   *Guided by Values*, The VanCity Social Report 1998/99, Vancouver, 2000.

88   Adapted from *How Do We Stand? People, Planet & Profits*, The Shell Report 2000, Shell International, London, 2000.

89   Oliver Dudok van Heel, Shelly Fennell, Franceska van Dijk and John Elkington, *Buried Treasure: Uncovering the Business Case for Corporate Sustainability*, SustainAbility for the United Nations Environment Programme, 2001. See also Buried Treasure Online web-site: www.sustainability.com/business-case.

90   See Colonel John Hughes-Wilson, *Military Intelligence Blunders* (Robinson: London, 1999).

92   Jay A Conger, David Finegold and Edward E Lawler III, Appraising boardroom performance, *Harvard Business Review*, January–February 1998.

93   John Elkington, Softly does it, *Tomorrow*, vol. 10(3), May–June 2000.

94   Kim Samuel-Johnson, An environmental scorecard, *Newsweek* special issue, December 2000–February 2001.

95   Morten T. Hansen, Henry W. Chesbrough, Nitin Nohria and Donald N. Sull, Networked incubators: hothouses of the new economy, *Harvard Business Review*, September–October 2000.

96   Joseph Jaworski and Claus Otto Scharmer, *Leadership in the New Economy*, Generon Consulting, May 2000 (www.generonconsulting.com).

97   Robert Buderi, Lucent ventures into the future, *Technology Review*, November/December 2000.

98   Clayton M. Christensen, *The Innovator's Dilemma: When New Technologies Cause Great Firms to Fail* (Harvard Business School Press, Boston, 1997).

99   Jon Swartz, Internet incubators get cold shoulder, *USA Today*, 31 October 2000.

100   Cover story, *Fast Company*, July 2000.

101   Ben R. Rich and Leo Janos, *Skunk Works* (Warner Books: London, 1994).

102   Scott Kirsner, Breakout artist, *Wired*, September 2000.
103   Tom Robbins and Andy Goldberg, Is this the revolution the world is waiting for?, *Sunday Times*, 14 January 2001.
104   Power players, *Wired*, January 2001.
105   Duff Hart-Davis, Eighth wonder, *The Independent*, 2 September 2000.
106   Stuart Birch, New capitalists, *Business Life*, October 2000.
107   Scott Kirsner, Design principal, *Fast Company*, October 2000.
108   Biomimetic design, in *More Than Meets The Eye*, exhibition at the Victoria & Albert Museum, London, September–November 2000.
109   Janine M. Benyus, *Biomimicry: Innovation Inspired by Nature* (Quill: New York, 1997).
110   Michael Ekin-Smyth, Budding business ideas, *Shell World*, September 2000.
111   Charles Fishman, Creative tension, *Fast Company*, November 2000.
112   Jeffrey Pfeffer and Robert Sutton, *The Knowing–Doing Gap* (Harvard Business School Press, Boston, 2000).
113   Vanessa Houlder, Business sees green controls as a prospect, not just a cost, *Financial Times*, 18 November 2000
114   Ray Anderson, *Mid-Course Correction* (Peregrinzilla Press, 1998).
115   Ray Anderson, *The Rest of the Story: Interface and Sustainability*, Interface, Inc., Atlanta, GA, 2000.

Notes to Part IV

1   More details at http://spaceflight.nasa.gov/station/index.html.
2   Michael Binyon, Blazing Mir's return trip could wipe out Sydney, *The Times*, 17 November 2000.
3   Joshua Watson, 2001 is here – just not as envisaged, *Fortune*, 13 November 2000.
4   Barnaby Conrad III, *Pan Am: An Aviation Legend* (Woodford Press: Emeryville, CA, 1999).
5   Hamel, *Leading the Revolution, op. cit.*
6   Betty S. Flowers, *Global Governance: Scenario Platforms*, World Business Council for Sustainable Development, Geneva, 17 April 2000.
7   *Exploring Sustainable Development*, WBCSD Global Scenarios 2000–2050, World Business Council for Sustainable Development, 1997.
8   See www.gbn.com.
9   This short section is extracted from *Cannibals with Forks, op. cit.*, pages 265–267.
10   Pierre Wack, Scenarios: uncharted waters ahead, *Harvard Business Review*, September–October 1985; and Scenarios: shooting the rapids, *Harvard Business Review*, November–December 1985. Reprinted as *Scenarios: The Gentle Art of Re-perceiving*, Shell International Petroleum Company Ltd: London, March 1986.
11   Kees van der Heijden, *Scenarios: The Art of Strategic Conversation* (John Wiley: New York, 1996).
12   WBCSD, *op. cit.*, 1997.
13   Dennis Meadows *et al.*, *The Limits to Growth* (Earth Island, 1992).
15   Peter Schwartz, Peter Leyden and Joel Hyatt, *The Long Boom* (Perseus Books, 2000).
16   *Four Futures for Organizing and Leading the New Economy* (Society for Organizational Learning: Cambridge, MA, 2000).
17   WBCSD, *op. cit.*, 1997.
19   Allen Hammond, *Which World? Scenarios for the 21st Century* (Island Press/Shearwater, 1998).
20   There is a discussion forum on the Internet.
21   Donald N. Sull, Why good companies go bad, *Harvard Business Review*, July–August 1999.
22   Mark Gimein, Has Tom Peters gone crazy?, *Fortune*, 13 November 2000.
23   Inside job, *Financial Times Weekend Magazine*, 6 May 2000.
24   Keith H. Hammonds, Practical radicals, *Fast Company*, September 2000. See also Debra Meyerson, *Tempered Radicals* (Harvard Business School Press: Boston, 2001)..
25   Jimmy Burns, Business learns the value of good works, *Financial Times*, 19 December 2000.
26   Michael Skapinker, A world away from Jo'burg, *Financial Times*, 23 November 2000.
27   Jonathon Porritt, Does working with business compromise the environmentalist?, *The Ecologist*, September 2000.

28 Peter M. Senge, From the chair, *Reflections*, vol. 1(4), Society for Organizational Learning, Summer 2000.

29 William McDonough and Michael Braungart, The next industrial revolution, *Atlantic Monthly*, October 1998.

30 Terry Slavin, People who live in grass houses, *The Observer*, 7 January 2001.

31 *Encyclopaedia Britannica*, 1983.

32 Alan Atkisson, *Believing Cassandra* (Chelsea Green: Vermont, 1999).

33 Peter Scott-Morgan, Eric Hoving, Henk Smit and Arnoud van der Slot, *The End Of Change: How Your Company Can Sustain Growth and Innovation While Avoiding Change Fatigue* (McGraw-Hill: New York, 2000).

34 C.K.Prahalad, Raising the bottom of the pyramid: strategies for sustainable growth, unpublished paper, July 2000.

35 Naomi Klein, *No Logo* (Flamingo: London, 2000).

36 Thomas Frank, *One Market Under God: Extreme Capitalism, Market Populism and the End of Economic Democracy* (Secker & Warburg: London, 2001).

37 Peter Marsh, A little goes a long way, *Financial Times*, 4 January 2001.

38 Eric Bonabeau and Guy Théraulaz, Swarm smarts, *Scientific American*, March 2000.

39 Francesco Guerrera, Bringing it all back home at ICI, *Financial Times*, 9 October 2000.

40 Edward Helmore, Old rockers don't die, they just sing for Microsoft, *The Observer*, 26 November 2000.

41 Robin McKie, 21 September 2030: the date scientists predict an asteroid will hit the Earth, *Sunday Times*, undated (see also the International Astronomical Union's website at www.iau.org/sg344.html).

42 Scott Freeman and Jon C. Herron, *Evolutionary Analysis* (Simon & Schuster: New Jersey, 1998).

43 Michael E. Porter, Hirotaka Takeuchi and Mariko Sakakibara, *Can Japan Compete?* (Macmillan: London, 2000).

44 Felipe Fernández-Armesto, *Civilizations* (Macmillan: London, 2000).

45 Paul R. Ehrlich, *Human Natures: Genes, Culture and the Human Prospect* (Island Press/Shearwater Books: Washington, DC, 2000).

46 Agencies, Concordes had 57 tyrebursts, *Financial Times*, 6 January 2001.

47 Edward R. Tufte, *Visual Explanations* (Graphics Press: Connecticut, 1997).

48 Fabio Casati, Visite d'un cockpit, *Air France Magazine*, 46, February 2001.

49 Martyn Turner and Brian O'Connell, *The Whole World's Watching: Decarbonizing the Economy and Saving the World* (John Wiley: New York, 2001).

50 Arthur Miller, Fantastic scoop, *Forbes ASAP*, 2 October 2000.

Index